D0269465

ASHES 2011:

England's Record-Breaking Series Victory

ASHES 2011:
England's Record-Breaking Series Victory

Gideon Haigh

First published 2011 by
Aurum Press Limited
7 Greenland Street
London NW1 0ND
www.aurumpress.co.uk

Copyright © 2011 Gideon Haigh

The moral right of Gideon Haigh to be identified as the author of this work has been asserted by him in accordance with the Copyright, Designs and Patents Act 1988.

All rights reserved. No part of this book may be reproduced or utilized in any form or by any means, electronic or mechanical, including photocopying, recording or by any information storage and retrieval system, without permission in writing from Aurum Press Ltd.

A catalogue record for this book is available from the British Library.

ISBN 978 1 84513 613 0

10 9 8 7 6 5 4 3 2 1
2016 2015 2014 2013 2012 2011

All interior images courtesy of *Getty Images* except p. 6: 'Australian captain Ricky Ponting' courtesy of *Newspix/Rex Features*

Typeset by SX Composing DTP, Rayleigh, Essex

Printed and bound in Great Britain by MPG Books, Bodmin Cornwall

Contents

Introduction

In the southern summer of 2010–11, England retained the Ashes in Australia 3–1. The novelty hasn't yet worn off that statement, and it might be a while before it does. Had you envisaged such a prospect this time four years ago, you would have been laughed out of whatever hostelry you proposed it in – because you would have needed a few drinks to work up the bravado to say it. At the time, England had been on the receiving end of the most thorough defeat in Test history. Australia faced a wave of retirements, but they had regenerated before, and were backing themselves to do so again.

The Ashes of 2009 were then played out by two battling, middling, sometimes shambling teams. But for the improbable resilience with the bat of James Anderson and Monty Panesar at Cardiff, Australia might have retained the trophy; as it is, an unlucky coin toss and poor selection cost them dearly at the Oval. In their summer of 2009–10, however, Australia won five of six Tests, a good summer's work even by the standards of their primrose path of the late nineties and early noughties. There was much talk of new fighting spirit, new talent like Steve Smith and Phil Hughes, new characters like Doug Bollinger and Ryan Harris. If not the magnificos of yesteryear, the Australia team still had a winning feeling about it, consolidated when they comfortably bested New Zealand in that country at summer's end.

What Masaryk said of dictators, then, can also be said to

apply to cricket dynasties: they always look good until the last minutes. Because cracks appeared when Australia went to England in the middle of 2010 to play Tests against Pakistan and one-day internationals against England; these were then widened by Tests in India and finally by one-day internationals against Sri Lanka at home. On the first day of the Ashes, an Australian bowler took a hat-trick; by the end, Australia had for the first time in the country's cricket history lost three Test matches by an innings. Had I not been there as eyewitness, I'd hardly have believed it; but I was, and the result is in your hands.

This book is a collection of my despatches. It interleaves the daily match reports I wrote for *Business Spectator*, and the daily columns I composed for *The Times*. They are unaltered from the form in which they were sent, so you can see when my forecasts were awry, often enough, as well as right, just occasionally, albeit probably by accident. Players don't have the luck of magisterial hindsight, rewriting events to leave out the bad shots they played, the long-hops they served up, the catches they dropped; it's fairest to be read in parallel. And let's face it: if you were right all along, where would be the point in watching?

One observation, however, may be pertinent. Reporting and analysing Test matches is both satisfying and deeply challenging, rather like trying to review a play at the end of each act, except from a distance of maybe a hundred metres, with little idea how the characters will appear and reappear, and no notion how the plot will unfold. With the online news environment having created a demand for round-the-clock content, both my report and my columns had to be filed within an hour of stumps, barely time to squeeze in the nightly press conference where a player from each side said not much about very little. I enjoy deadlines, and seeing something I have written posted within minutes of my completing it retains for me a heady novelty. Yet so heavily does the accent now fall on instantaneous judgement that the scope for considered journalism cannot but dwindle, with an impact on the way that cricket is perceived, understood and interpreted. *Caveat lector.*

This was a tough tour from a personal point of view also, given the separations from my wife Charlotte and one-year-old daughter Cecilia, for which even the wonders of Skype could not make up. I finally had them with me in Sydney, which meant that I ended the Test with my head ringing from both Barmy Army chants and songs from *In The Night Garden*, idly transposing Mitchell Johnson and Makka Pakka. In doing so I obtained a better understanding of what it takes for a cricketer to leave home and hearth for a foreign clime. If Andrew Strauss's tourists missed their loved ones half as much as I missed mine, they have my deepest sympathy.

It remains for me to thank my editors, Tim Hallissey at *The Times* and James Kirby at *Business Spectator*, for the opportunity to cover this constantly fun and fascinating series. I'd also like to acknowledge my estimable colleagues at *The Times* – Simon Barnes, Richard Hobson, Geoffrey Dean and especially the chief cricket correspondent Michael Atherton – for being a team scarcely less cohesive than England. I look forward to working with them all again.

GIDEON HAIGH

January 2011

Part I

KINDLING THE ASHES

Folie à Deux

The wife of Australia's longest-serving prime minister, Robert Menzies, saw two days of Ashes cricket, at Melbourne and Lord's, separated by eighteen months. On the first occasion, England's Jack Hobbs and Herbert Sutcliffe batted all day; at the beginning of the second, she was bemused to see Hobbs and Sutcliffe again coming out to bat. 'Well, I never,' she said. 'Don't tell me those two are still in?'

Good story – it also contains a kernel of truth. For those who don't understand it, but also for those who do, the Ashes is like one long, apparently unending, constantly fluctuating, seemingly unresolvable game – cricket's ultimate, insofar as even when a series is won or lost, that ascendancy is provisional until the resumption of competition. It never ends with 'goodbye', always with 'check ya later'.

And that it also is: a check. No matter where the two countries stand in cricket in other respects, Australia and England exhibit a perennial desire to ascertain where they rate in relation to one another. World Twenty20? A useful bookend. World Cup? Handy for keeping your cufflinks in.

But on the national mantelpiece, England and Australia keep space permanently cleared for the Ashes, even if there have been spells like the 1940s and 1990s when that area in England has grown a mite dusty.

There is something marvellous about this; also something quite mysterious. The Ashes is cricket's Stonehenge. Its origins are obscure. It was standing when we got here, and will outlast us all. Having outgrown its original purpose, its reason for being is not always entirely clear. Yet it goes from strength to strength, attracting more pilgrims than ever.

It is Test cricket's definitive rivalry, not because it has always provided cricket of the best quality, but because of two aspects integral to it. Firstly, continuity: since England came round to the five-Test format in 1899, it has been decided over a shorter distance on only a handful of occasions. Secondly, conduct: it is rough, tough, even sometimes bitter on the field. 'Test cricket is not a light-hearted business,' warned Sir Donald Bradman. 'Especially that between England and Australia.' Yet off the field, it has remained, with occasional exceptions that prove the rule, remarkably civil and companionable.

Not every English visitor finds Australia to their taste. 'Dear Father,' one of Douglas Jardine's team wrote home in 1932–33, 'this country is just hundreds and hundreds of miles of damn all, and then hundreds of miles more of it.' But the long distances and long durations involved in Ashes cricket beget hospitality: Alec Bedser and Arthur Morris played a decade's cricket against one another, then spent another five decades as friends and guests in one another's homes.

To the Ashes, there is also a pleasing equilibrium. Although their countrymen sometimes like to pretend otherwise, no two competitors in international cricket have as much common cultural ground: of language, history, institutions and even sporting values. The differences stand out the more for those surrounding similarities.

The conditions for cricket, for example, are radically dissimilar, and geography and meteorology have been hugely influential in the last five years: heat, harsh light and flat wickets in Australia, cloud cover and juice in England. And while globalisation should by rights be taking the edge off some of the distinctions between Australian and English cricketers, it's not doing so quickly. Ricky Ponting could be from no other country; Andrew Strauss likewise. Mitchell Johnson bounces it like an Australian; Jimmy Anderson swings it like an Englishman. From time to time, Australia and England eye one another with envious appreciation. Australians returned from England in 2005 wishing they had their own Andrew Flintoff; English spectators at the Oval Test of that series serenaded Shane Warne with a chorus of: 'We wish you were English'. But the fans of each country have ideas of the qualities in a cricketer they esteem.

What has changed about the rivalry? It originates, of course, from English colonisation of the Australian continent and from the desire to test the prowess of one society against the other. Sport, offering results in a fixed time on a superficially even footing, was an ideal medium for patriotic expression. 'Read the accounts of . . . the cricket matches,' opined Marcus Clarke in *The Future Australian Race* during the year of the inaugural Test match, 'and say if our youth is not manly.'

We sometimes think of this as all one way; that it was always Australians seeking an estimation of themselves against the imperial power. We should not underestimate how much the English enjoyed the challenge. The British historian David Cannadine has pointed out that the late Victorian age was one in which traditional power structures sensed menace from forces of equalisation – industrialisation, urbanisation, extensions of the franchise. Reminding an uppity colony who was in charge was therapeutic for the English too.

What is impressive about the first decade of Anglo–Australian competition is its sheer frequency. Tours were huge, complex, expensive and slow-moving undertakings, yet Australian teams toured England in 1878, 1880, 1882, 1884, 1886, 1888 and 1890, and English teams reciprocated in 1876–77, 1878–79, 1881–82, 1882–83, 1884–85, 1886–87, 1887–88 and 1891–92 – all of it without a single complaint of 'burnout'.

The seminal series was then the five Tests of 1894–95 in Australia, where the England team of Drewy Stoddart prevailed in the final match to secure the rubber 3–2, having won the first after following on. It was noteworthy not only for the drama and quality of the cricket, but the way in which the advent of the telegraph cable between the two countries permitted its following in both hemispheres.

Australians did not learn that their countrymen had won at the Oval in 1882 until ten weeks after the event; English cricket followers, which legend has it included Queen Victoria, knew within hours the fortunes of Stoddart's team. Over shorter routes, the telegraph offered ever more real-time thrills. Official telegraph traffic one afternoon in 1894–95 between the Melbourne and Ballarat stock exchanges consisted of single wire: 'Nothing doing. Cricket mad. Stoddart out.'

This took place against a backdrop of an evolving sense of distinct nationhoods, climaxing with Australia's Federation in 1901. In the nineteenth century, five players represented both England and Australia: Billy Murdoch, Billy Midwinter, Jack Ferris, Sammy Woods and Albert Trott. Murdoch, the first Australian captain to win a Test on English soil, was buried in it, having settled in Sussex; so was Fred Spofforth, his matchwinner in that fabled game, after putting down roots in Hampstead. Since Federation, Australia has chosen only a handful of players born elsewhere, and looked askance at England's partiality to cricketers from far away.

Then, and actually only really then, came the Ashes. As any fule kno, the symbol of cricket supremacy between England and Australia derives from that victory wrung for Murdoch by Spofforth at the Oval in 1882, after which a jesting obituary notice 'in affectionate remembrance of English cricket' was published in the *Sporting Times*, with the coda: 'The body will be cremated and the ashes taken to Australia.' The jest was double-edged, conflating two news events: the cricket, and cremation, the legality of which was being hotly debated in England.

This jest was then given physical form in Australia the following year, with the creation of an urn by a group of Melbourne society belles. They presented it to England's captain, the Hon. Ivo Bligh, in appreciation of his team's recent success in Australia. One of them, Florence Morphy, ended up marrying him too: they became Lord and Lady Darnley. But the original idea did not take off at once: it was, as it were, a slow burn. Not until Pelham Warner led an England team here in 1903–04 were the Ashes rekindled. For also en route to Australia aboard the *Orontes* was Lady Darnley, who so charmed Warner with her tale of her husband's cricket exploits that he adopted 'the Ashes' as a motif in the title of his tour book *How We Recovered the Ashes*. Even then, the urn itself did not come into the public eye until Lord Darnley's death in 1927, when it was bequeathed to the Marylebone Cricket Club.

So here's a puzzle. Some breathtaking relics survive from that epoch-making Oval Test 128 years ago. In the museum at the Melbourne Cricket Club, you will find the ball with which Spofforth conjured victory, adeptly scooped up by Australia's keeper, Jack Blackham; you will also find a brooch Blackham had made containing a fragment of the ball. In a sense, these are artifacts far worthier of our veneration than a joke urn inspired by a joke obituary revived by a forgotten cricket book: they are relics of the game that made Australia's cricket reputation in England, not an object twice removed from it. The Frank Worrell Trophy contested by Australia and the West Indies obtains its totemic significance from the placement of the ball from the first Tied Test; as the Ashes urn has never been opened, it could contain crack cocaine for all we know.

And yet . . . and yet . . . like I said, the Ashes is mystery as well as history. Perhaps we cherish it because among sporting trophies it is unique: not a dirty great shield or shining metallic art work, but a tiny frail terracotta. Perhaps we covet it because it can't be bought or sold, can't be replaced, can't be replicated. It is, in the original sense of the word, a myth – as mythic as the beast once imagined by an elderly woman who wrote to England's captain Norman Yardley sixty years ago after hearing on the radio that Ray Lindwall had two long legs, one short leg and a square leg: 'Tell me, Mr Yardley, what kind of creatures are these Australian cricketers? No wonder England can't win.'

That ineffability has survived enormous change in England, Australia, their relations, and in cricket itself. For in the century or so since it was successfully relaunched by Pelham Warner, the essence of Ashes competition has reversed, going from being regular because it is important, to being important because it is regular. But somehow the Ashes makes its own time, always coming up, even when it is over. And when it is happening you wouldn't be anywhere else.

12 OCTOBER 2010
THE ASHES

The Fourth Protocol

Cricket administrators nowadays are always prattling on about 'the three versions' of the game, trying to make it sound like evidence of marketing super-genius rather than of a Baldrickian cunning plan. You see, those clever johnnies in marketing know all about this stuff. There are Test matches, right? These appeal to . . . well, you know, the chap in the egg-and-bacon tie. Then there are your one-dayers. These appeal to . . . errrr, your average thirty-something binge-drinker. Finally, there are your T20s. These appeal to ten-year-olds – and doesn't cricket just love ten-year-olds at the moment? Complicated, eh? Are you still with me?

Of course, this is mainly cant, even without making a pedantic point about the regional variations in one-day cricket between 40-over, split-innings formats etc. For one thing, four-day, first-class cricket is always left out of these vauntings. Why? Probably as much of it is played as any of the foregoing. But somehow, cricket administrators keep forgetting about it. The impression you get is that they would just as soon it was not around, standing as it does inconveniently in the path of wringing the maximum money from everything. The other variation that has stealthily peeled off is Ashes cricket: the idea of five five-day Test matches, once the summit format of international competition, now kept alive only by Australia and England.

It's probably India who tolled the knell on this form of the game following the 1987 World Cup. Soon after, India hosted West Indies in a five-Test series, which while it was under way was reduced, over the visitors' protestations, to a four-Test series, for the sake of adding two further one-day internationals to a scheduled five. India has not staged a five-Test series since.

The West Indies' long-running Test supremacy fanned its interest in the five-Test series. They played South Africa at home in 1998–99 and away in 2000–01, Australia away in 2000–01 and India at home in 2001–02. But as its stock of talent dwindled so did dedication to the genre (five games were scheduled in the Caribbean early last year, only for the one on the ground better suited to cows than cricketers to be cancelled). Which left South Africa, until it lost to England at home in 2004–05. Since then the only countries to pursue the five-Test series have been its originators.

Why would one want to argue for five Tests as a variation distinguishable from the two- and three-Test series that have since proliferated? Short Test series are too apt to hinge on one-off performances or particular sessions to be completely satisfying; the Tests are often held on top of one another after minimal preparation, so that the possibilities of regrouping after a defeat, or significantly rethinking selection, are minimised; the chances of a player having impact are likely as not to be a factor of conditions rather than of all-round skill.

Yet India, the world's number one Test nation, likes its Tests in couplets – they are hardly worth the name 'series' any more. In order to keep its ICC rank, it squeezed couplets in against South Africa, Bangladesh and Australia, plus a three-Test series against Sri Lanka. All contained good cricket; all hardly seemed to start before finishing. What one would have given for more of the first encounter, after the rivals had taken turns knocking the stuffing from each other.

The five-Test series, by contrast, gives a cricketer's temperament, technique, endurance, versatility and resilience the most thorough work-out possible, in all conditions and match situations, against all skills and variations, as an individual and a member of a collective. To be genuinely consistent over this longest of courses, to maintain a positive frame of mind far from home through a campaign of such duration, is to achieve something genuinely rare. On the evidence of last year's Ashes, in fact, modern cricketers are struggling to meet the challenge.

This summer in Australia, furthermore, you may very well witness this event's last efflorescence: that is, five five-day matches as a season's centrepiece. If Cricket Australia has its way, by the time England is scheduled to return in 2013–14, international fixtures will be in competition with, if not overshadowed by, a supranational T20 competition. And that aforementioned Holy Trinity of formats might be looking more like the Odd Couple.

26 OCTOBER 2010
ENGLAND

Please Enjoy

Soon after arriving in Australia to follow Walter Hammond's English team of 1946–47, E.W. Swanton hailed a taxi. Swanton's plummy accent immediately gave him away. From England, eh? The cab driver was off. Well, Swanton simply had to do this. He must be sure to do that. He must go here, and be certain to visit there. In the course of the journey, Swanton barely slipped a word in, such was the torrent of information and recommendation. 'Yeah, it's a great country,' said the cab driver at last, setting his passenger down. 'Remember, it's yours as well as ours – and if you don't enjoy it here, it'll be your own ruddy fault.'

Swanton's story came to mind this week as England foregathered for its long flight to the other side of the world. 'There is nothing to be afraid of in Australia,' argued coach Andy Flower. 'It should be welcomed as one of the highlights of a cricketing career. Enjoying it means, yes, enjoying the challenges on the field, but also enjoying seeing another country, culture, and meeting new people. It is one of the best places to go. It should be a lot of fun.' It's almost a shame Flower felt obliged to enunciate something so screamingly obvious but it was a helpful point nonetheless. Australian cricketers exhibit an impressive unanimity in pronouncing England the best tour of all. English cricketers seldom display a reciprocal enthusiasm about Australia.

In one respect, this is easily explained. Australian cricketers have savoured a great deal of success in England, and enjoyment comes more naturally in such circumstances. English teams have achieved little in Australia for a generation, and there have been some spectacular misadventures: Phil Tufnell's panic attack in Perth sixteen years ago, Marcus Trescothick barely getting off the plane before he was back on it four years ago, and, perhaps ugliest of all, John Crawley being set upon by an unknown assailant as he returned to his team's hotel in Cairns in November 1998.

Yet other factors seem to play a part here. Australians are big travellers – they have to be, if they're to see any of the world. The English are accustomed to shorter distances, cosier ambiences. The gap year might be to the 21st-century student what the Grand Tour was to the 19th-century man of letters, but aspiring professional cricketers, in their hurry to get on, deprive themselves of such experiences. To indulge in some national stereotyping, too, Australians have a more extrovert culture, while the English are identified with reserve and understatement – well, in the books of George Mikes anyway.

There's reason to expect better of this England team. Seven players have toured before. Four have played first-grade cricket here, and the coach and his deputy have played Sheffield Shield cricket – the latter, David Saker, is, of course, Australian. Flower's seriousness about breaking past bad habits, of English players shuttering themselves in their hotels and socialising only among themselves, can be judged from his decision to delay the arrival of the team's wives and girlfriends until after the Second Test. And although such commandments always seem rather pettifogging where grown men and women are concerned, some evidence exists of their wisdom. When the Australians of 2005 placed no restriction on the comings and goings of partners, and even allowed players to set up separate lodgings outside the team hotel, the result was deep discord.

The other reason to expect better of England this summer is that the behaviours of previous teams are not bred in the bone. On England's last four Ashes tours, their fans have had a wow of a time. Say what you like of the Barmy Army, and many do, they know how to enjoy themselves, and their dedication has been unflagging: the way they roared England to victory in the 1998 Boxing Day Test remains for me a special sporting memory. They have taken their setbacks, like Cricket Australia's killjoy diktats, in good part too. And they have experienced the sincerest form of flattery in their emulation by Australia's Fanatics.

Sadly for the Barmy Army, the days of 'We're fat/We're round/Three dollars to the pound' seem a thing of the past, and word is that their numbers will be down. But England's cricketers should take their example to heart: the Barmy Army has always *paid* for the privilege they are about to be *paid for*. It is also hard to imagine a member of the Barmy Army remaining as mute as E.W. Swanton in the presence of a cab driver extolling Australian virtues.

1 NOVEMBER 2010
FORECASTS

Future Imperfect

Just as no battle plan survives contact with an enemy, few cricket predictions survive even a day of actual play. But the augurs of the forthcoming Ashes series are worth recording: England enter the series in the decidedly unfamiliar position of overdogs, forecast to ratify the possession of the urn they regained fourteen months ago.

When did this last happen? England arrived with the Ashes four years ago, but vestigial belief in their hopes lasted approximately one ball – the Steve Harmison wide that zeroed in on Andrew Flintoff's sternum at second slip. Even when England last prevailed down under in Australia, they were decidedly unfancied, their tri-cornered triumph of 1986–87 coming after an immortal three-pronged assessment of their capabilities from the *Independent*'s Martin Johnson: 'Can't bat, can't bowl, can't field.'

There was 1978–79, although the forecast that stands out from that series was Australian captain Graham Yallop's flippant prediction of a six-nil scoreline, which Mike Brearley's Englishmen almost entirely reversed. You must look back a further twenty years for a parallel with England's current favouritism, when Peter May's team of the talents arrived in Australia tipped to carry all before them – and were right royally ripped apart.

Expectations weren't ill-founded. It's hard to pick a bone with selection when you run your eye down the MCC team sheet, studded with such names as May, Cowdrey, Graveney, Bailey, Evans, Laker, Lock, Trueman, Statham and Tyson. As Jack Fingleton records in his classic account *Four Chukkas to Australia*, May's team was thought so strong that it would have 'played the Rest of the World and beaten them'; their 4–0 defeat duly became the 'biggest upset of modern cricket times'.

One individual not surprised was May himself. He embarked on the trip full of foreboding, believing 'we were always going to struggle'. The series was overshadowed by the Australian chuckers to which Fingleton's title slyly referred, but May declined to use this as an excuse, at the time or in retrospect: 'Australian cricket played on huge ovals is a young man's game and we had too many players on their last tour. If you have lost the keen edge, Australia finds it out.'

So how does an XI's reputation inflate beyond its abilities, and do any such considerations apply to the circumstances preceding this Ashes series? May points to one common mistake: the tendency to read teams on paper, rather than gauge the potentialities of individuals at particular stages in their careers and against particular oppositions.

Something similar applied ahead of the Ashes of 2005. On Statsguru, Ricky Ponting's team looked unassailable. McGrath, Lee, Gillespie and Warne versus Harmison, Flintoff, Jones and Giles? And had Glenn McGrath been injured at the end of the summer and Simon Jones at the start, what price the MBEs and open-top bus rides? Yet, as Adam Gilchrist has since admitted, the Australians, for all their battle honours, were an unhappy side, grumpily led by Ricky Ponting, absent-mindedly coached by John Buchanan. Andrew Strauss has also confided that a key conversation for him that summer was with Stephen Fleming after England's defeat at Lord's. Fleming urged Strauss to look past his chagrin – Australia were vulnerable, apprehensive about England's pace – and feeling turned out to matter more than figures.

An interesting aspect of the prognostications about the forthcoming Ashes is that they might be thought guilty of the opposite sin, of being intuitive rather than empirical. Alastair Cook, Paul Collingwood and Kevin Pietersen rather drifted through the northern summer, in Pietersen's case drifting out. Andrew Strauss averages less than 25 in Australia and barely 30 this calendar year. Of England's key bowlers, Graeme Swann took just six wickets in the first four Tests of last year's Ashes, while Jimmy Anderson has paid 56 runs for each of his Australian wickets and 82 runs for each of his wickets in Australia. The vibe around England is that of a resourceful, well-led and well-coached team rather than a particularly accomplished one. But from whom do we members of the media pick up that vibe? Often from others just like ourselves, where it's easy to fall in with a consensus.

How, meanwhile, does one read form ahead of an Ashes series? Ashes form seemed to point only one way in 1958–59. England had won the three preceding Ashes series; Australia had won only two and lost eight of the previous sixteen Ashes Tests. Yet there were other indicators. England had toured South Africa in 1956–57 and been well held; a year later, Australia had stuffed the Springboks out of sight, Richie Benaud and Alan Davidson, previously disappointments against England, suddenly coming of age. Why did observers choose to ignore this? Perhaps because of the Ashes' cultural hold on both countries – the sense that only what happened in Anglo–Australian competition counted. Perhaps also because overseas Test matches then took place well out of sight. Even their own countrymen were unaware what all-rounders Benaud and Davidson had turned into.

Those considerations do not apply today. The Ashes are no longer the only game in town, nor do the cricket teams of Australia and England disappear from the view of their own followers when abroad, even if it is true that foreign cricket feats still tend to be discounted, football lording it over the sporting winter of both countries. A kind of comparative indicator is available today in the respective recent meetings of Australia and England with Pakistan. But who can now say with confidence that performances against Pakistan are corroborative of anything?

The ultimate reason to distrust form seems to me to be just how different Ashes cricket has become from even the rest of Test cricket. The fashion nowadays is for two- and three-Test series; Australia last played a five-Test series against anyone other than England ten years ago; England last played a five-Test series against other than Australia six years ago. Test cricket over the shorter time span is often about winning first up, then attempting to live off that modish cricket concept of 'momentum'; Ashes cricket, over twenty-five days, fluctuates naturally, involves accepting that this will be so, and cultivating the competence of regrouping. It is also a different physical proposition. The world now seems to want its cricket games to end in three hours. Each day this summer, Australia and England will spend almost as long as that simply *preparing* to play; twice, they face back-to-back Tests. So this is not like wondering whether racehorses bred to gallop a mile have it in them to tackle ten furlongs; it's comparable to setting thoroughbreds the challenge of a fifteen-mile cross-country course lined with hurdles and equestrian hazards.

While contemplating the Ashes in advance might be confounding, it also reminds us of just how intricate are the contests within the contest of a team game played in changeable conditions over such a long duration. We are not simply looking at two teams; we are looking at two teams *against each other* and over the longest cricket haul of all. Swann has prospered against left-handers in his career, but how many will Australia pick? Strauss has fallen five times to Zaheer Khan in five Tests and four times to Mohammed Aamer in four, so how will he deal with the similarly left-armed Bollinger? And because England and Australia are now both middling international teams, it is almost the case that the longer you dwell on one or the other, the more palpable seem their vulnerabilities. England, you think, can't possibly be favourites – until you start looking at Australia.

8 NOVEMBER 2010
AUSTRALIA

66 and All That

At any one time in Australian domestic cricket, there are sixty-six players: eleven for each of the six first-class states. With the choice of John Hastings and Mitchell Starc for the last one-day international against India, preparatory to the Ashes summer, a curious symmetry was achieved. The number of Australian cricketers whom in the last two years have played Test matches, one-day internationals, T20 internationals, gone on tours or represented Australia A is . . . sixty-six.

When Bob Simpson became Australia's coach in the mid-1980s, he performed a similar exercise. On his figurings, there were forty-four players in the Sheffield Shield who had played some form of international cricket. This, opined Simmo, was 'a joke'. Numbers had blown out partly because of rebel tours and retirements, but he was adamant: 'There has never been a period in history when Australia had forty-four players good enough to play for their country.'

Has the game changed so much in the intervening period that this is no longer true? Workload is more sedulously managed by player rotation these days, even if this never seems to prevent anyone getting injured: in fact, if Doug Bollinger's breakdown in Bangalore is indicative, under-bowling is every bit as problematic as overbowling.

There are now three versions of the game where there were two, although on this list only three players have played T20 internationals alone. Fully forty-one players have played Test matches or one-day internationals, and there's actually a few more still involved in interstate cricket outside the sixty-six whom it could be argued deserve another look, including four very sweet strikers of a cricket ball in Brad Hodge, Mark Cosgrove, Phil Jaques and Luke Pomersbach. An honourable mention should also be made of Chris Rogers, with one lonely Test cap to show for almost 15,000 first-class runs at an average of 52.

So why is Australia cultivating selection habits that appear as random as Mitchell Johnson's pitch map? One reason – and this is hardly a phenomenon confined to Australia – is that first-class and top-class cricketers now mix like oil and water. Want to see whether Clinton McKay has what it takes to succeed at international level? You'll have to pick him at international level, because he won't encounter any Test-match batsmen in the Sheffield Shield.

One rationale, meanwhile, is that modern international cricket calls for strength in depth. Teams very seldom have the opportunity to select their first-choice XI. Rest is required. Injuries take their toll. Boot camps crop up. There's a logic to giving a taste of the big time to as wide a circle of players as possible, so that they are at least partly prepared when a more permanent turn comes.

Yet there's something more than a little disorienting about this turnover. Many hints have been given. Few cases have been made. In Australia's green and golden age, there was always a solid sense of who was next in the pecking order. But who is *primus inter pares* among Adam Voges, Callum Ferguson, Cameron White and David Hussey? Who is the next best thing out of Peter Siddle, Ryan Harris or Shaun Tait? Above all, where is the spin to come from, the incumbent Nathan Hauritz suddenly looking like an outcumbent?

This turnover coexists paradoxically with a sense of inertia where Australia's troubled batting is concerned. Since Matthew Hayden's retirement, Australia's top six has been occupied by only seven batsmen, and it is not as though any of them, save the ersatz openers Simon Katich and Shane Watson, has made an unassailable case for continued selection. The national selection panel – or the NSP as it is known in these acronym-happy times – has created not just a closed shop, but a closed shop without any opening hours on the front door, and precious little stock on the shelves.

For reference, here is our cream-of-the-crop elite sixty-six chosen for Australian representative teams in the last two years.

Chosen for Tests, ODIs or T20Is: Travis Birt, Doug Bollinger, Nathan Bracken, Daniel Christian, Stuart Clark, Michael Clarke, Callum Ferguson, Brett Geeves, Peter George, Brad Haddin, Ryan Harris, Shane Harwood, John Hastings, Nathan Hauritz, Matt Hayden, Josh Hazlewood, Moises Henriques, Ben Hilfenhaus, James Hopes, Phil Hughes, David Hussey, Michael Hussey, Mitchell Johnson, Simon Katich, Jason Krejza, Ben Laughlin, Brett Lee, Andrew McDonald, Bryce McGain, Clinton McKay, Graham Manou, Shaun Marsh, Dirk Nannes, Marcus North, Steve O'Keefe, Tim Paine, Ricky Ponting, Peter Siddle, Steve Smith, Mitchell Starc, Andrew Symonds, Shaun Tait, Adam Voges, David Warner, Shane Watson, Cameron White.

Also chosen in Australian touring teams: Burt Cockley, Jon Holland, Usman Khawaja, James Pattinson.

Australia A: George Bailey, Ryan Broad, Luke Butterworth, Beau Casson, Ed Cowan, Xavier Doherty, Brendan Drew, Luke Feldman, Aaron Finch, Peter Forrest, Jake Haberfield, Michael Klinger, Ashley Noffke, Luke Ronchi, Matt Wade.

9 NOVEMBER 2010
ENGLAND'S CAPTAINCY

For He Is an Englishman

No tribute to a foreign cricketer down under is settled so grudgingly but meaningfully as the one about them 'playing like an Australian'. Ian Botham was honoured with the description, and revelled in it. Likewise Freddie Flintoff. Darren Gough had his moments too.

Andrew Strauss has a head start. Born in Johannesburg, he was brought to Melbourne for two years by his father's career in insurance broking, and before the family relocated to London even developed an Aussie twang. He later wintered here, playing first-grade cricket in Sydney and undergoing elite coaching in Adelaide.

In the lives of both captains this summer, the rowdy, round-the-clock Bourbon & Beefsteak in Kings Cross, Sydney, has loomed large. It was where Ricky Ponting picked up a famous after-hours shiner from an off-duty bouncer; it was also where Andrew Strauss met the woman who would become his wife, actress Ruth McDonald, whose family come from outside Ballarat. Those with an eye for auspices will have noted that the first English captain to win the Ashes, Ivo Bligh, also married an Australian; mind you, so did the perennially unsuccessful Archie MacLaren.

Promising stuff – except Strauss spoils it by appearing every inch an Englishman, at the crease, in the field and behind the press conference microphone, twenty-five years having rounded the flat vowels he developed at Camberwell Grammar. No English captain since Strauss's Middlesex forebear, Sydney-born Gubby Allen, will have felt so instinctively comfortable with the country, the climate and the customs. Yet the three lions fit tight: expect no crowd-pleasing gestures, like affecting an Akubra or professing an appreciation of Kylie, from this verbal nudger and nurdler.

Thirty-three-year-old Strauss arrives in what should be his

cricketing prime. Captaincy has agreed with him. He has led England to thirteen wins and only four defeats in twenty-seven Tests, a win–loss ration superior to Richie Benaud's or Ian Chappell's – if not quite the equal of Ponting's. He has also accumulated six hundreds in the role, and opened a six-run edge on his average in the ranks.

It could easily have been otherwise. 'You might thank me for this one day,' Duncan Fletcher claims to have told Strauss after casting his captaincy vote as coach for Flintoff four years ago, ending Strauss's promising leadership audition. One wonders now how it bore on Strauss, to be part of a daily calamity where the only consolation was his not having to defend it.

Strauss's batting was slightly dispirited throughout that misbegotten sojourn, even a little disoriented. He perished hooking twice in Brisbane, which smacked of someone trying to make a point before it was quite clear in their own mind. Thereafter, he seemed almost astrologically cursed by poor decisions, and his average shrivelled to less than 25.

Memory of those travails has stuck. In a review of the English batting published in last week's *Sydney Morning Herald*, Stuart Clark, four years ago Australia's leading bowler, was dismissive of Strauss, rating him the least effective of the team's top seven. 'He hooks up,' said Clark, undoubtedly casting his mind back to the Gabba, 'and when playing forward his front foot goes straight down the wicket rather than to the line of the ball.'

Yet that method can't be said to have served Strauss badly. At his best, he is one of those players the sages routinely describe as 'well organised', as though batting was something to be learned from the *MCC Coaching Filofax*, and averages calculated by reference to the Dewey Decimal System. What it essentially means is that a cricketer has rationalised his game to within familiar and manageable limits, which in Strauss's case is verifiably true. He moves early then holds still, letting the ball come; he concentrates on scoring square of the wicket and off the pads; his strike rate hardly deviates from between the mid-40s and low-50s.

His organisation, in fact, is broader than technical. His economics degree at Durham University might have been a 2:1, but Strauss credits it with his unusual self-directedness: 'Having to revise for exams on my own enabled me to work on cricket without someone standing over me.' On the recommendation of his Australian-born ECB Academy coach Rod Marsh, he has for nearly a decade kept a detailed cricket diary. On meeting Alan Chambers five years ago, he was powerfully impressed by one of the polar explorer's aphorisms: 'Never put your body in a place your mind hasn't been first.'

So where his opposite number Ricky Ponting stakes the crease out briskly and busily, as though he can't wait to sort the bowling out and collar the contest, Strauss usually looks like a man settled into a comfortable routine, wearing the calm mask between deliveries of someone waiting in a queue – once again, a very English characteristic. You could arrive at a ground and not be sure whether Strauss had just taken guard or been batting a couple of sessions; you could meet him afterwards, it is said, and not be clear if he'd made a hundred or nought. Interestingly, in diary extracts published in his *Testing Times* (2009), he emerged as disarmingly susceptible to doubt, particularly during the eighteen months he went without an international hundred. But watching him from afar, you would not guess it; like one of those animals capable of controlling their heart rate and respiration, he appears to move only when he has to, and always with an end in mind.

As for that residual antipodeanism, Strauss should probably embrace it. Australians are fond of claiming success, and distancing themselves from failure. The story is told of the great racehorse Phar Lap, trained in Australia but foaled in New Zealand, that newspaper posters were prepared before its first American start covering both eventualities: 'Australian horse wins' and 'New Zealand horse loses'. The better Strauss does, the likelier the media is to stress his Aussie links; it will be in failure that he becomes just another lousy Pom.

11 NOVEMBER 2010
AUSTRALIA'S CAPTAINCY

Men in a Muddle

Australian cricket is sibilant with whispers. A newspaper article last week spoke darkly of the dissatisfaction of comrades with Michael Clarke and a push to promote Marcus North as a successor to Ricky Ponting, with Michael Hussey reportedly agitated at comments of Clarke's about the preference of some players for serving their IPL paymasters.

This being the way of things, the article set rolling the 24-hour juggernaut of talk radio, television and Twitter, gaining rather than losing momentum from the litany of denials. An opinion poll in a weekend paper proved Clarke's approval rating to have slumped to Obama levels, with only 28 per cent of respondents preferring him to follow Ponting – Cameron White had more supporters.

In one respect, Clarke should feel reassured. If his chief rivals to Australian cricket's number one job are either barely in the side (North) or out of it (White), then it is surely his for the asking. Yet not since Australian cricket's *anni horribili* in the 1980s, when at one stage a lobby for Dirk Wellham thrust him into the role of Allan Border's deputy for exactly five days, can I recall advocacy for a candidate for national captaincy outside the starting XI. Clarke can be thankful he's not competing in *The X-Factor*.

At the very least, it is a poor start to the summer's relations between the Australian cricketers and their media, who mix at the best of times like oil and water. Where the relatively wealthy English cricket press has a strong core of well-credentialled ex-players, Australia's journalists tend to be all-sport roustabouts specialising temporarily whom players keep at arm's length with the aid of a courteous but protective public affairs cadre and a phalanx of zealous agents. The players go through their motions grudgingly, bound only by a contracted minimum of appearances: there was amusement at Cricket Australia earlier this year when Clarke asked that a glossy mag photoshoot be deemed one of his gigs.

Team members are consequently seldom seen other than in the regimented and formulaic environment of media conferences, where the questions hardly rise above the level of the cricket equivalent of their favourite colour and what's on their iPod. Shane Warne and Glenn McGrath, superb extempore performers, are sorely missed; there is certainly nobody in the Australian setup as consistently engaging as Graeme Swann.

The results are plain to see. In coverage terms, the summer game languishes by comparison with the football codes, masterful at promoting their players even out of season – the Australian Football League's annual draft, for example, will squeeze cricket off the sport pages when it is held on the Gold Coast next week. And cricket writers fed up with mushroom treatment start speculating, as they seem to have here, on the basis of an unsourced mutter, a sideways glance and a theory or two.

Is Clarke's position as Ponting's dauphin in jeopardy? Is his place in his team-mates' esteem secure? The rumours predate this summer, dating back to a widely reported dressing room contretemps between Clarke and Simon Katich after last year's Sydney Test, when the former's keenness to slip away with his celebrity girlfriend offended the latter's obeisance to post-match rituals.

Rumours resumed after Clarke's muted tour of India. Other players were said to have 'issues' with him. Perhaps the highest kite flown was a newspaper article suggesting that South Australian Callum Ferguson – five centuries in forty-eight first-class games and an average of 36 with Adelaide

Oval as his home pitch – was an Australian captain in the making.

Frankly, who can tell? Dressing rooms are curious places. Dissimilar personalities can get on. Too-similar individuals can clash. A losing team need not always be on the point of insurrection, and a winning team need not be concordant – for proof, see the Yorkshire XIs of the 1960s, recently brought to life in Andrew Collomosse's excellent new book *Magnificent Seven*. Steve Waugh and Shane Warne won a lot of Tests together without liking each other all that much.

Nor is it as though the Australian media have an ear to the dressing room keyhole. Thanks to Cricket Australia's public affairs *cordon sanitaire*, they have their ear to the keyhole of six-inch-thick steel double doors separated by a moat from the Australian team's gated compound where the fences are topped with barbed wire.

But therein may lie the problem. Australian cricket now wears such a banal, expressionless face that it leaves the journalists to make their own suppositions, while the choreographed denials invite the scepticism of Mandy Rice-Davies: 'Well, he would say that, wouldn't he?' The other factor is that, just for once, two teams are about to undertake a Test series with a reasonable period of preparation and premeditation. Such hiatuses demand interim narratives, preliminary judgements, questions to be answered, answers to be questioned. There actually used to be more of this. Nowadays the calendar is so congested that speculation is usually the stuff of a day or two at best. Is Ponting finished? Oh, now he's got some runs. Is Steve Smith a top-class leg-spinner?

Errr, no. Nothing puts rumour and innuendo to flight like real runs and wickets – and it's not long to wait now.

17 NOVEMBER 2010
AUSTRALIA'S SQUAD

17 Again

Bismarck commented famously that there were two things the public must never see made: sausages and laws. Had he known of the game, he would surely have added cricket teams. Albeit unintentionally, Cricket Australia has just demonstrated why.

For some time, CA has been squirming about the encroachments of the football codes on summer. Although of limited actual significance, the Australian Football League's national draft has come close to eclipsing concurrent cricket news; the League's PR flaks boast of 'owning' November, and not idly.

Thus the scheme, driven by CA's marketing department, of bringing forward the selection of the Australian team for the First Test, just ahead of the draft, and turning it into a public event, in the lunch hour at Sydney's bustling Circular Quay, in sight of the Opera House, the Harbour Bridge and various other visual clichés. Ricky Ponting and some of his men could also be presented to the media, and even mingle with the public – a rare experience for them nowadays, when for much of the time the players might as well be holograms.

Unfortunately, the days when the Australian cricket team chose itself are a thing of the past; likewise the era when Australian cricketers were physically susceptible only to kryptonite. The selectors, chaired by Andrew Hilditch, did not want to commit themselves. Three Sheffield Shield games loomed. New South Wales were hosting Tasmania at the SCG, Queensland entertaining South Australia at the Gabba, Victoria tackling Western Australia at the MCG. Likewise was Australia A due to throw the gauntlet down to England at Bellerive Oval in Hobart. It made as much sense to announce the Test team so ahead of time as it did to include whodunit in the programme for *The Mousetrap*.

So it wasn't only the climate that made the event a damp squib. When the moment came that only a handful of spectators were waiting for, Hilditch temporised. He started to read. The list went on . . . and on. It stopped at last, almost arbitrarily, at seventeen names. Tension? You could barely have heard a piano drop. As a moment of buttock-clenching bathos, it ranked with the England and Wales Cricket Board preening themselves around Allen Stanford's box of bucks. Ricky Ponting doesn't faze easily, but even he was nonplussed: 'It's a different feel. Unfortunately, that's what we've got. For some reason, Cricket Australia wanted to name the squad as early as they have. We've just got to get on with it.'

In fact, it was the selectors who needed to be getting on with things, winnowing this down to something more properly resembling a cricket team – as indeed they will. In one sense, it was quite an instructive exercise, like watching the rushes of a film or reading the first draft of a book. One was admitted to the selection process at a preliminary stage, with all compositional options still open, and before the consideration of factors like conditions and overall balance. On the other hand, there are reasons all this is usually screened from the public gaze.

For a start, the selectors have sent a garbled communiqué to those involved in the Australia A game in Hobart. The team's captain Cameron White, who has led his state to consecutive Sheffield Shields, has learned he is not in Australia's best seventeen. Ditto, *inter alia*, opening bat Phil Hughes, opening bowler Peter George and keeper Tim Paine. As motivation, it is notivation.

For those who have been chosen, meanwhile, the message is ambiguous. The selectors are standing for continuity *and* change, past performance *and* future potential, which implies not flexibility but suggestibility. Surely, for instance, the relative abilities and ripeness for selection of Michael Hussey and Usman Khawaja will not be altered by the events of one round of games.

Yet the squad of seventeen seems to set up comparisons that might be difficult to ignore. Suppose that Doug Bollinger bowls like a drunk in Sydney while Peter Siddle rests in Melbourne. Suppose that, in the great Sheffield Shield bowl-off, Nathan Hauritz is tidy but luckless while his new shadow Xavier Doherty gathers a few wickets; Kevin Pietersen then throws his hand away in a Red Bull rush at Bellerive Oval to either Steve Smith or Steve O'Keefe.

How does one rank the respective merits of such

performances? Does it become difficult to persist with Johnson, despite his unvarying selection for two years, and not to commit to Siddle, despite the recency of his return from injury? Does then choosing Hauritz invite the criticism that the selectors have ignored a contest they set up? Above all, are players to infer that they have not a considered judgement of their ability to thank for their baggy greens, but the luck and chance of a single game?

In bygone days, of course, selectors pronounced ex cathedra. Players heard of inclusion, and omission, via the media – a cruel fate, if at least a shared one. In more recent years, in the spirit of inclusion, transparency and all those feel-good things beloved of New Labour sloganeers, selectors have become more accessible, to players and media – some have even grown quite talkative.

But this week's exercise in Sydney was a frankly odd contrivance – as odd, in fact, as projecting Ricky Ponting's face on Big Ben, an idea of the same marketing department. It revealed little that an observer could not have gleaned from afar. As an exercise in selection, it invited charges of both premature adamance and insufficient conviction. As a marketing ploy, it smelled of desperation, of the attitude that any publicity is good publicity. It looked, jarring as it sounds in the context of Australian cricket, phoney and unserious.

23 NOVEMBER 2010
PREPARATION

Yes, No, Wait

R.C. Robertson-Glasgow, universally known as 'Crusoe', who sixty years ago was *The Times*'s eyewitness for an Ashes series in Australia, once asked a girl he fancied to accompany him to the cricket. 'No, thank you,' she replied. 'Cricket is all just waiting.'

Unkind but not unfair. The girl would certainly have felt vindicated by the preamble to the Ashes of 2010–11, which, proceeding at a very twentieth-century pace, has just moved its location to a fourth Australian state. The tour hasn't been quite as leisured as Crusoe's journey, which commenced when England left Tilbury aboard the *Stratheden* on 14 September 1950 and took seventy-eight days wending its way to the First Test at Brisbane. Yet by contemporary standards, which view anything beyond 140 characters as needless rattling on, this is a slow-dawning pleasure indeed: the standard tour today involves no preparatory game at all, and as a result often seems to finish almost before it has started.

Graeme Swann, who toils as long on his turn of phrase as his turn of off-break, put it nonetheless neatly at the weekend: 'When we first got over here I daren't think of the first Test match, because I was like a kid on the first of December, with an Advent calendar. I couldn't wait for the twenty-fifth to come along. It's really building now, less than a week to go, and I go back to my room at night and I smile like a lunatic and bounce off the walls. It's going to be amazing come Thursday – I just can't wait.'

Happy the cricketer who can cope with delayed gratification in times that are a stranger to it. Others haven't handled it nearly so well. Cricket Australia, ever-so-slightly desperate about maintaining the attention of an easily distracted public, has staged a succession of mainly pointless pseudo-events and pranks. So ceaseless has been the bombardment of promotional media releases that it has almost been necessary to don a helmet before checking one's email.

Channel Nine were doing their bit on Sunday night, using the innings break in the underwhelming All-Stars game at the Gabba to talk up the Ashes, albeit in much the same tone as they adopt when promoting *Top Gear* or *CSI: Miami*. It is also hard to tell from Nine whether they regard the week's key event as the Ashes or Shane Warne's new talk show, which commences the night before.

England, by contrast, have been an impressive unit, doing everything so far asked and more. By this stage on previous English visits, two or three cricketers have usually flown home injured, half a dozen Aussie bolters have smashed them all over the park, and the red-tops have their talons in up to the cuticle. This time, Strauss's men could but for weather have had three victories. Local journalists, apt to write English teams off on the basis of their deportment in the customs hall, have had none of the succulent stories that have sustained them in past years: defeats sustained against Australia A, Steve Harmison's Lilac Hill wides in 2002, Marcus Trescothick's boomerang journey four years ago.

England have also stayed away from the big cities, Sydney and Melbourne, with their more numerous distractions and disturbances. The world has changed since Mike Brearley likened cricketers on tour to a Victorian family, challenged always to provide their own entertainment. But especially early on a trip, having to fall back on one another's devices is no bad thing for a team's members.

The only aspect lacking from England's preparation has been a game on the Gabba itself prior to the First Test, which used to be de rigueur, but which the hosts haven't actually offered for a generation. Thus bowling coach David Saker's exploratory reconnaissance last week with Swann, Jimmy Anderson, Stuart Broad and Steve Finn. The lack should be felt less by the batsmen, of whom only Jonathan Trott has not previously batted in Brisbane.

In the meantime, it has been Australia that have not looked the part, unaccustomed to English guests making themselves so comfortable. Issues have accumulated, lately round Nathan Hauritz. Injuries have lingered, like Ryan Harris's, and cropped up, like Tim Paine's. One suspects that Ricky Ponting will be as happy as Swann come Thursday. No more seventeen-man squads, fluctuations of form, favour and fortune, or content-free press conferences.

When the series begins, this leisure of the present will quickly become a thing of the past. Touring Australia can be a hurried, hugger-mugger experience, thanks to an innovation that actually began on that tour of Crusoe's sixty years ago of flying between cities rather than taking the train (back then it was not compulsory: Warwickshire's Eric Hollies, averse to flying, was excused it). This is a correspondingly intensive series: twenty-five Test days in forty-four, interrupted only by a three-day game against Victoria, with lots of opportunity to repeat ad nauseam clichés about 'momentum', as though Newton's Second Law formed part of the Marylebone code.

Recovery time, physical and psychological, will be at a premium. In the last two Ashes series in England, the hosts had the good fortune of ten-day breaks following both its defeats: Lord's at 2005 and Headingley in 2009. They recuperated well, and bounced back convincingly. Wound licking will need to be a good deal slicker this southern summer. As the hosts this time, Australia will enjoy the traditional advantage of being able to choose from players in the pink of domestic form, although England have counteracted it somewhat by the expensive but prudent expedient of keeping their 'shadow' squad in Australia until a week before Christmas.

Come Thursday, then, all the waiting will be over – for we spectators, anyway. For the players, waiting will continue, of a rather more nervous kind – waiting to go in, waiting to bowl, waiting for snicks, waiting for the opportunity to parade their skills. Cricket is increasingly agitated by waiting, preferring its pleasures more instantaneous, explosive and lucrative, so it can better appeal to those like the object of Crusoe's interest. But we've already seen, and I suspect will continue to see, how much can happen in cricket when all one seems to be doing is waiting.

Part II

FIRST TEST

The Gabba, Brisbane
25–29 November 2010
Match drawn

Gabba Jabber

The Gabba has always seemed a suitable location for an Australian ambush, and not only because its address on Brisbane's Vulture Street summons up visions of Dead Man's Gulch or the OK Corral. Visiting cricket teams usually roll in about half ready, out of season, out of synch, and are soon out of time to come back. Hit by Australia's full force, they have managed to draw only four of the last twenty Tests here; the rest they have lost. In the last decade, Australian batsmen have accumulated eighteen hundreds and averaged almost 50 at the Gabba; their bowlers have conceded only three hundreds while gathering their wickets at an average of 21.

It says much about the respective recent fortunes of Australia and England that this history hasn't simply killed speculations about tomorrow's First Test stone dead. Not in years, in fact, have predictions before an Ashes series ranged so widely – while remaining, let it be said, mainly partisan.

The usual Australian gauntlets have been thrown down: Glenn McGrath has uttered his reflex prediction of 5–0, making Merv Hughes look like a big girl's blouse for countenancing a single draw. But other Australians are more circumspect, with 2–1 a popular margin, and Ian Chappell deeming his countrymen only 'slight favourites'.

Just for a change, too, English critics are joining in the fun, with Ian Botham gathering supporters for the idea of a comprehensive visitors' victory. Others claim to have discerned cloying insecurities behind Australian triumphalism, and had a flutter before English odds came in sharply after their ten-wicket victory over Australia A at Bellerive Oval, with the result that almost two-thirds of the money wagered on the Brisbane Test is on England, and less than a third of the money on the series has been wagered on Australia.

So why is the expectation suddenly of two-way traffic on Vulture Street, when for so long it has been a dead end? For one, Ricky Ponting's Australians have acquired a losing habit. Their three consecutive Test defeats have not been stuffings, but they have had their stuffingesque moments: being bowled out for 88 in 33 overs at Headingley, allowing the last two Indian wickets to add 92 at Mohali, and squandering their last seven for 97 at Bangalore.

Their decline has been precipitous. When Australia last met England, they were still rated the world's number one Test nation; not much more than a year later, they have declined to fifth. Last year, it was common to talk about the Australians having lost their 'aura'. This year they seem to have lost something less fanciful, more fundamental, equivalent in cricket terms to their credit rating or their eligibility for life insurance.

For another thing, England look this summer to have actually come to play rather than merely to participate.

Before the series of 1998–99, Alec Stewart startled onlookers by saying that England's objective was to be 'competitive': the Ashes barely smouldered and were extinguished before Christmas. On this tour, it has been possible to use about an England preparation adjectives like 'meticulous' and 'effective', rather than preparing for the standard allusions to Captain Mainwaring's Home Guard and Fred Karno's army.

Standing in their way is what might be called Fortress Australia: that sense of unassailability, real and imagined, about Australian teams in their own backyard. On pitches with more bounce and in conditions with less swing, English batsmen used to playing with low hands and bowlers accustomed to healthy sideways movement have habitually struggled – far more so than Australians going to England.

The strut of Australians under their own skies shows up statistically. In the cases of Ponting (an average of 60 at home versus 48.7 away) and especially Michael Hussey (62.65 versus 39.75) and Michael Clarke (58.56 versus 42.52), one is almost considering different players. Mitchell Johnson is a similar homebody, paying 25.59 per wicket here compared to 31.1 overseas, and his humours are of particular importance. Although no cricketer looks quite so forlorn in failure, Johnson on his occasional day can take on the world. If he brings to the Gabba the all-round excellence he exhibited at the MCG last week, Australia will be that much more formidable.

Among the visitors, by contrast, only Kevin Pietersen and Paul Collingwood can claim to have developed happy memories of Australia, and these lasted all of three days. It was England's capitulation four years ago on the last day at

Adelaide after this pair had added 310 on the first and second that confirmed the suspicion nothing would go right for Andrew Flintoff's outmatched combination.

Australia also have a talent for winning first-up, taking four of the last five opening Ashes Tests, and being just a ball away from a clean sweep. England's habits are opposite. They went four years between winning the first Test of a series in 2005 (against Bangladesh) and doing it again (also against Bangladesh). A slow start in Brisbane has cruelled many a hope: not for fifty-six years has the victor at the Gabba not gone on to claim the Ashes.

All the same, strange things have been happening lately: Australia hadn't lost at Lord's since 1934 when they succumbed last year. Yesterday's weather was delightful, but showers are predicted for the next few days, and the resumption of more familiar conditions, ideal for the propagation of orchids, and thus also for the swing of Jimmy Anderson. Twenty Australian wickets may be easier to take here than later this summer, Johnson's footmarks also providing fourth- and fifth-day opportunities for Graeme Swann.

It has also been an odd few days in Brisbane waiting for this series to move out of the subjunctive mood, with players 'targeting' one another left and right, and Shane Warne's Twitter account seemingly set to go in number three for Australia; Warne's dutifully reported call for the captains to show some 'cojones' suggests he might have played one hand of Texas Hold 'Em too many.

Australia's preparations have been clouded by the dicky back of Michael Clarke, probably not as bad as thought, and the allegedly dicey Gabba pitch, probably the same, despite its preparation being impaired by rain. England, meanwhile, have gone about their business under relatively little pressure, apparently spending as long on their sprinkler dance as their slip catching. Australia's advantages remain considerable, but this will be no ambuscade.

25 NOVEMBER 2010

Day 1

Close of play: Australia 1st innings 25–0
(SR Watson 9*, SM Katich 15*, 7 overs)

A Test hat-trick almost defies logic. At the top level, good batsmen on good pitches almost should not permit three wickets to fall in three balls. But it's that 'almost' that matters. In squeezing the daylights from England's lower-middle order at the Gabba today, Peter Siddle made obtainable the very nearly unthinkable; as part of six for 54 from sixteen sizzling overs, it left logic looking a little the worse for wear.

The Test had been slumbering when Siddle entered his twelfth over. Alastair Cook and Ian Bell had added a calm-browed 72 in twenty-five overs. Siddle's earlier dismissals of Kevin Pietersen and Paul Collingwood had been to that stage relatively isolated highlights for Australia.

Cook, whose judgement had hitherto been unerring, felt for a ball slanted away, which settled in Watson's muscle-bound midriff. Blood up, Siddle arrowed the next ball into

Matt Prior, attacking the stumps that England's keeper is sometimes casual about defending, and scattering them.

It's an ill wind, Siddle might have reflected at this point. Had Cricket Australia not cajoled Doug Bollinger into representing the Chennai Super Kings in the Champions League a couple of months ago, he might have been properly prepared for Australia's Test in Mohali, might not have sustained a side strain, might not have looked rather underwhelming in the recent Sheffield Shield match at the SCG, and might as a result have squeezed Siddle out of the eventual XI, rather than becoming the squad's specialist national anthem singer.

Siddle might have thought that but he didn't. He confessed modestly afterwards that he planned simply to hit 'top of off'. What he bowled was closer to 'bottom of leg', but it was too quick for Stuart Broad, who stumbled into a 90mph yorker. For the fourth time during the day, umpire Aleem Dar's decision was challenged; for the fourth time, it was upheld. If more umpires were as competent, referrals would not be needed at all.

The obligatory scenes of man-love that ensued were perhaps more than usually heartfelt. Siddle is a popular, hard-working, blue-collar cricketer, with no airs and graces, and a dirty great Southern Cross tattoo on his back. He has been out of Test cricket since January with a stress fracture of the back, after toiling manfully much of last year. Today was his twenty-sixth birthday; he won't forget his hat-trick's anniversary.

With Australia making short work of the tail, and Shane Watson and Simon Katich breezing through the final ten overs, the opening day of the series could hardly have unfolded more deliciously for the capacity crowd. Two hundred and thirty-five runs in arrears at the close with all their wickets in hand, the hosts would have felt on their way to ratifying the Gabba's reputation as Fortress Australia.

The ghost of first overs past had been a pre-match talking point, Steve Harmison's wide in 2006 and Phil De Freitas's long-hop of 1994 being widely recalled; those with a memory for such things recollected that the second ball of the Test here in 2002 ran between Michael Vaughan's legs at gully.

The action today was again in the gully, with Andrew Strauss destined to relive the third ball of this series for years to come. From Hilfenhaus, it bounced a little, came back a tad, and was chopped rather than cut to Michael Hussey, who caught it in front of his own disbelieving eyes. Strauss reeled back, placed his hand to his head like he'd just remembered leaving the gas on at home, and returned to a dressing room where his initial instinct might well have been to stick his head in the oven. After forty minutes, he re-emerged on the players' balcony behind oversized sunglasses, as though loath to be recognised. Nobody should envy the captain cum opening batsman.

It was fourteen deliveries before the first English runs accrued, from Jonathan Trott's deadened edge to third man, a flick off the pads soon after providing the series' first healthy boundary. Trott's pedantic rituals – he marks his guard obsessively, as though fearful of the stumps moving – have clearly attracted Australian attention: Hilfenhaus charged halfway in at the beginning of the seventh over, even as Trott immersed himself in head-down fussings, and pulled up grumpily. This cat-and-mouse game could be set to last all summer long.

The Gabba was uneasily quiet throughout, as if people could not quite believe that cricket had actually begun after a month of punditry and prognostication. There were some home-town cheers when Johnson replaced Hilfenhaus at the Stanley Street end, and some pantomime boos later for the coming of Pietersen; otherwise the tension in the middle was contagious.

The match had settled into a lulling rhythm when Shane Watson came on and promptly bowled Trott through a beckoning gate. Before lunch, in fact, Australia's relief bowler looked as likely as anyone to break through. His sightscreen-broad shoulders held the promise of great velocities; in fact, he operated at the pace at which Stuart Clark was so effective here four years ago, and to a full length.

Siddle watched and learned. After lunch, rolling his fingers over the seam to good effect, he drew Pietersen and Collingwood into injudicious push-drives. But when, some-what surprisingly, Siddle was relieved after four overs by Johnson, Alastair Cook redoubled his application, and Ian Bell settled in quickly.

Cook played the innings England needed – almost. Although he has the left-handedness, slim physique and some of the self-containment of David Gower, he is as technically busy as Gower was physically minimal. He wears his method, with its double foot movements and double backlift, like a shabby but comfortable jacket, too-long sleeves worn through at the elbows, yet imbued with pleasant associations.

Because he can be ungainly, Cook often appears when dismissed to have been completely defeated, in veritable disarray. In this, he is a contrast to Bell, a batsman of comparable ability and record, who usually seems to get out while in nonetheless perfect position, bat straight, feet ideally spaced and balanced. Cook looks as though he's gotten himself out, Bell like he's been defeated by something special, Cook to have failed because of his method, Bell in spite of his. The contrast is seductive, and tends to shape the way they are criticised: Cook is always being enjoined to work on his technique, Bell to toughen his temperament.

For his part, Bell looked by far the most complete of England's batsmen, a far cry from the soft touch of 2005, playing with time to spare, and with far better awareness of the game unfolding around him than has been his habit. Of Bell, Australians have been inclined to reprise Shane Warne's comment regarding Monty Panesar: that he hasn't played fifty-eight Tests, but the same Test fifty-eight times. Out of Aussie sight, however, he has matured into a flourishing Test batsman, who finally overreached himself only when the circumstances compelled it.

When Cook succumbed to Siddle after almost five patient hours, the bowler charged down the pitch into the welcoming arms of the slips cordon, which joyously engulfed him. His head emerged from the huddle bearing a smile, which was as jagged as a crocodile's and broad as the Harbour Bridge. He looked like a man for whom life could simply not get better. It was a logical inference to draw. He was wrong.

25 NOVEMBER 2010
PETER SIDDLE

Up and at 'Em

Peter Siddle's first ball in Test cricket hit Gautam Gambhir on the helmet. During his recent interstate comeback, he hit Phil Jaques on the helmet too. A disciple of the blood-and-thunder school of fast bowling, he looks like he'd be happier knocking your block off than your stumps over. Yet he proved in Brisbane today that he can work both sides of the street. On a surface seemingly yellowing by the hour and that should tomorrow be ideal for batting, pitching it up was the way to go, so pitching it up was the way he went. To show for it, he had that rarest of cricket feats, a hat-trick.

Not long before he died, Donald Bradman was asked by Greg Chappell which deliveries had troubled him most in his career. After at first waving the question away, Bradman came up with an interesting and inherently authoritative answer: the full ball attacking the stumps that might go this way or might go that but at all events compelled a stroke was, even at his peak, a challenge.

What was good enough for Bradman those many years ago proved today more than enough for England. The third ball of Siddle's twelfth over was sharp and tight on off stump. When he entered Test cricket three years ago, Siddle rather struggled with left-handers, and lost knots and accuracy when bowling round the wicket. From over the wicket, this ball demanded a defensive bat from Cook, and snagged an edge as it angled away.

Siddle found the right solution for Prior too, who for a batsman with an average above 40 is bowled too often – 28 per cent of his dismissals. The ball was again full. It found bat and pad not just ajar but almost at odds.

The younger Siddle might at such a point have bowled a bouncer, into the ribs, maybe at the helmet. But it was Siddle's twenty-sixth birthday today. This is his eighteenth Test. He is in his fast-bowling prime, coming into savvy to go with the sizzle. In the nets before the game, both Tim Nielsen and Troy Cooley were entreating him to bowl a fuller length – as he did so, he was excited to find the ball swinging. So for his hat-trick ball, he aimed again to skid the ball from the otherwise disobliging surface, to take advantage of slow-moving feet and an uncalibrated eye.

Stuart Broad's preparatory rituals were as elaborate as those of a prize fighter shadow-boxing in his dressing gown: stretching, skipping, fiddling and generally farting around. His failure was almost foreordained. Siddle's yorker was rather like the jubilant sandshoe crusher with which Jeff Thomson at the Gabba thirty-six years ago upended Tony Greig; it is destined to be replayed as often. Broad legged it from the scene of the crime like an urchin spied stealing an orange, but was collared by the long arm of the lbw law, personified by Aleem Dar and ratified by Tony Hill.

Here was the delayed gratification of Test cricket at its best. In the hour before it, the Test had slipped from a restless doze into REM sleep. Alastair Cook and Ian Bell were restoring

English heart, ticking over calmly enough, if not threatening at any stage to break away. The commentators were chatting. The crowd was a little listless. Marketers were busy thinking about how to squeeze in another T20 international. They were disturbed in their machinations by the sound of celebration reverberating around the concrete crucible of the Gabba, by the outbreak of cricket worth waiting for.

Australia had special need of Siddle under the circumstances. The attack was generally persevering rather than consistently penetrative. Shane Watson chipped in, but Ben Hilfenhaus was no better than adequate, and Xavier Doherty was rather flattered by a couple of tail-end wickets.

Debutant Doherty came on to bowl the 21st over with a slip, a bat-pad and, after his first ball bit and bounced promisingly, a short mid-on. Except that he struggled with his line to Cook, asking too little of the left-hander's cover drive and offering too much to be nurdled round the corner, a bread and butter shot that sustained the batsman when his vital signs, every so often, showed signs of failing.

The comparison was unfair but inevitable. Four years ago, Warne let Pietersen know there would be no gimmes with a waspish throw back to the keeper that struck his old mucker's bat, following up with some pantomime huff-and-puff. Doherty's response in his third over to stopping Pietersen's crisp straight drive was rather less assured: his throw bounced at the edge of the cut strip and would have vanished for four overthrows had Haddin not darted quickly to his left.

A moustache has made Mitchell Johnson look a little more like Dennis Lillee, meanwhile, but it hasn't enhanced the bowling resemblance. His arm still swings through like a roundhouse punch, leaving little margin for error with his release, and his general presence remains rather less than menacing: as he pauses at the end of his run, it still looks as though he's trying to remember the last five things Troy Cooley told him.

Bowling to Bell during the afternoon, Johnson was at one stage nudged to mid-on. When he proceeded to hare after the ball himself, it looked a little odd, like the act of an overactive boy in a backyard; it was not an action one could have expected of Glenn McGrath, who would have chuntered about bloody short leg or bloody mid-off bloody well doing what they were bloody well paid for.

Johnson was the only bowler to make a pre-match prediction, talking up the need to be aggressive, and his intent to bombard Andrew Strauss. How long ago these prophecies and prognostications already seem. As Siddle might have said: 'The only way to go is up.' The same sentiment now applies, in a somewhat different sense, to England.

26 NOVEMBER 2010

Day 2

Close of play: Australia 1st innings 220–5
(MEK Hussey 81*, BJ Haddin 22*, 80 overs)

In Australia's great period of ascendancy, Michael Hussey was a talisman – a symbol of Australian cricket's panache, vitality and fertility. The dwindling of his average from its zenith of 80 to a more mortal 50 has been a leading indicator of the country's cricket decline. Today he found a new role, shoring up the order of a rebuilding team with batting in some of his best vein, ending the day undefeated on 81.

Likewise unfinished, Hussey's partnership of 77 with Brad Haddin allowed Australia to feel ever so slightly ahead at the end of day two of this First Test at the Gabba. Still 40 in arrears of England, Australia will want a lead. Although Kevin Mitchell's surface will not deteriorate badly in the unseasonally mild weather, the hosts would not relish a substantial fourth-innings chase after three consecutive Test defeats.

England opened the day in search of early wickets, but with the sun out struggled even to generate appeals, let alone beat the bat. Stuart Broad's spell was like a pat-down airport search: invasive but not particularly effective and chiefly irritating. His best moment was a bouncer which Watson bore beneath the left arm, and at which the batsman, anxious to defend his stumps, issued a fresh-air kick as it fell. Otherwise there was too much to shoulder arms to and sway away from, which was nonetheless applauded monotonously in the slip cordon. A couple of clumping drives early on, including an on drive that Watson drilled down the ground from Finn's fifth ball, seemed to have the effect of discouraging the bowlers from pitching up, despite Siddle's first-day example. A run-out opportunity went begging; overthrows were conceded. This was not the New England so widely praised, but a hint of Ye Olde England during the long Australian ascendant.

Between times, nonetheless, Anderson picked up Watson with a good one, nicking to slip, and Ponting with a bad one, feathering down the leg side. Australia were glad of some stern resistance from Katich, a turtle of a batsman, who retracts his head at the first hint of danger and always has the long view in mind. His stabs, jabs and back-and-across step are not a method you'd recommend anyone emulate, but his head is still when he plays the ball and he defends right under his nose. The South Africans and Englishmen had some success bowling outside his eyeline last year – Flintoff picked him up in the gully at Lord's. For whatever reason, there seemed no such plan today. His eventual fall, bunting back a low caught-and-bowled, surprised the batsman almost as much as the bowler: it was his first such Test dismissal, as well as a useful first Ashes wicket for Finn, whose stoop to conquer involved almost all his 6ft-6 frame.

At 100 for three, there was abruptly the hint of danger. Hussey nicked his first ball just short of Swann at second slip, and Clarke ducked unblinkingly into a Broad bouncer. From Clarke, in fact, emanated signals of some distress, which cannot help but be interpreted in light of his chronic back problems. He never achieved fluency in a fifty-ball stay, and set off without looking at the umpire when he nicked a half-hearted pull as though glad the interlude was over.

When Swann resumed after lunch, Hussey came down the track to shovel him back down the ground for six and rocked back to pull three early boundaries. It evinced less a concerted plan from the batsman than erratic length from the bowler, perhaps from an excess of sprinkler dancing. Actually slightly flattered by three overs for 34, Swann looked momentarily vulnerable. He perked up finally when able to bowl to the left-handed North, whom he dismissed for the fourth time in six matches. Suddenly his bowling acquired a little more loop and shape, a mix of speeds, and greater economy: after his early prodigality, he gave away just two runs an over.

In the on-going battle between man and machine that is the referral system, meanwhile, Aleem Dar was outdoing Garry Kasparov against Deep Blue. For the fifth time in the game, Tony Hill upheld his judgement when England appealed for a catch at the wicket against Clarke (then on 1). Snicko later detected a tiny, indeterminate click, although this said little – studying the Australian vice-captain's struggles, you half imagined the noise to have come from his creaking back.

Australia's backbone was Hussey. He was unbending, the slow pitch feeding the pull shot he favours, the bowlers' inconsistency of line allowing him the singles he likes. He found a trustworthy partner in Haddin, who belied his reputation for peeling off exotic 40s with a strait-laced 22 in 105 minutes. England were on the brink of a new ball at 4.20 p.m. when the heavens suddenly opened, finally reminding us that we were in Brisbane rather than the milder south. The forecast for the next three days suggests few further problems overhead; England have a few at ground level to dispose of first.

26 NOVEMBER 2010
MICHAEL CLARKE AND MICHAEL HUSSEY

Two by Four

Number four is the hinge point in any batting order. Think Tendulkar, Lara, Pietersen. In days bygone, think Greg Chappell and Graeme Pollock, David Gower and Colin Cowdrey. If your number four is making runs, your team is probably ticking over nicely. If not, his failures can reverberate down the order.

In England last year, Australia's number four Michael Hussey could barely buy a run until the Oval Test. It seemed to set his team-mates' teeth on edge. The tale of Australian batting in Brisbane today was accordingly bittersweet. Hussey made a sterling undefeated 81. The trouble is that he is now batting at number five; a version of his earlier malaise has enveloped his successor at number four, Michael Clarke.

First the good news – for Australia anyway. Early on, Channel Nine's protractor, which measures the alleged deviation of balls after pitching, and is studied as seriously as ballistics testimony before the Warren Commission, had little to do. By the time Hussey took guard, however, the game was in the balance at 100 for three. He propped forward to his first ball from Steve Finn, which arced from a tentative edge towards Swann at second slip. On a quicker deck, the snick would have carried comfortably; here it fell tantalisingly short. Some batsmen in this match will blame the slow pitch for their dismissals; Hussey is one who should bless it.

For the last eighteen months, of course, far less has been coming out of Hussey's batting than has been going in. A cricketer with a Stakhanovite ethic, he reminds one of the comment attributed to his former state team-mate Graeme Wood after he was advised to relax: 'I'm working really hard on this relaxation business.' But the dwindling dividends of that physical and mental investment have sorely puzzled him. In the middle, Hussey has been lurching back and forward between strokeless defiance and headlong attack. In Mohali, he grafted almost three hours but scored from only every fifth ball he faced; in Bangalore, he played a sparkling cameo then chased a wide one. Returning home, he indulged his taste for pop philosophy by saying that he didn't 'feel the talk' about his place, and expressing the view that he was 'playing well inside myself'. Outside himself, he commenced the domestic season with three runs in three innings.

Then last week at the MCG, Hussey peeled off a domestic hundred, and a positive hundred at that, with 72 in boundaries. It's debatable whether such performances can be deemed to represent a restoration of that precious state of grace called 'form'; Mitchell Johnson, who took a fast, furious five-for in the same game, has here bowled like a drain. But at the very least it hinted that batting proficiency is only ever an innings away.

Here, as in Melbourne, Hussey set quickly about punishing even minor errors of length, the trampolining bounce tending to make short balls sit up for a batsman's delectation. He pulled Swann thrice early, Finn twice more, each shot comfortably controlled and kept to ground. After tea, Swann bowled to him with a deep mid-on and a deep mid-wicket, which he still bisected: in all, nine of Hussey's thirteen boundaries were cross-batted to leg. He seized on opportunities to drive too, and responded to a glare from Stuart Broad, which seems roughly equivalent to getting an earful from Aled Jones, by stroking him soundlessly through the covers – perhaps the shot of the day.

Now for the bad news. Clarke also made a hundred in the first innings of his most recent Sheffield Shield game, but when he batted low in the order in the second innings to save the aching discs in his lower back was gingerly walking singles as he drove the ball into the deep. Clarke told anyone who would listen that he was fine coming into this Test, giving himself a clean bill of health even on Shane Warne's new talk show, but his performance today suggested that you can't believe everything you see on television.

When Clarke's back first played up five years ago at Old Trafford, he batted like a man in a full body cast. Today he seemed resigned to limited mobility, and to be trying to play accordingly, but the conditions did not suit his forward press or his limited footwork. His travails against short-pitched bowling were painful for onlookers, and for him as well, especially when he nodded into a Broad bouncer as though he simply couldn't avoid it.

Clarke has made himself Australian cricket's marathon man – the only player being consistently selected in all forms of the game. He is trying to prove a point, but is now in danger of proving another. A year ago, Clarke seemed a banker to replace Hussey in the number four slot, yet his average since assuming the position as of right is just 20. Thirty in April, he should be in his batting prime. Australia needs more from number four: it will have to find it from somewhere.

27 NOVEMBER 2010

Day 3

Close of play: England 2nd innings 19–0
(AJ Strauss 11*, AN Cook 6*, 15 overs)

The first hour of the third day of the First Test contained 21 runs and the last hour 19 runs, although they were in their ways as integral to a fascinating contest as the 240 runs between times. Australia's survival of the first hour without losing a wicket was crucial to their dominance; England's similar survival at the end offers some hope for the morrow.

The balance of the day was almost entirely Australia's. Michael Hussey, 'Mr Cricket', fell five runs short of a double-hundred in five minutes short of 500 minutes, an innings encompassing 330 deliveries, a six, 26 fours, four threes, ten twos, and 53 singles – and which was as impressive as those vital statistics sound. It was model batting from a model professional. His head was bent as low over the ball at the end as at the start, like a schoolboy swotting over his homework.

With the bustling Brad Haddin, Hussey constructed a record-breaking 307-run stand on sturdy foundations, taking a careful 299 balls over their first hundred runs, 158 balls over their second, and 84 over their third. England now need to bat perhaps 150 overs, about twice as long as in their first innings, to salvage a draw; it is not beyond them by any means, but nor theoretically is a political comeback by Margaret Thatcher.

What will gall them is that it could easily have been otherwise. The first hour of the third day was the Test's tensest so far. Channel Nine are introducing new batsmen and bowlers this season with quaint identification portraits: Englishmen and Australians pose uneasily in strangely washed-out colours, which lend them the exsanguinated pallor of the stars of *Twilight*. Just for once, James Anderson bowled as menacingly as promised on screen, hungry for blood. He bent the ball both ways, used the full width of the crease, and beat the bat almost as often in eight overs as bowlers had in the rest of the game. There will be few better spells this summer, and few better unrewarded ones ever.

Again, the referral system was on trial – and, frankly, flunked. After fifteen hesitant and nervous minutes, Hussey (82) was hit on the pads by Anderson and given out immediately by Aleem Dar. When Hussey challenged, replays suggested that the ball would have hit the stumps but had landed a micron outside leg. If you recall, the referral system was meant to counteract umpiring 'howlers'; this was the kind of fifty-fifty lbw decision that batsmen would once have accepted as their occasional lot, hoping for better luck another day. Yet it was overturned.

Worse was to follow in Anderson's next over, when he bent a ball back into Hussey and hit him on the knee roll on the line of leg stump. This time Dar shook his head slightly;

so did Strauss, rather more wearily, having deployed his two referrals unsuccessfully the previous day; Anderson's head was sunk in his hands. It was hard to avoid the sense that Dar, like many an umpire before him, was erring on the side of caution, fearful of another mistake. In doing so, alas, he had perpetrated another, for replays showed the ball to be bisecting middle and leg. And so the endless quest for 'perfect' umpiring led to compound injustice, undermining an excellent official and cheating a deserving bowler. Strauss had previously come out agin the referral system. 'Cricket is about the umpires making decisions,' he observed last year, 'and players living and dying by those decisions.' Nothing occurred here to change his mind.

England did a reasonable job of keeping their cool under the circumstances, although some chagrined and martyred looks were exchanged, and a few words escaped the normally taciturn Anderson and the never knowingly outtalked Broad. The match at this stage was still finely poised. But as the sun emerged, the ball lost its shine, the fielders' legs grew heavy, and Australia began to pull away.

Hussey greeted Swann with dancing feet, launched him down the ground for four to go to 96, then drilled a hole in the covers with a well-timed jab at Broad to attain his twelfth Test century, second in consecutive first-class innings and second in consecutive Ashes innings – heavens, fans were wondering by now, what had all that fuss over his position been about? There was more to it, of course, and none knew better than Hussey, who celebrated with unusual abandon, including a fist-pump from the Lleyton Hewitt playbook. In doing so, he probably infringed all manner of trademarks – a cease and desist order from Hewitt's intellectual property lawyers is probably in the post.

What was perhaps just as interesting was that Haddin was very nearly as animated, giving his own punch of the fist as he ran through, and joining Hussey in a husky embrace. Cricketers enjoy a redemption story even more than fans; it's how they dream that their own bad luck/bad form will end. They see themselves routing their doubters amid standing ovations, making it all up to their suffering families – whom Hussey did indeed salute, with a wave to his wife (Mrs Cricket, presumably) and children.

Perhaps Haddin had his own situation in mind. No questions had been raised about his selection prior to the game, but this was his first Test match since March, and some critics had taken a shine to his proxy Tim Paine in England and India, as they had earlier talked up rivals like Darren Berry, Wade Seccombe and Graham Manou. Haddin resumed in the subdued mood in which he'd left off the night before, England restricting him by bowling wicket-to-wicket, although they needed to, because he unfailingly penalised deviations from the plan by the inexperienced Finn. It was by slashing a wide one from Finn backward of point then punching the overpitched follow-up forward of point that Haddin reached fifty in 134 balls and 190 minutes. He will seldom have batted longer for the milestone.

With that, Haddin upped the tempo. He scores in unusual areas: he drives straight, he cuts late, he hits on the up through cover, he wellies through mid-on with a strong bottom hand. He has an appealing laconicism: he doesn't fidget or filibuster; between deliveries, he usually holds his ground; between overs, he holds smiling mid-pitch chats. During one longueur today, he engaged Broad in a chat in the middle which seemed pleasingly expletive-free.

Haddin got into trouble only when he attempted to manhandle Collingwood, whose relief overs the Australians were intent on minimising in order to maximise the load on England's four specialist bowlers. On 63, he hit high rather than long down the ground, and the ball descended through the fingertips of Cook running back. But once bitten never shy, he carried on playing with freedom, using his feet and the air to collar Swann, and finally flat-batting down the ground for six to achieve his hundred, the second fifty of which had taken 88 balls.

Thereafter the partnership began accumulating decorations: biggest here, longest there, among most exasperating to England anywhere. When it reached 276, it became the highest of all time in Gabba Tests, in addition to being 200 more than England's longest collaboration in this game. Convinced by now of *Survivor*-like immunity, Haddin (114) top-edged a cavalier pull shot from Broad, which Anderson made a meal of at mid-wicket. England was not to see Haddin's back until Australia's lead was 189, when Collingwood caught sharply at slip, whereupon there was a belated and irrelevant clatter of wickets.

One of these was Hussey, swallowed at deep mid-wicket as he pulled for once in the air; another was Mitchell Johnson, who by rights should have been in after twenty minutes, and showed how this mattered by being bowled rather lamely. Steve Finn finished with his best Test figures, six for 125, although as a consolation this rather fell into the 'Apart-from-that-what-did-you-think-of-the-play-Mrs-Lincoln?' category.

To the first ball of England's second innings, Strauss padded up to Hilfenhaus, and for a batsman on a pair waited with impressive insouciance while the excited Australians referred Dar's not-out decision: it was, just, too high. The visiting captain and vice-captain negotiated the last hour dourly, only reducing the lead to 202 but avoiding further alarums. The first hour tomorrow should be at least as tense.

28 NOVEMBER 2010

Day 4

Close of play: England 2nd innings 309–1
(AN Cook 132*, IJL Trott 54*, 101 overs)

The first sound I heard on approaching the Gabba on day one of the First Test were the strains of 'The Great Escape' played for a radio station by the Barmy Army's trumpet sergeant Billy Cooper. Surely, I thought, they couldn't be rehearsing for strategic withdrawal already. The English press seemed so convinced of their own team's favouritism that surely the theme from *Rocky* would have been more appropriate.

For members of England's cricket community, though, a little barminess is never misplaced. Just like the last time, a strategic withdrawal is what this opening of the Ashes is proving to be, England having retreated so far for 101 overs and sustained only a single casualty. At stumps, having been outplayed for two and a half of the first three days, they led by 88 runs with a day to play. The effort was undergirded by Andrew Strauss and Alastair Cook's partnership of 188 in 398 balls, England's biggest in Ashes cricket at the Gabba for any wicket, although Cook's fluent two-hour century stand with Jonathan Trott was little less crucial, putting distance between the visitors and their hosts once England had erased their arrears.

The tension and hurry of the first day seemed long ago. In the first innings, Siddle felt close to wickets so constantly that he almost added a cradling of his head to the end of his regular follow-through. Today there was as little encouragement for the bowlers as there was lateral movement, save when a ball every so often hit one of the cracks marking the pitch darkly like fading operation scars on a pale abdomen.

Siddle's eighth over was Australia's best of the pre-lunch session. Strauss cover-drove a fullish ball for four to raise England's hundred in two and a half hours, but inside-edged the next to fine leg, then was hit on the gloves protecting his clavicle; he looked momentarily nonplussed. A quarter-hour later, he came down the pitch to Doherty and miscued as the ball hit the rough, but Johnson, advancing overexcitedly, floored the catch.

The moment passed. The pair buckled down anew, constructing their partnership as painstakingly and collaboratively as English journalists construct their expenses. Strauss looked less like a batsman avoiding a pair than one coming off back-to-back warm-up hundreds, neat and economical in everything he did, even in the perfunctory retracing of his guard between deliveries. Getting out to Marcus North will have annoyed him, but he is not the best batsman to do that, Sachin Tendulkar having contrived it eight weeks ago.

Compared to the callow youth of 2006–07 and the limited and somewhat vulnerable figure of last year, Cook was a revelation, accumulating invisibly but invincibly. In addition to his usual repertoire of cuts and nudges, he displayed a pull shot almost as powerful and fluent as Hussey's the day before, and even the occasional unostentatious cover drive. Four years ago in Perth, he marred his only previous Ashes hundred by falling late in the day. Here his concentration was cast iron to the last ball, and his fitness irreproachable.

Bowling circumstances today were not unfavourable. It was warm but not hot; with plenty of runs to play with, there was ample scope for attack. But conditions were very different to those that pertained a year ago when Hilfenhaus won the man-of-the-match award against West Indies. Today he seemed to lack some variety, a bouncer, or an extra turn of speed. In fact, according to Channel Nine's patented Gator Tracker, with which they monitor players' vital signs during the match, Hilfenhaus's heart rate varies more than his pace. At one stage, he was so grooved at 84mph that it was like he had slipped into cruise control.

Johnson was the gravest disappointment, his arm reaching Malinga-like lowness, with the result that, at his natural length, most deliveries were reaching England's batsmen, who tend to hang back anyway, at a comfortable waist height.

There was ample geeing-up for him. After one over, no fewer than seven team-mates ran past to ruffle his hair, pat his backside or maybe compliment him on his moustache. But he is wicketless so far here, and has taken three for 328 since his successful first innings in Mohali.

Watson, by contrast, was probably underbowled, despite his qualities as perhaps Australia's most consistent and certainly luckiest bowler of the last year. And it was a day on which Australia needed better luck than that they made themselves. Four years ago they were catching the chances put down by Johnson, by Clarke when Trott (34) square-cut Siddle in the air, and by Siddle when Cook (103) mishooked Hilfenhaus. The outstanding fielding effort of the day was a headlong dive to save a boundary by Queenslander Lee Carseldine, substituting for Katich, who was recuperating from an Achilles strain. The rewards for desperation otherwise accrued to England alone. It isn't an escape yet. But it has been great.

28 NOVEMBER 2010
PARTNERSHIPS

The Power of Two

The first day of the Gabba Test was crowned by cricket's supreme individual feat, the hat-trick, which for an instant makes the spectator forget the other twenty-one players involved in a game. It has been overshadowed since not by individual virtuosos but by partnerships – alike, different and intriguing.

On Saturday, Michael Hussey and Brad Haddin shut the light from England's bowlers, and eventually England's hopes. They were a study in contrasts: intense and driven left-hander, breezy and laconic right-hander. Today it was the turn of Andrew Strauss and Alastair Cook, captain and vice-captain, leader and heir, and rather more similar players.

That's not entirely a coincidence. Australians tend to believe in the principle of opposites attracting, and also causing bowlers problems of adjustment in line and length. Katich and Watson are the latest of many left-hand/right-hand opening combinations, including Morris and Barnes, Lawry and Simpson, Marsh and Boon, Slater and Taylor.

The last of these represented another classic and more general contrast, dasher and foil, known in England too. In fact, when two English openers last scored hundreds in the same innings of an Ashes Test, at Trent Bridge in 1938, the perpetrators were Charlie Barnett and Len Hutton, amateur aggressor and professional pragmatist. Barnett was 96 when the penultimate over of the opening session ended, but he was a man who suited himself. 'Don't worry about trying to give me the strike, son,' he told Hutton. 'We've given them enough cause for indigestion.'

Strauss and Cook are peas in a pod by comparison, left-handers strong square of the wicket and off their pads. They are accumulators rather than stroke-makers. Both fancy the pull shot. They run similarly between wickets, rather better than their Australian counterparts, neither pushing particularly hard, but alert for singles. Even their records run parallel, Cook's average being a run greater, Strauss's strike rate two runs faster.

They look so comfortable and complementary in each other's company it is a surprise to find that their average first-wicket stand is just over 40 – compared, for example, to Katich and Watson, who in twenty-six partnerings together have a mean stand of 55. Too often to be quite satisfactory, then, they have been like Cox and Box, one coming when the other is going.

Strauss, however, has argued that their similarity as batsmen is a strength of the partnership, that they understand one another's cues and watchwords: 'Being similar has helped us spot each other's difficulties more quickly.' Both, too, have come to Australia with a kindred sense of mission.

Today's killer stat was that Strauss commenced his second innings with an average in Australia (22.45) poorer than Mike Brearley's (22.7) – a failure or two away, perhaps, from becoming the butt of that standard Australian jibe about English specialist captains. Had he misjudged that first ball of the second innings even slightly, moreover, his record against Ben Hilfenhaus would have been six dismissals for 116 runs in 273 deliveries. He was possibly six inches away from turning a presumed weakness into a downright hoodoo.

Cook's Test record ex Australia of 3,866 runs at 46.57 suggests a player of pedigree; an Ashes average 20 runs less before this Test implies room for improvement. Like Strauss, too, he has played grade cricket in Australia, for Willetton in Perth. It will have left him with friends here in front of whom he would wish to do well.

Both have gone a way today not only to saving England's face, but to answering questions about themselves. Strauss scored almost half as many runs as he managed in the whole summer four years ago; Cook drew the sting from Ponting's pre-Test barb about him 'hanging on to his place by the skin of his teeth'.

For all the dissimilarities of the players involved, one feature of both the key partnerships of this Test has been their obvious personal harmony. When Hussey gave his roar of triumph on reaching his hundred on Saturday, Haddin gave a fist-pump of little less gusto. Having endured through the perilous morning to savour the sunny uplands of the afternoon, there was a sense of completed and shared journey. Strauss and Cook communicate by word, gesture and touch – their frequent little consultations, their fussy glove touches. They seldom say much, but seem to like the other to know that they are there, shortening the odds of the contest from eleven to one to eleven to two.

Batting – and, to a lesser degree, bowling – are tackled together. The contribution partners make to one another is not measured and has no obvious material reward, but is an index of cohesion. Interviewed before play today, Justin Langer talked about partnerships being integral to every great team. But this is axiomatic: partnerships are no less important, and perhaps more, to every more modest team that has aspirations to punch above its collective weight. A lot of this series will be about what players help others achieve – Cook and Strauss, and also Hussey and Haddin, have made positive starts.

29 NOVEMBER 2010

Day 5

Close of play: Australia 2nd innings 107–1 (26 overs)

Nobody was badly injured. The Movember moustaches of Mitchell Johnson and Peter Siddle may have raised some money for charity. Apart from that, today's final day of the First Ashes Test had virtually no redeeming feature for Australian cricket.

Alastair Cook and Jonathan Trott, meanwhile, batted as they might in their dreams, compiling the highest English partnership in Australia: Cook made the highest Test score at the Gabba, breaking the record set by Bradman in the ground's inaugural Test against Trott's native land.

The pitch wasn't quite as benign and featureless as all that. Long parallel lengthways cracks had opened, almost as though Jonathan Trott had taken his serial guard-marking on tour, and the ball jagged about when it hit them. There were chances, too, both from the bowling of Shane Watson. When Trott was 75, Clarke dropped the kind of slip catch for which the description 'regulation' was devised; when Cook was 222, Ponting dropped the kind of difficult, full-stretch slip catch which he used to make look 'regulation'.

But nothing is 'regulation' for this Australian cricket team, even the regulations. At 457 for one, Cook (209) turned Doherty in the air to short mid-wicket, where Ponting pitched forward to intercept at grass level. Ponting claimed the catch, albeit without much conviction, and the game ground to a halt while replays revolved inconclusively above. Having acquitted Hussey by a sliver of doubt on the third day, the system similarly exonerated Cook – again, it was probably a miscarriage of justice. Otherwise, the Gabbatoir was under new management, this sense consolidated by the probability that at least 90 per cent of the small crowd were English, sequestered in the southern corner of the ground once occupied by its raucous hill and raising a racket to match.

Cook played shots he can hardly have played for years. It was like someone rummaging through their favourite old clothes and deciding: yes, I used to really like that. Straight drive along the ground off the left-arm spinner? Might try that on. Feather fine-leg glance for four? Hmmm, still fits. Not that Cook ever became much more elegant for that. Even in complete control, he seems to be tucked up by the short ball, to jump in the air in defence, to stumble slightly as he turns to leg. Nor is his cover drive a thing of beauty: it relies too much on his hands, too little on the recommended transference of body weight, and involves him reaching for the ball. But the method is his, and it works. Cook zipped through the 190s with a scissor-sharp back cut from Doherty and a muscular hoick from North, becoming the fourth English double-centurion in Australia with a nurdle round the corner made easy by a misfield. His record, meanwhile, underwent a total makeover. His Ashes average went into the Test a meagre 26; it came out a neat 40.

Trott, meanwhile, became only the third batsman for England – one still hesitates to deem him an 'Englishman' – to commence an Ashes career with hundreds in back-to-back

Tests. The other two were archetypal Yorkshiremen, Herbert Sutcliffe and Maurice Leyland, at a time when it was proverbial that when Yorkshire was strong, England were strong. Cynics might say that the correlation is now between the strengths of England and South Africa.

Trott has been typed a one-pace batsman, but it is a pace a team could learn to love, and he essayed some shots of the highest class, in particular a back-foot drive and back cut off Doherty, which somehow threaded their way between a wide first slip and a deepish backward point for consecutive boundaries. His straight drive back over Watson's head for a one-bounce four bordered on impudence.

In the media box there was a great deal of record-delving. Parallel scorecards are few indeed. At their zenith in Melbourne in February 1912, England were 425 for one. It was while Australia were labouring in that Test match that a mannequin fell from an advertising blimp onto the outfield. 'Another bowler for you, Clem!' cried a wag in the crowd to the local captain, Hill. Ponting might have wished a similar intervention. Brisbane today turned on its most enervating weather of the Test match, the kind that has the shirt clinging to your back within minutes of moving outdoors, and after an hour or two becomes downright soporific. England's plan was clearly to weary the Australian bowlers ahead of the ensuing Adelaide Test, and the futility would have been as depleting as the physical exertion.

Strauss then declared at a mountainous 517 for one, hoping to take a few cheap wickets, and would have been disappointed that Collingwood dropped a catchable nick from Watson (17) from Swann's fifth ball. As it was, Strauss's counterpart made some golden hay, a crunching straight drive and a vintage pull shot from Finn's first two deliveries getting him under way, and a resounding maximum over mid-on from Swann speeding him to a forty-ball half-century.

Thus ended a Test match that seemed to last longer than its five days, so markedly was it divided between the first fifteen wickets falling for 403 and the last seven for 962, between the Australian ascendancy and the English – a draw, but one in which the register of redeeming features trended only one way.

29 NOVEMBER 2010
MITCHELL JOHNSON

Scarred for Life?

Journalists at the Gabba today found relief amid the relentless accumulation of statistics by chortling over the story of a hapless woman in Westfield, Massachusetts, who because of her Twitter handle of @theashes has found herself trapped helplessly in online banter about the series, despite her protestations: 'I am not a freaking cricket match!!!' and 'What the hell is a wicket?'

The latter question has probably also crossed the mind of Mitchell Johnson, who for five days has found himself likewise ensnared with no hope of escape. And for all his effectiveness in the First Test – none for 170, a duck, a costly dropped catch – he might as well have been half a world away on the internet.

Like Longfellow's archer, who shot an arrow into the air that fell to earth he knew not where, Johnson seems only to have the foggiest notion where the ball is going any more – one arrow today fell to earth in the gutter at fine leg. Bowled round the wicket from wide on the crease, it was comfortably the worst Ashes wide since Steve Harmison's went down in infamy, and the most egregious Australian wide for twenty years before that, when Chris Matthews dramatically lost his bearings on the first morning of the Ashes in Brisbane – the last time, not coincidentally, Australia had a team as modest as this one.

Australian cricket has tried just about everything with Johnson. At first, in search of a ready-made replacement for Glenn McGrath, it promoted him to the hilt, entrusting him with the new ball and the role of new enforcer, with some success. In South Africa last year, he suddenly began bringing the ball back in to right-handers, late and at pace – the left-arm quick's version of the philosopher's stone.

Then it went awry, in a small way at Cardiff, and in a big, short, wide way at Lord's. 'I was surprised at how big the Ashes were in England,' he said later, explaining things so ingenuously as to deepen the puzzle. Some ascribed it to a low front arm; others blamed domestic tribulations; still others sensed a kind of friction between id and superego, with Johnson letting thought intrude on instinctual processes.

As a result, Australian cricket began hiding Johnson, or at least relieving him of some of his responsibilities, again with some success. One of the many quirks of Johnson's record is that he performs best as a second-change bowler, when he has obtained 33 wickets at 23, compared to 133 wickets at 32 the rest of the time. But this could only ever have been an interim measure: the whole point of Johnson, in an increasingly medium-paced country, is to bowl fast, for which he needs a new, hard, shiny ball.

So Australian cricket has recently begun vaunting him again. 'Our leading bowler for a long time and one of the leading bowlers in world cricket,' said chairman of selectors Andrew Hilditch in announcing his inclusion for this Test. But leading them where? At the press conference before this game, Johnson talked up the idea of bombarding England's captain because . . . well, it sounded like because someone, a ventriloquising coach or an official, had told him this was a good idea. It was far more in character for Johnson when he began expanding on the detail of his tattoo, during which he drifted into a metrosexual reverie, leaving himself open to the urging that he spend less time worrying about what is on his arm and more on where it is pointing.

That would be unfair. Johnson is a hard-working cricketer, dedicated, team-oriented and formidably fit. Alone among Australia's attack for the last two years, he has kept himself on the park and ready for action at all times. And it is not his fault alone that when he is exposed at Test level, he is revealed full frontal. For there is one solution to the Johnson enigma that Australian cricket has not pursued, and that is actually letting Australian cricket sort him out as it does others and always has – by forcing him to work on his game at first-class level.

Johnson was spotted early, designated a 'once in a lifetime' bowler by Dennis Lillee, sent to the Academy, funnelled through the Centre of Excellence, introduced to international cricket at under-19 level and handled with gloves of the softest and most expensive kid throughout. At some stage in this process he ceased being Mitchell Johnson the cricketer and became the Mitchell Johnson Project – a kit of components with instructions, made to measure for the twenty-first century by a retinue of coaches and consultants to spare him the rigours of figuring the game out for himself.

In a country that prides itself on a Darwinian sporting culture, he has become a strange anomaly, Australia's most inexperienced experienced cricketer. In his thirtieth year, although he has earned thirty-eight Test caps, he has played only sixty-nine first-class games in all; at twenty-one, by comparison, Steve Finn has already played forty-eight.

His returns to domestic cricket are only ever brief and hardly ever indicative: he came into this game off a hundred and a five-for in Melbourne. But if the selectors crave consistency from him, why do they not let him find it, by playing interstate cricket for a prolonged period, and by solving the game according to his own lights?

The day at the Gabba ended with two unrelated announcements, the first that Qantas had offered the hapless Massachusetts tweeter a free trip to Australia in order to experience the game so perplexing her, and to answer her questions about what a wicket is. The second announcement was that while Australia's Gabba XI was being transferred intact to Adelaide, pace bowlers Ryan Harris and Doug

Bollinger have been added to the squad. Mitchell Johnson's chances of rediscovering what a wicket is during the Second Test thereby narrowed quite sharply.

FIRST TEST   Brisbane Cricket Ground, Woolloongabba, Brisbane
25–29 November 2010
Toss   England   **Match drawn**

ENGLAND 1st innings			R	M	B	4	6	SR
*AJ Strauss	c Hussey	b Hilfenhaus	0	2	3	0	0	0.00
AN Cook	c Watson	b Siddle	67	283	168	6	0	39.88
IJL Trott		b Watson	29	62	53	5	0	54.71
KP Pietersen	c Ponting	b Siddle	43	95	70	6	0	61.42
PD Collingwood	c North	b Siddle	4	9	8	1	0	50.00
IR Bell	c Watson	b Doherty	76	183	131	8	0	58.01
†MJ Prior		b Siddle	0	1	1	0	0	0.00
SCJ Broad	lbw	b Siddle	0	1	1	0	0	0.00
GP Swann	lbw	b Siddle	10	21	9	1	0	111.11
JM Anderson		b Doherty	11	38	22	2	0	50.00
ST Finn		not out	0	1	0	0	0	–
EXTRAS	(lb 8, w 7, nb 5)		20					
TOTAL	(all out; 76.5 overs; 360 mins)		260	(3.38 runs per over)				

FoW	1-0	(Strauss, 0.3 ov),	2-41	(Trott, 13.6 ov),
	3-117	(Pietersen, 37.3 ov),	4-125	(Collingwood, 39.5 ov),
	5-197	(Cook, 65.3 ov),	6-197	(Prior, 65.4 ov),
	7-197	(Broad, 65.5 ov),	8-228	(Swann, 69.2 ov),
	9-254	(Bell, 76.1 ov),	10-260	(Anderson, 76.5 ov)

BOWLING	O	M	R	W	ECON	
BW Hilfenhaus	19	4	60	1	3.15	(2nb, 2w)
PM Siddle	16	3	54	6	3.37	(2nb, 2w)
MG Johnson	15	2	66	0	4.40	
SR Watson	12	2	30	1	2.50	(1nb, 3w)
XJ Doherty	13.5	3	41	2	2.96	
MJ North	1	0	1	0	1.00	

AUSTRALIA 1st innings			R	M	B	4	6	SR
SR Watson	c Strauss	b Anderson	36	113	76	6	0	47.36
SM Katich	c &	b Finn	50	159	106	5	0	47.16
*RT Ponting	c †Prior	b Anderson	10	34	26	1	0	38.46
MJ Clarke	c †Prior	b Finn	9	76	50	0	0	18.00
MEK Hussey	c Cook	b Finn	195	462	330	26	1	59.09
MJ North	c Collingwood	b Swann	1	6	8	0	0	12.50
†BJ Haddin	c Collingwood	b Swann	136	374	287	16	1	47.38
MG Johnson		b Finn	0	32	19	0	0	0.00
XJ Doherty	c Cook	b Finn	16	43	30	2	0	53.33
PM Siddle	c Swann	b Finn	6	7	11	1	0	54.54
BW Hilfenhaus		not out	1	16	10	0	0	10.00
EXTRAS	(b 4, lb 12, w 4, nb 1)		21					
TOTAL	(all out; 158.4 overs; 662 mins)		481	(3.03 runs per over)				

FoW   1-78   (Watson, 25.2 ov),   2-96   (Ponting, 33.2 ov),
      3-100   (Katich, 36.1 ov),   4-140   (Clarke, 51.2 ov),
      5-143   (North, 52.5 ov),   6-450   (Haddin, 145.3 ov),
      7-458   (Hussey, 148.6 ov),   8-462   (Johnson, 152.3 ov),
      9-472   (Siddle, 154.4 ov),   10-481   (Doherty, 158.4 ov)

BOWLING	O	M	R	W	ECON	
JM Anderson	37	13	99	2	2.67	(1w)
SCJ Broad	33	7	72	0	2.18	(1nb, 1w)
GP Swann	43	5	128	2	2.97	
ST Finn	33.4	1	125	6	3.71	
PD Collingwood	12	1	41	0	3.41	(2w)

ENGLAND 2nd innings			R	M	B	4	6	SR
*AJ Strauss	st †Haddin	b North	110	267	224	15	0	49.10
AN Cook		not out	235	625	428	26	0	54.90
IJL Trott		not out	135	362	266	19	0	50.75
EXTRAS	(b 17, lb 4, w 10, nb 6)		37					
Total	(1 wicket dec; 152 overs; 630 mins)		517	(3.40 runs per over)				

FoW   1-188   (Strauss, 66.2 ov)

BOWLING	O	M	R	W	ECON	
BW Hilfenhaus	32	8	82	0	2.56	(3nb, 1w)
PM Siddle	24	4	90	0	3.75	(3nb, 2w)
MJ North	19	3	47	1	2.47	
MG Johnson	27	5	104	0	3.85	(1w)
XJ Doherty	35	5	107	0	3.05	
SR Watson	15	2	66	0	4.40	(2w)

AUSTRALIA 2nd innings			R	M	B	4	6	SR
SR Watson		not out	41	119	97	4	0	42.26
SM Katich	c Strauss	b Broad	4	22	16	0	0	25.00
*RT Ponting		not out	51	96	43	4	1	118.60
EXTRAS	(b 4, lb 1, w 1, pen 5)		11					
TOTAL	(1 wicket; 26 overs; 119 mins)		107	(4.11 runs per over)				

FoW   1-5   (Katich, 5.2 ov)

BOWLING	O	M	R	W	ECON	
JM Anderson	5	2	15	0	3.00	
SCJ Broad	7	1	18	1	2.57	(1w)
GP Swann	8	0	33	0	4.12	
ST Finn	4	0	25	0	6.25	
KP Pietersen	2	0	6	0	3.00	

Part III

SECOND TEST

Adelaide Oval
3–7 December 2010
England won by an innings and 71 runs

Winds of Change

An old joke runs that it is harder to get out of the Australian cricket team than into it. The word in Adelaide today was that it is ripe for reconsideration.

Due for makeover in the Second Test is Australia's four-member specialist attack, which toiled fruitlessly for the better part of two days of the First as three English batsmen broke three figures. Andrew Hilditch's selection panel looks set to drop Mitchell Johnson for the first time in his three-year career. Ben Hilfenhaus, who is said to have twinged a hamstring in Brisbane, may also make way.

That entails Test recalls for Doug Bollinger and Ryan Harris, who were added to the squad in the aftermath of the draw at the Gabba. It is not an altogether easy fit, with Johnson, a Test centurion, probably giving way at number eight to Xavier Doherty, who has two first-class half-centuries in 59 innings and an average of 13.7. But teams generally find themselves shorter of wickets than runs at Adelaide, and it is the kind of bold selection many have called for, showing what Shane Warne now describes as 'cojones'. In long-term prognostications, in fact, most pundits deemed Adelaide Oval the likeliest venue for a draw in the Ashes summer. But then, they also deemed the Gabba the likeliest place for a result, and the sides took eleven wickets each.

This result has confounded most everyone. An hour after stumps at the Gabba when I checked *The Times* website, the headline read 'England Triumphant'. Steady on, I thought, and so did someone else, because an hour later it had been scaled back to 'England escape with draw'. Hmmm, still not quite right. By now curious, I returned in another hour to find the report of my esteemed colleague Mike Atherton bearing the headline 'England's ascendancy'. Probably a little closer to the mark – the last two days, anyway. 'Australia's descendancy' would also have fitted the circumstances.

Quite what the result means in the balance of the series may not actually be much. Australia had much the better of the first draw of last year's Ashes then were soundly beaten at Lord's; England held a decided edge for much of the second draw at Edgbaston, then were utterly monstered at Headingley. Players are rather more practical than onlookers. They are apt to draw lines beneath games and start afresh, leaving it to the likes of us to speculate about 'momentum'.

In truth, the slowness of the pitch at the Gabba tended to obscure the shortcomings of both teams. The majority of players in both sides had modest to poor Tests. Cook, Strauss, Trott and Bell impressed, but Anderson looked the business only for an hour and a half, and the rest of the attack was inconsistent. When Pietersen donated a lazy four overthrows in Australia's second innings, it looked like someone a little frustrated by a lack of attention.

Apart from their star turns, Hussey, Haddin and Siddle, the Australians performed humbly, struggling to get into the game. Although it is Johnson's psychology that is presently being pulled apart as if he were an episode of *Oprah*, Hilfenhaus was perhaps as much a let-down, with a wicket after three deliveries, no more from the remaining 303, dropping generally a yard and a half short, and exhibiting little variety. An opening bowler need not be the fastest, Glenn McGrath being a classic instance of making up in nous what he lacked in knots. But he needs to have a presence, disturbing to opponents and reassuring to his captain, and this, in Brisbane, Hilfenhaus conspicuously lacked.

The other player to arrive in Adelaide on seemingly borrowed time is Marcus North, still to find a neap tide in his batting after the flood of five hundreds and the ebb of seventeen single-figure scores in his first twenty Tests. 'I'm a big fan of loyalty,' said his captain of North during the preliminaries to the Gabba Test, as though the only alternative was disloyalty. But if we're to use such emotive phraseology, what sort of loyalty is being shown Usman Khawaja, Callum Ferguson or even Cameron White when their way is barred by a batsman with a home Test average of 20.8?

Hilditch and his colleagues may also be missing a trick. In the last few years, perhaps because of a general decline in overall quality, perhaps because the incessancy of international cricket is depreciating its assets faster, debutant players have had disproportionate impacts. Consider the current England team. Andrew Strauss, Alastair Cook, Jonathan Trott and Matt Prior all made hundreds in their first Tests; Kevin Pietersen top-scored in both innings of his; Ian Bell made 70 in his. Likewise did Australia's one real experiment of the last two years, Phil Hughes, have an immediately rejuvenating effect on Australia's top order, even if the bush telegraph soon spread the word about his technical shortcomings.

Such case studies argue not for continuity, but turnover, against a 'loyalty' that phases into obstinacy, and in favour of choosing hungry cricketers whose methods have not been heavily scrutinised by opponents and whose physiques have not been ravaged by nonstop competition. To be fair, Australia's selectors did introduce a new cap at the Gabba in Doherty, even if the theory Hilditch espoused that a left-arm orthodox bowler would be a 'better option' against 'a predominantly right-handed English middle order' remained untested when 156 of his 210 second-innings deliveries were to left-handers Cook and Strauss.

Rain fell in Adelaide yesterday and thunderstorms are predicted today, but the expectation for the next five days is congenial to uninterrupted play, with the probability that the two teams will need every minute in which to conjure a result from new curator Damian Hough's pitch. The batsmen who had no impact in Brisbane will be eyeing it covetously, particularly Michael Clarke, who averages 102.4 here, and Paul Collingwood, who averages 228, albeit from one Test. The bowlers? Two already look like they will be otherwise engaged.

Day 1

Close of play: England 1st innings 1–0 (AJ Strauss 0*, AN Cook 0*, 1 over)

It was the battle of the losers in Adelaide today, between the two countries who would not be hosting the football World Cup for the foreseeable future. Misery loves company, and there is something consoling about tradition too: no matter how many brown paper bags change hands at FIFA, Australia and England will always have each other. So there was something rather warming and reassuring about the preparatory rites of the Second Test: all rise for the national anthem, and let's salute the red, white, blue and green, the last provided by the Milo munchkins, lined up to mix their corporate message with the patriotic ones.[1]

There had, however, to be a winner from between the losers, and on this first day that was emphatically, irrefutably and astonishingly England, despite them losing what looked like a handy toss, despite their middling-to-poor record at this ground, and despite it being not ten days since they were dumped on their backsides at the Gabba by a marauding Peter Siddle – an event that now seems almost like it occurred in a previous series.

Such are Adelaide's genteel customs and its reputation for flat pitches that it hosts the kind of Test you might be tempted

---

[1]For those uninitiated in Australian culinary culture, Milo is a chocolate powder made by Nestle that makes milk more congenial to the juvenile palate; the nearest English equivalent would be Ovaltine. The traditional green of its can has been adopted as the colour of Milo In2Cricket, the littlies' form of the game, representatives of whom lined up with the respective teams at each playing of the national anthem, and played in luncheon intervals.

to wander into a little late. If you did this morning, you never will again: the first ten minutes were electric, involving more wickets than fell on the last two days at the Gabba.

From Anderson's fourth ball, Watson set off for a nervous single on the on side, catching Katich slightly unawares, but not Trott, who darted quickly to his right, and threw the stumps down from side-on with the Australian not even in the frame. In front of Chappell Stands solid with St George Crosses, English fielders piled on like footballers celebrating a World Cup hat-trick.

Early losses are one thing; self-inflicted wounds another. Katich's was the sort of death by misadventure that rocks a dressing room, still to seat itself comfortably, still to obtain the day's first cups of tea or sports drinks, maybe still straining to detect early movement on television. Passing a batsman yet to face a ball was certainly not the manner in which Ponting would have imagined batting in his 150th Test.

In the recent stages of his career, Ponting has sometimes looked overanxious to make early contact with the ball. The South Africans two years ago worked on the theory that the right avenue to Ponting in his first half-dozen deliveries was just outside his eyeline, where his tendency was to push with hard hands: they had him caught in the cordon first ball at Perth and Sydney. Ponting's first ball from Anderson was even better, tight on off stump, compelling a stroke and eliciting an edge. Both captains on winning the toss this series have now been out within five minutes of the start.

Over the last couple of days, Michael Clarke has been a model of fastidious professionalism, undertaking lengthy net sessions, tiring out arms with his avidity for throwdowns, talking about his technique in a press conference, generally announcing himself ready for a big one. Last out of the practice area yesterday, he chirpily thanked the net bowlers whom he'd politely enslaved. His hundred here was instrumental in Australia's Ashes triumph four years ago and he has added two more since.

Again, though, Anderson found close to the ideal length, Clarke rather sauntered into his drive, and Swann collected a second catch. To think that there had been so much learned debate before the series about Anderson's ability to swing the Kookaburra: here he was making it laugh. His bowling coach David Saker has described him as a potential challenger to Dale Steyn as the world's number one quick bowler. On the evidence of today, he might soon be more than a challenger.

The match was ten minutes old, and three batsmen with a total average at Adelaide of 234 had been removed. Two for three was the worst start to a Test by Australia against anybody. The Adelaide Oval's defiantly analogue 1912 scoreboard was somehow apposite for the scoreline: this was no time for a noisy advertisement or a pop video. It brought to mind the famous photograph of Australia's second-innings nought for three at the Gabba sixty years ago. That, though, was in the middle of a match on a mudheap; here we were on the first morning of a Test on reputedly Australia's most benign cricket surface; here the Australian contingent on the hill cheered the first boundary as though Mafeking had been relieved.

Australia would have been 12 for four had Anderson held a return catch low to his left when Hussey (3) chipped one back.

But it was blindingly hot, Broad and Finn struggled with their lengths, and Hussey and Watson put the pitch in truer perspective by scoring with impressive fluency, even panache; indeed, with the bowlers pitching up in search of swing, and fields configured to attack, there were ample scoring opportunities.

Hussey looked at his compact, industrious best, turning the strike over busily, while Watson drove five boundaries in his first 30 with that confident two-stage front-foot stride, then sent Australia to lunch in good heart by pulling Finn off the front foot for four to reach his half-century. But, as here last year, he drove carelessly at Anderson soon after resuming, a shot as arrogant and foolhardy as lighting a cigar with a $100 note, and Australia were almost back where they started. For although Hussey was by now deeply entrenched, his state colleague North is taking baby steps towards form. The run rate dwindled, as Swann was treated with caution and Anderson with downright suspicion; the wicket fell, as it sometimes does, to the bowler least fancied, Finn, who drew from North a shot without a name, a poke very nearly an afterthought, followed instantly by a pang of regret.

As at the Gabba, Hussey looked to Haddin to help him pick up the pieces. There were now rather too many. Hussey used his feet vivaciously to Swann, but fell after five hours' hard graft, and Haddin provided some delectable shots, then was perplexed how to operate in the company of Australia's elongated tail – Johnson's batting, or at least the promise of it, had provided some lower-order ballast. Haddin reached a fluent fifty by hoisting Anderson over fine leg but was bounced out soon after by Broad.

Late in the day, Xavier Doherty drove Anderson through the covers on the up for four. Nice shot for Doherty, but not a bad indication for England: if Doherty is confident enough to have such a dart, then there is nothing much amiss with this pitch. Australians will need a lot to go right for the general national sporting outlook to improve in the next week.

3 DECEMBER 2010
ENGLAND IN THE FIELD

Killer Looks

Adelaide is burdened with a reputation – unfortunate, unfair but also kind of fun – as the serial-killer capital of Australia, the 'City of Churches' doubling as the 'City of Corpses'. Bowlers would probably agree. The average first innings of the last fifteen Tests here is a bloodstained 517; four sadistic double hundreds have been committed since 2003.

Which doesn't mean it is impossible to claim twenty wickets. But it does mean you must seize every opportunity, lest batsmen dash you against its short square boundaries, and cook you in its enervating heat. England's accomplishment today was not necessarily to generate more wicket opportunities than usual, but to accept all but one very difficult chance, and between times to keep the game fantastically tight.

The first thirteen deliveries of the Second Test, as will long be remembered, especially by those who arrived a little late, presented three chances: a run-out and two nicks to second slip. Most England sides in Australia in my lifetime would have missed one at least; a few would have missed the lot, and spent the rest of the day kicking the ground, cursing the gods and mentally preparing excuses for their ghosted columns. Today you could call to mind that worn-out word of modern coaching, 'execution', because it could also be applied in a colloquial sense. Katich, Ponting and Clarke could not have been despatched more peremptorily had they been lined up against a wall and shot.

As the day unfolded, England were hardly less impressive in the field. Chases were full tilt. Diving saves were routine. Bell, despite glasses that look less suitable for fielding than for watching *Avatar* in 3D, made one electric interception at point; even Finn threw himself around, looking like a frisky antelope.

There was some sloppiness in Brisbane, Anderson's drop in the first innings and Pietersen's all-too-casual four overthrows in the second innings the most heinous lapses. Today, both were on top of their form. When Strauss called Anderson in from deep backward square leg to a close-to-the-wicket on the on side, he fairly sprinted in, despite the heat, despite his overs. Pietersen also took a smart catch, only his fifth against Australia, and used his huge reach at gully effectively.

Shane Watson endured through the early chaos. Sometimes against Swann he was stretching so far forward as to touch the knee roll of his right pad on the ground, as though he was proposing marriage, or maybe genuflecting to Warnie. As Swann approached, too, Watson looked to be shuffling his feet in the crease, as if to disrupt the spinner's length; he undertook this challenge still more decisively ten minutes from lunch when he slog-swept in the direction of the statue of Adelaide's founder, Colonel Light, atop the hill overlooking the ground. It testified to the power of modern bats that Watson imparted the force of a flail without significant wind-up or follow-through. But England were ready for Watson, posting two gullies in anticipation of his hard hands and poor concentration around breaks.

Again, the go-to guy Hussey was gone-to. His shouldering arms no longer sends a tremor down Australian spines, as it did in England last year, and his defensive bat now seems to descend in ample time, and almost to be waiting for the ball. As at his zenith, he is acquiring busily, advancing a few paces with every nudge and nurdle, as though a single is his default setting. Shortly before tea, he worked Finn to leg and set off at such a gallop that he almost lapped his partner in completing three.

Yet England's bowlers, commendably full, made Hussey work for every run. Adelaide's boundaries beckoned, shaved still further by a boundary rope for the sake of additional advertising, but there was little on offer to cut or pull. Having made the pull shot his signature in Brisbane, Hussey played it today just once, for a single off Finn.

It is in the final sessions of hot days in Australia that attentions often stray and fielding teams unravel. England remained on the qui vive. Collingwood had stood at slip to Swann for twenty-six overs when he finally received a nick from Hussey; he caught it. Strauss was at short mid-wicket for the low-flying catch when he sprawled to make a save, and took advantage of Doherty's double hesitation to run him out from the prone position; short-leg Cook rugby-passed the return to

Prior even though he had his back turned on the runners.

The Australia of old made a leitmotif of such quicksilver routines. The Australia of new dropped five catches in England's second innings in Brisbane, and it is England that are becoming the streamlined and efficient unit, performing their tasks not just well but easily, as if it were second nature. Despite the city's reputation, this bore no resemblance to the work of a serial killer. It was, instead, that of the most clinical and cold-blooded assassin.

4 DECEMBER 2010

Day 2

Close of play: England 1st innings 317–2
(AN Cook 136*, KP Pietersen 85*, 89 overs)

First, some background. Four years ago, England dominated the first two days of the Adelaide Test. Two batsmen made fat hundreds. McGrath and Warne took a solitary wicket between them. The Barmy Army swooned with admiration. Three days later, England lost – worse, they were disgraced.

OK, although it will never be entirely unnecessary where England are concerned, that's the cricket-is-a-funny-game stuff out of the way. England are as far ahead in this Second Test as it is almost possible for a team to be after two days, and Australia will have the devil's own job avoiding defeat – there is, of course, no Warne and McGrath now, nor miracle-working Langer, Hayden and Gilchrist either.

Alastair Cook played in that game four years ago. He made 27 and 9, part of a decidedly modest series for him and rather a lot of his mates. He has so far been on the field for all but sixty-six minutes of this series, faced 842 balls, made 438 runs and been dismissed once – on 25 November, for the record, which if things go on this way might almost be declared a national holiday.

The Cook of today is no more obtrusive than four years ago. He plays plainly, almost politely, refraining from such impertinences as reverse sweeps, ramps and dilscoops, and with a straighter bat than a Foreign Office spokesman. He moved to 47 with three boundaries in four deliveries from Bollinger. He went to 78 by cutting three consecutive boundaries from Doherty, and proceeded to his century with a wristy slash for four from the same bowler. Otherwise he ticks over at one steady, solid, soothing pace – and just doesn't get out.

Actually, he *was* given out today, at 64, by Ray Erasmus, having taken his eye off a Siddle bouncer that had grazed his arm. He sought the referral instantly, even assertively, using the bat as the upright of the 'T' symbol. 'Out? Ump? Come, come. I don't think so. Very well, we shall have to sort this out.' Third umpire Bill Doctrove promptly did so. Cook continued – as, in roasting temperatures, did the cooking.

The first few minutes of the day were almost as eventful as yesterday's, with both captains guilty of misjudgements – small but significant. Just as his rival late in his career has developed the tic of going searching for the ball early, Strauss has become a little cute about letting the ball go, wafting his bat over the ball like a matador caping a bull. It cost him at Lord's last year, when he let the second ball of the second day clip off, and did again today, when he allowed the third ball of the day from Bollinger clear passage, only for it to snip the off bail.

Because it is necessarily exploratory, opening the batting is full of such infinitesimal judgements. Strauss could even claim that his non-shot selection was vindicated by Hawk-Eye, which mysteriously pronounced that the delivery would barely have grazed the target. But leaving on length – as Strauss also did to the first ball of the second innings in Brisbane – is frankly better left until a proper evaluation of bounce is made, particularly when one is unfamiliar with the bowler, as Strauss is with Bollinger. England's captain has missed few tricks in this game, but this was one.

Australia's captain may have missed one soon after, when Trott (6) set off skittishly after thick-edging to square leg, the same environs he had been patrolling yesterday when Watson called Katich through fatally. This time the outcome was different. Cook turned his partner sternly back, and the fielder at mid-wicket was a left-hander, Doherty, who had to run around the ball before collecting it, and whose unavoidably hurried throw missed the stumps. When the ball is new and hard, and the ball is likelier to travel square than straight, mid-wicket should really be right-handed: Trott the fielder would have comfortably run out Trott the batsman.

The morning's other opportunity was not a matter of inches, or even of feet, but of hands, Hussey's, whose failed to close around a thick edge at gully offered by Trott (10) from Bollinger; his legs closed too late to prevent two runs being taken too. Beaten by the ball's slight arc? Defeated by sweaty palms? Whatever the case, Hussey, never po-faced, looked up like he'd seen a ghost. Had Johnson grassed it, he would have been placed on suicide watch.

England would have been, and should have been, 21 for two, with the mercurial Pietersen to follow. As it was, one could feel the hiss of the pressure drop. As numbers two and three at Brisbane, Cook and Trott looked prepared to bat for a week had not Strauss declared. They suggested similar permanence here, and have now added 543 runs for the second wicket from 874 deliveries in the series for twice out.

Encouragement for the bowlers lasted the first hour, Siddle gaining appreciable sideways movement when he pitched the ball up. In his sixth over he was driven imperiously on the up through point for four by Cook, and followed up with a peach of a ball that pitched leg and detoured round a groping bat to miss off. Great *mano e mano* stuff, this: the bowler prepared to be driven in order to draw the batsman forward; the batsman prepared to drive. Cook let the next go as it sizzled through at sternum height – détente resumed.

After lunch, Siddle tried a different approach, bouncing Cook with two men back, while Harris tried something similar to Trott with Ponting camped at leg gully. After his early tremors, in fact, Trott experienced some aftershocks involving the bouncer. To a rearing delivery from Bollinger on 44, he repeated the cramped, almost involuntary pull shot that cost him his wicket against Australia A, which this time fell safely. When Trott was 76, Haddin also parried rather than held a flying top edge from Harris.

Trott was actually somewhat less fastidious than in

Brisbane, where he was taking longer to get ready than a supermodel, although this only limited the distance by which he has been the match's fussiest batsman rather than threatening his status. He marks his guard with a long repeated scrape of his right boot, which is becoming as much his signature as the Moonwalk was Michael Jackson's. He even marked his guard at the end of the last over before lunch: again, three slow, deliberate scrapes as if to mark a spot under which treasure was buried. As it was, Australia's short-pitched policy paid dividends when Clarke dived smartly to his left at mid-wicket to hold a shot off the hip – Trott can expect to see rather less bowling in his own half of the pitch this tour.

The sight of Pietersen wafting down the wicket to Doherty excited Australian thoughts of further inroads. Pietersen stood tall to cut his second ball for four, and sent the next floating over point from a thick outside edge. There was a flurry of interest in his patchy record against slow left-armers, who have dismissed him seventeen times in sixty-seven Tests.

In fact, Pietersen has an attribute which should by rights serve him well against left-arm spin, which is a huge front-foot stride, using all his 6ft 4in. He succumbed to Steve O'Keefe at Bellerive by failing to use his full stretch. He did not make that mistake here. In fact, say it soft, because Pietersen really needs no more encouragement than is absolutely necessary, but he looked, at times, a little magnificent, the reach providing the half-volleys, the wrists providing the batspeed. He whisked two not dissimilar balls from North through cover and just forward of square leg for four – the kind of shots that don't just disarm a bowler but mortify him. Where to bowl next?

Pietersen ended the day fifteen runs short of his first hundred in eighteen Tests, Cook with his third hundred in four Tests, Australia having taken three English wickets in their last 241 overs of bowling in this series – about one per new ball. They will have the opportunity to bat again on this blameless pitch, but England could keep them waiting a very long time indeed.

4 DECEMBER 2010
RICKY PONTING

Little Big Man

'Australia will fight back today!! No other choice . . .'

'Patience is the key for Australia and must stick to it and have good body language!!!'

If Ricky Ponting was following Shane Warne on Twitter this morning – and one suspects he enjoys nothing more – he'd have appreciated Warnie's jaunty tone, but perhaps hoped for a little more content. Fight back? Stick to it? Well, yeah. Hey, mate, how about some of that advice on field placement that you offered so helpfully in India?

Alas, Warnie was unable to provide Ponting with further elaboration, being too busy swapping tweets with Piers Morgan and vaunting his underpants (seriously, he has a brand, called Spinners). So Ponting was on his own – and frankly, when a captain has made a first-baller in a total of 245, and seen the opposition rack up 317 for two in reply, leadership must be a very lonely life indeed. The talk today was all of Cook – but spare a thought for the cooked.

As far as his captaincy was concerned, Ponting did not have an altogether bad day. Had Hussey held Trott in the gully and reduced England to 21 for two with Pietersen to come, Australia would have felt themselves well and truly in the game; likewise had one of Cook's early gropings elicited an edge.

When the Australians laid into Trott after lunch from short of a length, they also showed semblances of a scheme which could serve them well this series. Trott plays the hook in the two minds of a smoker who can't quite decide whether to give up: he knows it is bad for him, but also that there is a packet in a kitchen drawer. He should either renounce it, like Steve Waugh, or learn discretion, like . . . well . . . Cook.

Even late in the day, Ponting set what for him were some original fields, including a screen of three catchers at intermediate distance on the off when Cook faced North, when there was just the chance he would drive tiredly. But what can you do as captain if you set an off-side field, and the bowler serves up a half-volley on leg stump, or if your allegedly economical left-arm spinner keeps dragging the ball down on a ground with square boundaries so short? Tweet for your life, and don't all answer at once.

Nor, it must be said, is this one of the more naturally mobile Australian sides. Katich jogged after a three down the ground during the afternoon, handicapped by his aching Achilles tendon, at not much greater pace than he showed between wickets yesterday. Watson, too, stands at slip for a reason, because when he chases the ball he resembles a circus strongman who has borrowed a unicycle from one of the clowns. He caught up with a flick to leg of Pietersen's on the boundary under the Chappell Stands today only to find he had conceded an all-run four. Coming on to the field after tea as Australia's best-paid thirteenth man, Mitchell Johnson dived headlong after a ball that had comfortably beaten him to the mid-off boundary – it looked almost like an act of deliberate self-harm.

It was enough to make a captain tear his hair out, were that hair not itself quite expensive. A man who turns thirty-six in two weeks might almost be wondering how much longer he can go round like this. To his credit, Ponting has kept all such thoughts to himself. He still looks like a man engaged and absorbed in his task, however gruelling that may sometimes be, and however vicious the criticism. 'Clueless', read one headline after Brisbane; it was by no means the most hostile, merely the shortest.

For most of his career, Ponting has looked younger than his years, fresh-faced, nearly cherubic. The decades, and maybe cares too, have caught up with him. It is a leathery, stubbly face that peers from beneath his weathered baggy green, which itself is in conspicuous contrast to the bottle-green bonnets of his younger comrades. Eschewing the sunglasses that this Australian team would no sooner go without than would the Rat Pack, he is now a figure who could have stepped from the 1950s. Ricky? Surely he is overdue redesignation as Richard Ponting.

Ponting was a savvy enough cricketer to see change coming. In Matthew Hayden's new autobiography, he recounts a remark of his captain in the Australian slip cordon at the SCG in 2008 as India piled up a 500-plus score. Suddenly, sotto voce, to nobody in particular, Ponting said: 'So this is life without Warnie.' It was not a complaint, or even a sigh of resignation – just an empirical observation. Yes, life had changed. Yes, things would be different in future. Ponting would adapt – he would have to.

In fact, Australia won that Test, to reassure themselves. But they lost the next: the first defeat in which the coach and more than half the team had played. Later that year they gave up the Border–Gavaskar Trophy; a year later they surrendered the Ashes. As the trophy cabinet at Cricket Australia has taken on an antique look, Ponting has grown more grizzled and gritty.

Ponting has looked undignified in this series only when he has aped old Australian behaviours, like chuntering around umpires, and singling out individual opponents: he may never live down describing Cook before the series as 'hanging on by the skin of his teeth'. But lambasting him for being an insufficiently aggressive captain is a little like complaining that he is not taller.

It is Ponting's misfortune to be effectively repeating Allan Border's captaincy career in reverse. Border inherited a poor team and left it on the brink of greatness; Ponting has watched a great team grow ordinary around him. But it has not been for want of trying. There he was throughout the brutally hot afternoon, even at the end, throwing himself around at short mid-wicket, shuffling his fielders, consorting with his bowlers, desperate but not despairing. As stumps were drawn, he walked unselfconsciously to the head of his tired team and led them off as unit: they had struggled but would not straggle.

About twenty minutes later, with the ground empty, a suited Warne descended from his commentary eyrie to kick an Australian rules football around with members of the Channel Nine camera crew. Maybe even he had run short of opinions. Ponting does not have that option.

5 DECEMBER 2010

Day 3

Close of play: England 1st innings 551–4
(KP Pietersen 213*, IR Bell 41*, 143 overs)

Kevin Pietersen made a chanceless double hundred today, England's first for six whole days. Then it rained, long and persistently enough to scotch the session after tea. On which of the two events is more significant in the context of the Second Test, the outcome of this Ashes series may hinge. England were 306 runs ahead of Australia with six wickets in hand at the premature close, but there is the chance of further thunderstorms. As far as the hosts are concerned, they cannot be too Biblical.

Pietersen's undefeated 213 featured today only one very minor flutter, when Harris insisted on referring an lbw appeal in the morning's fourth over; the batsman was then 91. It was perhaps for the sheer novelty of having something else to think about other than Pietersen's weight of stroke and level of intent, and quickly dismissed.

The ursine Harris, who continued barrelling through the crease all day, also tested Pietersen with a couple of early bouncers, the first of which descended safely from the slice, the second causing the batsman to pirouette out of danger. Other than that, Pietersen cast a lengthening shadow over bowlers and fielders alike, tackling Ponting's seven–two dispositions by quickstepping to flick through the untenanted on, carving up the callow Doherty, the flagging Siddle and the failing Bollinger at will. He used every stroke in his repertoire, explored every quadrant of the field, and restored his Test average to within a whisker of the 50 below which it fell for the first time a year ago. This was only his second Test hundred since the ECB busted him to the ranks at the end of 2008 – but he is not finished yet.

England resumed this morning with Cook and Pietersen in harness, Cook having now batted on seven of the eight days of the series, Pietersen ominously threatening parallel permanence. The crowd were subdued – quite possibly hung over too. After forty-five hard-charging minutes, Harris seamed one back through Cook's defence, and Haddin doubled back to snare the inside edge. Haddin had made a point of shaking Cook's hand at stumps the previous evening – his were appropriate hands for the batsman's seven-and-a-quarter-hour 148 to end in.

Siddle could not obtain the same lift, consecutive half-pitchers in his first over arriving at a friendly waist height. Pietersen pulled both majestically, like baseball grounders, and they bisected boundary fielders who hardly had time to move. The only movement Siddle obtained today was after the ball passed the bat, one veering so violently that Haddin could only brush it with the tips of his gloves as it sped to the long-leg boundary.

Bollinger, meanwhile, looked to be running in faster than he was bowling, and at unjustifiable length. Belonging to the Australian park cricket condition of playing cricket to get fit rather than getting fit to play cricket, he has been found short of a gallop here, and given away no fewer than eighteen boundaries. On present indications, his will be a brief international career, if not so brief as Xavier Doherty's.

Each time an English batsman hit a boundary, the big screen overlooking the Hill flashed up the smiling face of Shane Warne, flogging a new fast food item a little less healthy than a deep-fried doner kebab; it also offered a periodic reminder of the chief reason for Australia's toils. Pietersen found Doherty tasty indeed, while Paul Collingwood also tucked in with relish. The captaincy was average. The fielding was average to terrible. The scenario was just terrible. Mitchell Johnson came on as a substitute again, for the visibly limping Katich, and started whirling his arms, seemingly perchance to bowl. A little part of him must have been just a tiny bit happy that he didn't have to.

After lunch, Watson found a hint of reverse swing, and brought one into Collingwood, back when he should have been forward. But the crucified looks exchanged when Pietersen (140) slashed wide of North's right hand at gully implied a team feeling itself at odds with the fates. Pietersen marched on, moving into the ball with predatory intent, content to defend only when every possibility for attack was categorically denied him.

In Ian Bell, Pietersen found the perfect foil in a stand of 99 at four an over. Bell still looks like a Lego figurine, his stroke production seemingly the outcome of various plastic pivots and swivels. This does mean, however, that he seldom mistimes or tries to hit too hard. When the ball is in the slot, it is cover-driven sweetly. When it is short outside off, it is cut unerringly. He has none of Pietersen's originality, but wouldn't keep next man in on tenterhooks like his team-mate either – his only mannerism is fiddling with the shoulders of his shirts, as though his tailor uses too much starch. Other than that, he provides England with the security at number six that North signally does not.

Rain began to descend at tea. It fell not heavily but sufficiently and, for Australia, relievingly. Pretty soon there were covers on the centre, videos on the big screen and several damp games of cricket on the Hill; the weather may yet have the final word here. But even if it does, some long, weighty and rather intimidating words have already been uttered.

5 DECEMBER 2010
KEVIN PIETERSEN

KP or Not KP

In all the pre-Ashes soundings among former Australian greats, even those involving a pro forma prediction of 5–0, there was one common denominator. Whenever an opinion was sought about the identity of England's key player of the coming summer, the answer came back the same: the kp was KP.

Part of this was probably general ignorance. Australians have grown used to letting English cricket look after itself. Some pommy bloke making runs? Some promising new bowler? Yeah, well . . . wait till they get out here. But Kevin Pietersen? Hard to forget him getting the better of Australia at the Oval in 2005; hard to forget Australia getting the better of him at Adelaide in 2006. Looks a bit of a show pony, but Warnie likes him – that's gotta count for something.

It's still arguable that Australians in underestimating England overestimate Pietersen: he forms part of a more consistent and uniformly competent visiting unit than that which he joined. But, especially after today, you will never convince those grudging Australian admirers otherwise. His undefeated 213 was Pietersen *in posse*, *in esse* and in total command – of himself, not least of all.

That meant it was not quite the Pietersen that Australians first saw. He offended no orthodoxies. He cut no capers. He met Xavier Doherty with a defensive bat so doornail dead and plumb-line straight that it bordered on parody, although it wasn't – this was meaningful deliberation. At last. He'd worked it out at last. To think, after all his travails against it, that left-arm spin was *this* easy to play.

When Pietersen then went after Doherty – indeed, took 57 from his 58 deliveries, including nine fours and a six – it was hard to avoid the sensation that the hapless Tasmanian was paying for Pietersen's previous indignities at the hands of other members of the genre. That Ponting entrusted North with

eighteen overs to Doherty's twenty-four suggests that the ninth
Australian post-Warne spinner is about to go from being a
Test cricketer to part of the answer to a trivia question.

All the same, Australians saw again the qualities in
Pietersen that first caused them discomfiture. A Pietersen
playing soberly is still like a conventional batsman spontaneously brainstorming. Thanks to wrists that rotate like
gimbals, he scores in more areas of the field than perhaps any
other contemporary batsman. Most wagon wheels tell you
not much. Batsmen score in different directions: who knew?
But Pietersen's formed almost a complete asterisk. He does
not have one sweep, for instance, but many. He swung
Doherty as fine as forty degrees to square leg, then North as
much as thirty degrees in front, all along the ground.

This latter shot, played in the over before lunch and taking
England's lead to 200, was followed by a similarly confounding
boundary that split Bollinger and Hussey, meant to be protecting the leg-side boundary, but each aborting approaching the
ball out of consideration for the other – commendable from an
occupational health and safety point of view, but evidence of
the confusion and dismay an in-form Pietersen can spread.

When Doherty resumed to Pietersen after lunch, it was
with six men deep: Siddle at deep mid-on, Watson deep mid-
off, North deep mid-wicket, Bollinger deep backward square,
Harris deep point, and Ponting deep trouble. They were
brought in as Pietersen's double-hundred loomed, but he was
not to be denied, dropping to his knee as he completed
the climactic single as though about to receive the Order of
the Garter on the spot.

Pietersen's boldness and ingenuity was brought to the fore now and again when he advanced on both Bollinger and Siddle to pick them off through the leg side from off and middle. But a subtler feature was Pietersen's strength straight: more than 30 per cent of his runs were acquired in the 'V' demarcated by mid-off and mid-on, often by no more than leaning on the ball and harnessing the transference of his weight as propulsion for the stroke. When the ball ducked around a little after lunch, his perpendicular bat and front-foot launch stood him in good stead.

One is never permitted to speak solely of Pietersen the batsman. No member of the current England team is the subject of more cod psychology. Twenty-eight innings without a Test hundred has left plentiful opportunities for sentiments like 'he needs to feel loved', as though this is a breakthrough insight about Pietersen rather than an embarrassing channelling of Oprah.

It's true that Pietersen has caused England team-mates to sigh with exasperation almost as often as to gasp in astonishment. Just over three years ago, for example, he promised that his team would 'humiliate' Australia in the World Twenty20, only for the promise to boomerang. 'Kevin's obviously Kevin,' was Paul Collingwood's Gertrude Stein-esque explanation, amid sage nodding. Born to tweet, he has, of course, tested the limits of the ECB's social media policies in Adelaide.

Yet Pietersen's analysts sometimes seem to reveal as much about themselves as their analysand. John Buchanan and Shane Warne both addressed themselves to his status in the England line-up before the series, Buchanan opining that he was potentially a 'major problem' where England's 'strength and unity' were involved, Warne that he was being treated as 'a bit of an outcast': 'KP might be the walking ego with the way he struts around, and sometimes he is unpopular with his own team-mates, and he can rub people up the wrong way. But he has to be made to feel important and like he is the man. If he feels like that, he will give you everything.' It was the bureaucrat ruminating about the presence of the occasionally disruptive virtuoso, the occasionally disruptive virtuoso raging against bureaucracy. It sounded like Buchanan talking about Warne, and Warne talking about . . . well, Warne.

Does any of this matter? There is a cast of mind that thinks every cricket team must harmonise like the Mormon Tabernacle Choir, that all traits of individuality must be effaced for the sake of a uniform whole. Cricket – and team sports in general – are more complicated. In any event, what today attests is that Pietersen's most significant psychological impact this summer will not be on his own team but on the Australians. They saw today coming – perhaps more clearly than the English.

6 DECEMBER 2010

Day 4

Close of play: Australia 2nd innings 238–4 (MEK Hussey 44*, 79.2 overs)

England stand on the brink of a famous victory in the Second Test at Adelaide Oval. But the brink lies beneath an inky vault of cloud, storm warnings for tomorrow likely to render the game's final day a stop-start affair – assuming it starts at all.

At stumps tonight, Australia were 138 runs from making England bat again, with six wickets remaining, Michael Clarke, after his best score in thirteen Test innings, having succumbed to the day's very last ball, turning a high-bouncing delivery from Kevin Pietersen to short leg Alastair Cook. Pietersen and Cook had already shared the match's highest partnership; they may well remember this instant better. Four years ago, Australia raced time to win here, and beat both England and the clock. Now the roles are reversed – as they are in so many other respects in this series.

Resuming after yesterday's early finish due to rain, Pietersen drove the day's second ball to the cover fence with a flourish. 'As I was saying before I was so rudely interrupted . . .' it seemed to announce. England carried on another forty minutes and eleven overs, hastily adding another 69, losing Pietersen for his best Test score to perhaps the first shot he premeditated, but rubbing their ascendancy in just a little deeper. Bell played the shots of the day, and some of the best of the series, in his unbeaten innings: a double-fisted forehand over cover off Siddle; an exquisitely fine reverse-sweep for four and a imperious lofted drive for six off the seemingly doomed Doherty. The sole impediment to their breezy progress was a failure of the River End scoreboard to dissolve to white from its hamburger advertisement – perhaps one day the burger advertisements will be permanent and players will have to play on regardless. Australia's nadir was reached when Prior's top-edged sweep from Doherty fell safely between Ponting and North, who decided individually that the other could take the catch and chose effectively that neither would.

Strauss's declaration left Australia 375 in arrears with most of two days to play, weather permitting. The Test match improved for Katich when he reached the other end for the first time – three days after starting, as it were. But with his aching Achilles tendon, he moved between the wickets like an elderly man trying out new orthotics. Having brought the injury into the game, he was not entitled to a runner under Law 2.1 (a), even if the Australians might reasonably have pointed out that Marylebone's statutes are silent on the subject of Zimmer frames.

Swann's arrival for the tenth over then involved what might have been taken for a meeting on a building site, with four hard-hatted figures in close proximity: batsman, short leg, silly point, keeper. In a cap, first slip Collingwood looked as though he was living a little dangerously. Australia's relatively straightforward progress to that point abruptly became a challenge. Compared to Swann, previous English spinners have barely revolved the ball at all; with the momentum of his double-whirling arms, he gives it a mighty rip, and the ball leaves his hand seething with spin.

Katich sent a leading edge just beyond Strauss's reach at short cover. Both batsmen then paused in their parlay of a run: had Anderson directed his throw to the striker's rather than the non-striker's end, Watson (25) might well have come up short. Watson's stand-up sweep at the next ball then sent a bat-pad chance looping over Bell at silly point. There were half a dozen half-chances in the session – which, in cricket currency, unfortunately for England, does not translate as three chances. But they promised a lot for the afternoon, as did the darkening footmarks outside a right-hander's off stump, loosened by Bollinger's front footfall. Katich was duly caught behind lunging at the second ball after the break.

This brought Ponting to the wicket, on not just a pair but a king pair. I could get a king pair in a Test; so could you. Swann went past his outside edge at once, turning crimson with suppressed excitement, and Australia's captain was kept waiting on a pair for a dozen deliveries. He then swept a ball from outside the off stump for four, a resounding but not necessarily a reassuring shot, for in his 150 Tests it is one he has seldom played. The next ball did not deviate far from the straight, Ponting played towards mid-on, and Collingwood scooped at slip, inches from the grass – he rose, with his team-mates, performing transports of delight.

Watson looked in his usual reasonable fettle before nicking a ball from Finn that held its line. What has been to this stage treated as impressive consistency in Watson's record is becoming increasingly problematic. In thirty innings since his restoration to the Australian team as an ersatz opener, he has fallen on seventeen occasions between 30 and 65, and progressed further only five times. And people thought John Howard was stuck in the 50s . . .

Clarke found the right moment and occasion to attain something like his best form, justifying his pre-match bullishness. His footwork to Swann was sparkling. He never allowed Anderson to settle, and he survived Broad, in whom has clearly been vested responsibility for roughing him up. At one stage, he struck four boundaries in eight balls, all of them legitimate disposals of errant deliveries. England thought themselves entitled to celebrate when a ball from Swann looped to slip after worming its way between bat and pad, but Clarke (69) referred promptly and pooped the party – the replay was inconclusive.

Either side of fifty-seven minutes lost to a squall, the half-chances continued their non-accumulating occurrence. Clarke was 72 when he steered another from Swann into Cook's knee at short leg. The fielder did not flinch, but nor did he really move, and the ball dropped safely amid anguished glances. Hussey was 27 when he drove out of the rough just wide of Anderson at slip. Collingwood might have caught it – had he not been bowling at the time. Hussey was 41 when his miscued sweep wafted across the face of the stumps but spun wide.

It was looking very like Australia would begin the last day with their fourth-wicket pair still in harness, when Strauss threw the ball to Pietersen, who had not taken a Test wicket since July 2008 – after thirty-four consecutive overs from Swann, it was an unexpected gambit, and a smart one. Like Watson, Clarke has a reputation for being vulnerable around breaks, and his fall to the last delivery of the penultimate day at Edgbaston in 2005 may even, at a stretch, be said to have cost Australia the Ashes.

Pietersen's eighth delivery turned, bounced, and emerged from a flurry of bat, pad and body, whereupon Cook took the catch, and umpire Tony Hill declined to adjudicate. This time it was England's turn to refer promptly – in fact, in an impressive act of synchronised signalling, virtually every member of the fielding side seemed to be forming the 'T' symbol. When the replay confirmed the presence of an edge, England drew to the brink of its brink. The final step awaits.

6 DECEMBER 2010
DRAWS

What Are They Good For?

Just before 4 p.m. at the Adelaide Oval today, there was a sight for the ages. It was quite dark. Rain-bearing clouds were progressing slowly across the skies, ominous as zeppelins. Below, a captain of England was trying to disabuse two umpires of their conviction that the light was too poor to permit a continuance of play in an Ashes Test. Two Australian batsmen, meanwhile, were already three-quarters of the way to the boundary gate, refusing to look over their shoulders in case their rival had his way.

The Ashes of 2010–11 remain nil-all. If the weather warning is to be believed, that scoreline might still apply at the end of this match. In the interim, the aforementioned events are worthy of remark. Even five years ago when England restored Ashes parity after a long interval, the prevailing emotion was one of blessedness. *Is It Cowardly to Pray for Rain?* was the title of Rob Smyth's wonderfully droll retelling of the series, inspired by the weather at the Oval rather than the wickets. The answer was: yes, a bit. But, well, you know . . .

This English affinity for the draw might be said to stem from ancient roots. It's their game, after all. Incorporating it as a potential outcome was a conscious decision; some have always rather liked it. In a famous report for the *Spectator* of the Lord's Test of 1964, Neville Cardus contrasted the atmosphere in the Long Room during the game's intermittent periods of play and much longer rain-induced pauses. While cricket was in progress, Cardus reported, frustration seethed. Poor bowling was censured; ill-judged shots deplored; damn near everything was said to be going to the dogs. Whenever the players sought shelter from the elements, in comparison, merriment broke out, and conviviality prevailed. He had not, thought Cardus, seen Londoners so united since the Blitz. Could there, he wondered, be a market for cricket grounds at which it was guaranteed no play would take place, with perhaps a band on hand for general good cheer? One day, perhaps, a revisionist historian will acclaim Cardus as the forefather of 'cricketainment'.

At the time, England were midway through a long period in fruitless pursuit of the Ashes. They had just lost to the West Indies; they were about to lose to South Africa too. They were, in modern parlance, a 'mid-table' side. No wonder, perhaps, that inactivity was not an entirely unwelcome state. That state of mind certainly applied through the decades that followed Australia's 1989 cakewalk. A draw was received as manna; 'being competitive' was the repeated ambition.

Australians, by contrast, do not believe in 'honourable draws' – the very expression seems to them a contradiction in terms. There is probably some deep cultural reason for this that is above my pay grade to explicate: our distrust of ambiguity, perhaps, or our dislike of form and protocol. Whatever the case, we pine for results. Until World War II, all our first-class cricket, including Tests, were timeless. Most of Australian club cricket is played over two days and to a result. It does not rely on declarations, target setting and cooperating captains.

So here is a role reversal in a series already replete with them: England pressing for victory, Australia thinking that maybe 'match drawn' is not a profanity after all. After the Adelaide Test eight years ago, Melbourne's *Age* newspaper headlined its front-page report: 'Ho-hum, we've won the Ashes again.' You don't require a long memory to appreciate the piquancy of the turnabout.

For England, of course, the reverse in thinking must be decidedly encouraging. They came to Australia needing only to share the series in order to regain the Ashes. It would have been easy to slip into the frame of mind that the running was Australia's to make. Instead they have come to win the Ashes again, not simply to defend them.

For Australia, this shift in power may be a greater problem than is fully grasped. The whole of the Australian ascendancy was designed with results in mind. Aggressive batting; aggressive bowling; aggressive aggression, with its kit bag of verbal abrasion, extrovert body language and 'mental disintegration'. Yet Australia have now lost three of their last four Tests, which means that their problems are more than simply 'putting teams away', as they were interpreted originally, but concern basic matters of security and stability. Their batsmen

Australia Felix: For three days, the home side dominated the First Test, Andrew Strauss (above) perishing in the first over, and Peter Siddle (left) obtaining Australia's fifth Ashes hat-trick later on the first day. Michael Hussey's 195, full of pulsating pull shots (below), then placed his team in the lead by 221 runs.

Turn, turn, turn: After Mitchell Johnson's crucial reprieve for Andrew Strauss (left), Alastair Cook (below) combined with his captain then with Jonathan Trott to bat England to safety, eventually spending all but an hour of the match on the field.

Outrageous fortune: Jonathan Trott's run out of Simon Katich in the first minutes of the Second Test blew Australia's first innings wide open (left); Kevin Pietersen's dismissal of Michael Clarke with the last ball of the fourth day (middle) did the same to the second.

One Step Ahead: As James Anderson celebrated dismissing Brad Haddin on the last morning (below), victory was minutes away – rain wasn't far behind.

A Lot of Hard WACA: Ricky Ponting's fall to an outstanding slip catch by Paul Collingwood summed up Australia's first day in the Third Test (left).

Mitchell Johnson's peremptory lbw dismissal of Kevin Pietersen was at the centre of Australia's fightback on the second day (above); on his home ground, Mike Hussey (left) was one of few batsmen to conquer the conditions.

Under Siege: The Fourth Test, Ricky Ponting's last of the summer, was costly to his pocket and reputation. He incurred a heavy fine for a second-day altercation with umpire Aleem Dar (left) and finished a parlous season with the bat on the third day by playing on after a painful second innings to Tim Bresnan (bottom). In between times, Phil Hughes was another victim of Jonathan Trott's deadly arm (middle).

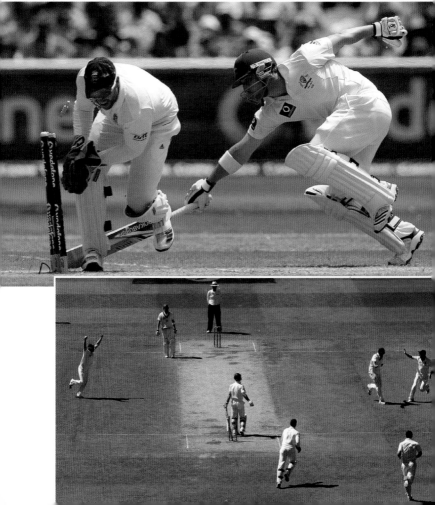

Vanquished: Graeme Swann's sprinkler dance (above) and the Barmy Army's reciprocal exultation (below) marked the retention of the Ashes in Melbourne, while Australia's captain (middle) pondered the turn of cricket's cycle.

ENGLAND
RETAIN
THE ASHES

Old Caps, New Heads: In the injured Ponting's absence, spinner Michael Beer and batsman Usman Khawaja made their debuts for the Fifth Test (top left), Khawaja impressing with his instant strokeplay (middle). But first Phil Hughes (top right) then stand-in skipper Michael Clarke (bottom left) fell cheaply to weaken Australia's first innings.

Old Heads, New Attitudes: On the ground on which England's humiliation had been made complete four years earlier, Alastair Cook (left) and Ian Bell and Matt Prior (below) completed effortless hundreds. Bell completed a season of decidedly mixed results from the referral system by successfully challenging a decision that was almost certainly correct (bottom).

design: www.timpeters.co.uk

are failing to turn fifties into hundreds; their bowlers are unable to bowl maidens. They are therefore not taking long enough to be bowled out, and are letting oppositions score too quickly. Ian Chappell, entrusted with rebuilding the Australian team in the early 1970s, had a nice way of putting it: before you can start winning, you have to stop losing. And there won't always be friendly cumulonimbus to come to Australia's aid.

7 DECEMBER 2010

Day 5

Close of play: Australia 2nd innings 304 (99.1 overs)

The clouds at the Adelaide Oval this morning were high, tufty and really rather pretty, especially to English fans, concerned that the climate would cheat their cricket team of what nobody could deny were just deserts. Once it had been confirmed that the storms stalking South Australia would not arrive at the Second Test until later in the afternoon, they could relax and enjoy the view. There was no escape for Australia, and an early start was followed by an early finish, England's margin of victory coming out at an innings and 71 runs after an hour and a half.

It was better than that – or worse, depending on your point of view. England lost just five wickets in the game, and have made 1,137 runs for the loss of half a dozen batsmen since their Gabba first innings. Not since Australian cricket's dog days in the Packer era have the hosts been so utterly outplayed in their own backyard.

In truth, Australia had been behind since the first thirteen minutes of the game in which they disintegrated to 2 for three. Their last seven wickets in the first innings added 243. Had they done so from a position of 300 for three, they would have approached something like a par score for this very good Test match pitch. As it was, they didn't have a big enough total for bowlers who probably wouldn't have been good enough to defend anyway – like I said, this was a very bad Test match indeed.

At least the end was quick, as England looked confident it would be. When Hussey (50) bent forward to Swann's twelfth delivery, the ball gripped the footmarks but evaded the grip of Prior, who was surprised by the edge and bounce, and proved unable to recover the rebound from his shoulder. Yet Prior made it look like he had just been advised that the label was protruding from his shirt collar – no harm done, easily fixed.

If he brooded at all, it was only for fourteen deliveries. As Finn took the new ball, Hussey misjudged a pull shot – the same stroke he had played with profit and impunity for nearly eight hours in Brisbane – and Anderson calmly caught the top edge at mid-on. Anderson then zipped one away from Haddin that Prior took joyously.

Perhaps nobody had more riding on this final day in a personal sense than the embattled Marcus North. He could argue that in this Test he overcame his all-or-nothing habits, for he made starts in both innings and today struck three attractive boundaries in an hour's stay. But Swann further bolstered his stats against left-handers and his habit of obtaining lbws by turning one down the line of off-stump.

With the ball, Harris had quite a good Test. With the bat, his fortunes have been altogether bizarre. He called confidently for the referral of his first-ball lbw decision in the first innings, only to find it upheld. He requested the same after padding up to his first ball in the second innings, albeit somewhat more hesitantly, as though he simply could not believe how cricket apportions luck. It was to no avail: he was sent on his way for a king pair – the system showing the ball to be just grazing the off bail – thereby completing the surely unique experience of being given out four times in two deliveries. It was a shame for Harris that the system could not also immediately open a trapdoor beneath his feet to enable a prompt, private exit. As it was, he traipsed from the arena, feeling, as a batsman at least, acutely overdressed.

The luck denied Harris might be said to have settled on Siddle (0), who watched, mesmerised, as an inside edge on to his bat from Swann back-spun into the base of the stumps without loosening a bail let alone dislodging it. This backspin of Swann's is a remarkable feature in an English spinner. When they drop from a dead bat, his deliveries tend to fizz and whiz around the batsman's feet like a child's top – it testifies again to just how huge a rip Swann gives the ball, in contrast to English off-rollers of the past too many and mediocre to name.

The rest came quietly – as quietly as Strauss spoke during his post-match press conference. He was quiet *and* deliberate. 'When you're confident, things start happening for you as a matter of course,' said Strauss. 'You don't have to push it . . . Even when Hussey was getting them back in the game, they weren't going anywhere.' For Strauss, who normally addresses his interlocutors in a mild-mannered monotone, this virtually constituted fighting talk.

'We've got to go away and do some soul-searching,' mused his rival, as well as using the word 'execute' more often than a Texan politician. The rain? Ponting insisted that it hadn't come into Australia's calculations. 'If you start thinking about that, you're beaten already,' he averred. Yet at 2 p.m., clouds which had cast the ground into darkness exploded with their watery freight, and in half an hour had transformed the outfield into a shallow lake. Adelaide itself was under water. Rather like Australian cricket.

7 DECEMBER 2010
SIMON KATICH AND STUART BROAD

Collateral Damage

Yesterday, Simon Katich and Stuart Broad, opening batsman and opening bowler, were young men in the fight of their lives, a cricket contest for which both have effectively spent their whole lives training. Today, both learned that it was a contest in which they would play no further part.

Katich had waited more than nine years from his Ashes debut in England to actually playing an Ashes Test at home. Broad had arguably bided his time still longer. In his autobiography, father Chris Broad described how his then-wife missed hearing him attain a maiden Ashes century at the WACA in December 1986 because she was busy changing four-month-old Stuart's nappy. 'Stuart can be very insistent!' he wrote. Umpires and match referees the world over would agree.

Katich now has an Achilles tendon injury that reduced him to batting in Australia's second innings as though he had a club foot. Broad may have damaged his abdominal muscle in the act of striving to exploit Katich's immobility. While it is, as often remarked, a cruel game, the cricket gods sometimes sprinkle their cruelty with a pinch of whimsy.

In the media conferences after the game, their respective captains paid Katich and Broad heartfelt tribute. Both also took turns stating what on the face of it is the bleeding obvious – that England and Australia had so far played only two Tests in a five-match series in which there was therefore three to play.

If it sounded a little like *Sesame Street*, there was a point beyond the mathematical reinforcement of the understanding that five minus two equals three. Over the course of cricket's longest distance, vicissitudes of fitness and form take their toll. And in this an enormous amount of luck is involved. Surely one of the most freakish aspects of the preternatural summer of 2005 was that England made only one forced change in the whole series; one of the others was that Australia were deprived of their key bowler by their own hand, as it were, or ball, to be exact. Neither England nor Australia were ever likely to reach the end of the Ashes of 2010–11 with their first-choice sides intact; now they know they won't. Both will feel these losses.

For Katich, now thirty-five, this might be the end of a long, hard, rutted road. His wife is expecting their first child; he is known to be committed to home and hearth. Facing the media this afternoon, he pointed out that he had been regarded as finished three years ago, and that his resurrection as an opener had owed a lot to happenstance, the epilogue to his career being richer than the first draft. It sounded a little like someone thinking back rather than forward.

Katich has made eight hundreds and averaged 50 in thirty-three Tests since returning to Australian colours, and formed an unexpectedly adhesive opening combination with Shane Watson. Of Ponting at number three they have been contrasting protectors, Katich stepping across his stumps like a secret serviceman guarding a president, Watson more like a bouncer in a swanky nightclub. They have been the most reliable part of Australia's top order, even if of late they haven't had much to compete with on a scale of reliability.

Broad has also had a two-stage career, at least in a statistical sense. He arrived at last year's Headingley Test with a bowling average over 40; since providing England with its sole semi-competent performance there, his average has been under 30. Until that Test, Broad had looked to Australians like a Hugo Boss clotheshorse; he has become in the last year the bowler to whom Strauss looks for a bit of brass-knuckled bravado. 'I don't think he meant to hit him,' Strauss said after Broad threw the ball that struck Zulqarnain Haider at Edgbaston in August – perhaps a semi-conscious ambiguity.

So although it looks like one-all in the injury Ashes, the absence of Broad will hurt England more than the unavailability of Katich hampers Australia. Broad is one of four specialist bowlers, Katich one of six specialist batsmen. England must choose from within their squad, which contains no like-for-like replacement; Australia have, at least notionally, a whole country of batsmen, and indications of form by which to judge them.

It is evidence of England's preparedness that, learning from past misadventures, they brought to Australia their 'shadow' squad, from which the team itself has since drafted Ajmal Shahzad. When England last won in Adelaide, in 1995, it was with an XI cobbled together from an ensemble through which no fewer than twenty players passed, Mark Ilott's sole contribution being his appearance in the team's Christmas panto. But it is the lot of touring teams everywhere to be at a slight disadvantage where drumming up reserves is concerned. Broad's return to England, in fact, probably constituted Australia's best news of the day – by being the only development that was in any way favourable to them.

Here was a reminder, too, that the five-match series knows no equal as a test of physical firmity, mental resilience and professional organisation. Other fine cricketers will also fall by the wayside this summer; who fills that wayside may exert a considerable influence over the Ashes' final resting place.

SECOND TEST   Adelaide Oval 3–7 December 2010
Toss   Australia   **England** won by an
innings and 71 runs

AUSTRALIA 1st innings			R	M	B	4	6	SR
SR Watson	c Pietersen	b Anderson	51	127	94	7	1	54.25
SM Katich		run out (Trott)	0	2	0	0	0	-
*RT Ponting	c Swann	b Anderson	0	2	1	0	0	0.00
MJ Clarke	c Swann	b Anderson	2	7	6	0	0	33.33
MEK Hussey	c Collingwood b Swann		93	299	183	8	0	50.81
MJ North	c †Prior	b Finn	26	100	93	4	0	27.95
†BJ Haddin	c Finn	b Broad	56	148	95	3	1	58.94
RJ Harris	lbw	b Swann	0	4	1	0	0	0.00
XJ Doherty	run out (Strauss/Cook/†Prior)		6	25	19	1	0	31.57
PM Siddle	c Cook	b Anderson	3	24	21	0	0	14.28
DE Bollinger		not out	0	7	3	0	0	0.00
EXTRAS	(lb 6, w 1, nb 1)		8					
TOTAL	(all out; 85.5 overs; 377 mins)		245	(2.85 runs per over)				

FoW	1-0	(Katich, 0.4 ov),	2-0	(Ponting, 0.5 ov),
	3-2	(Clarke, 2.1 ov),	4-96	(Watson, 28.3 ov),
	5-156	(North, 54.4 ov),	6-207	(Hussey, 73.3 ov),
	7-207	(Harris, 73.4 ov),	8-226	(Doherty, 79.3 ov),
	9-243	(Siddle, 84.3 ov),	10-245	(Haddin, 85.5 ov)

BOWLING	O	M	R	W	ECON	
JM Anderson	19	4	51	4	2.68	
SCJ Broad	18.5	6	39	1	2.07	
ST Finn	16	1	71	1	4.43	(1nb, 1w)
GP Swann	29	2	70	2	2.41	
PD Collingwood	3	0	8	0	2.66	

ENGLAND 1st innings			R	M	B	4	6	SR
*AJ Strauss		b Bollinger	1	4	3	0	0	33.33
AN Cook	c †Haddin	b Harris	148	428	269	18	0	55.01
IJL Trott	c Clarke	b Harris	78	213	144	11	0	54.16
KP Pietersen	c Katich	b Doherty	227	428	308	33	1	73.70
PD Collingwood	lbw	b Watson	42	92	70	5	0	60.00
IR Bell		not out	68	151	97	8	1	70.10
†MJ Prior		not out	27	25	21	2	0	128.57
EXTRAS	(b 8, lb 13, w 8)		29					
TOTAL	(5 wickets dec; 152 overs; 673 mins)		620	(4.07 runs per over)				

FoW   1-3   (Strauss, 1.3 ov),   2-176   (Trott, 48.3 ov),
3-351   (Cook, 96.4 ov),   4-452   (Collingwood, 117.4 ov),
5-568   (Pietersen, 146.2 ov)

BOWLING	O	M	R	W	ECON	
RJ Harris	29	5	84	2	2.89	(1w)
DE Bollinger	29	1	130	1	4.48	(2w)
PM Siddle	30	3	121	0	4.03	(1w)
SR Watson	19	7	44	1	2.31	
XJ Doherty	27	3	158	1	5.85	
MJ North	18	0	62	0	3.44	

AUSTRALIA 2nd innings			R	M	B	4	6	SR
SR Watson	c Strauss	b Finn	57	174	141	10	0	40.42
SM Katich	c †Prior	b Swann	43	108	85	6	0	50.58
*RT Ponting	c Collingwood	b Swann	9	21	19	2	0	47.36
MJ Clarke	c Cook	b Pietersen	80	170	139	11	0	57.55
MEK Hussey	c Anderson	b Finn	52	154	107	5	1	48.59
MJ North	lbw	b Swann	22	56	35	3	0	62.85
†BJ Haddin	c †Prior	b Anderson	12	24	21	2	0	57.14
RJ Harris	lbw	b Anderson	0	1	1	0	0	0.00
XJ Doherty		b Swann	5	17	9	1	0	55.55
PM Siddle		b Swann	6	28	22	1	0	27.27
DE Bollinger		not out	7	14	16	1	0	43.75
EXTRAS		(b 5, lb 1, w 5)	11					
TOTAL	(all out; 99.1 overs; 392 mins)		304	(3.06 runs per over)				

FoW   1-84   (Katich, 29.2 ov),   2-98   (Ponting, 35.2 ov),
      3-134   (Watson, 46.2 ov),   4-238   (Clarke, 79.2 ov),
      5-261   (Hussey, 85.2 ov),   6-286   (Haddin, 90.5 ov),
      7-286   (Harris, 90.6 ov),   8-286   (North, 91.2 ov),
      9-295   (Doherty, 95.1 ov),   10-304   (Siddle, 99.1 ov)

BOWLING	O	M	R	W	ECON	
JM Anderson	22	4	92	2	4.18	
SCJ Broad	11	3	32	0	2.90	
GP Swann	41.1	12	91	5	2.21	
ST Finn	18	2	60	2	3.33	(1w)
PD Collingwood	4	0	13	0	3.25	
KP Pietersen	3	0	10	1	3.33	

Part IV

THIRD TEST

The WACA Ground, Perth
16–19 December 2010
Australia won by 267 runs

Post-Warne Society

Shane Warne is not playing in the Ashes of 2010–11. This somehow needs stating, because it often seems otherwise. At Adelaide Oval, fully four years since his Test retirement, he was more visible than ever. Every other over, a burger superimposed on his face materialised on the River End sightscreen. Every boundary was toasted by Warnie on the replay screen brandishing something as much a part of a balanced diet as a deep-fried Mars bar. Every other commercial break, his talk show was plugged on Channel Nine: Warne with a smile so luminous it could be read by at night.

The man himself was there commentating, which he does so naturally well it is almost like playing alongside him, while his Twitter feed was being followed by a quarter of a million close friends and acquaintances. Footloose, fair-haired Aussie rebels can make a dangerous mix with new technology, even if Warnieleaks, as it were, has no pretensions to being other than a forum for mutually admiring glances with celebrity pals and a jumble of product placements, interspersed with gusts of electronic laughter ('Hahahahahaha' etc.). Yet whenever

Warnie says something about the cricket, the scene in the media box resembles the scattering of cockroaches as a door opens, grumbling hacks scrambling to solicit comment.

So, to paraphrase Norma Desmond, Warnie is still big; it's the cricket that got small. 'Like a room with the light turned out,' was the great Australian cricket writer Ray Robinson's description of the game in his country after the retirement of Sir Donald Bradman. The post-Warne game is more akin to a television studio in which the autocue has failed, leaving captain Ricky Ponting to keep filling time while it is fixed by endlessly repeating the word 'execute'.

The vacuum is so palpable that 71 per cent of respondents to a recent online poll wished that Warne, now forty-one, would return to the colours. One should be wary of the results when self-selecting samples pass for mass opinion, but it has provided a storyline beguiling even to Warne. 'There has been a bit written in Australia and people have been asking me about making a comeback,' he wrote yesterday. 'All I can say is that it is very flattering to hear those words.' That's surely *not* all he can say. He could, for example, say it won't happen, as it really can't; he is now, in any case, in London, interviewing for his talk show. But that would spoil the game, and Warne's spirit is above all playful, his perennial gameness the perfect complement to his extraordinary skills.

Two years ago, it might have been a possibility. When Australia struggled in India in 2008, Ponting is known to have been in touch with Warne about Australia's slow-bowling woes, and there were low-level murmurings of a return.

Two years later, Warne is a very part-time cricketer, with a last season ahead at the Rajasthan Royals, and full-time media act.

Most publicly, there is *Warnie*, in which Australia's greatest leg spinner is cast in the role of vernacular Michael Parkinson, and in which the result is probably a little more successful than if Parky took up leg-spin, but not much. The first show brought to mind the exchange in Terry Zwigoff's movie *Ghostworld* where the girl protagonists are debating the awfulness of the band at their school dance. 'This is so bad, it's good,' says one. 'This is so bad,' corrects the other, 'it goes through good and back to bad again.'

With all the surrounding programmes so slick, planned and predictable, *Warnie*'s artlessness is very nearly endearing – you watch because you cannot imagine what on earth could be the next idea the producers come up with that sounded funny after six beers. But there's a limit, and Australians appear to have reached it quickly: the show's audience halved after the first week.

Also underestimated is Warne's attachment to his three children, of whom he is far more protective than he is of himself. It was for their sake he forsook the game; he is as doting now as then. There is a touching vignette of Warne in the recent autobiography of his erstwhile Hampshire team-mate Shaun Udal. In August 2006, Udal learned that his son was autistic. The first person he bumped into was his Aussie skipper, in front of whom Udal burst into tears. Warne – 'a good man, a softer soul than the public perception,' according to Udal – was immediately solicitous. 'I could not bear it if anything happened to my kids,' he confided. 'That is the one thing that has not happened to me.'

The nub of the will-Warnie-won't-Warnie story, however, is not the possibility of his presence but the perplexities of his absence. For there is no escaping the hole in Australian cricket; it is just that Warne's existence gives it a shape that bears his likeness.

Ponting's Australians are playing with something not associated with cricket in this country in a generation: a fear of doing the wrong thing. They have taken refuge in a bureaucratic cast of mind, in which the system is all, and nobody seems capable of thinking for themselves. 'In the end,' said Mitchell Johnson after his omission in Adelaide, 'I need to work things out, go to net sessions, get back in the gym, get my head straight, and get back into the team.' Follow the system, have a bit of a trundle, do a few ab crunches, and all will be well.

Everyone talks about 'plans' and 'executing' them, but when events occur outside the plan, nobody seems to have a clue what to do. At least John Buchanan only asked his charges to 'control the controllables'; his successor Tim Nielsen, whose contract was quietly renewed for three years back in August, declines to acknowledge that uncontrollables exist.

Warne, of course, never had a plan in cricket; no more so has he had a plan in life. His philosophy reminds you of the scene in *Peep Show* where the incorrigible Jez realises he is about to sleep with his flatmate Mark's girlfriend: 'This is almost certainly the wrong thing to do. But if I don't do it, how will I know?'

Warne would almost certainly hate to be a member of this Australian side – not because they are losing games, for his career contained its share of failure, but because they are going about their tasks so predictably, so mechanically, so joylessly. It is not simply his playing skills that Australians miss, but his infectious, irrepressible, irreverent spirit. If Warnie could be bottled – and surely an advertiser will find a way eventually – then the Australian team would be first in the queue to partake. But it is not at all clear they could enjoy the taste.

13 DECEMBER 2010
AUSTRALIA

The Recession We Had to Have?

Abject defeat at England's hands. Test grounds in which the majority of fans seem to be English. The choice of a spinner with six first-class games behind him, and the recall of an opening batsman yet to score a half-century in this season's Sheffield Shield. Any or all the foregoing would be enough to plunge Australian cricket into a bout of introspection – were it not already there.

Back in August, Cricket Australia held a five-day state-of-the-nation conference which heard disturbing truths about the game's health in this country. Attendances, delegates learned, were marking time. Television audiences had tailed off over the decade by a quarter. There was a marked drop-off in junior participation after the age of thirteen, while female fans were staying away in droves.

When the discussion paper elaborating on these problems found its way into the media, a degree of green-and-gold garment-rending ensued, although the leak may also have had the desired effect: Cricket Australia's board agreed soon after to an expansion in 2011–12 of the so-called Big Bash League, Australia's T20 domestic competition. This would entitle the state associations that compose CA to sell off minority stakes in putative city-based teams, and beget two further privately owned franchises. But apparently excluded from the discussion was the actual quality of Australian cricket, which, it seemed to be assumed, would simply take care of itself, as it always had.

A decade ago, that certainly seemed to be the case. Australia's Cricket Academy, based in the Adelaide suburb of Del Monte, had made it the envy of the cricket world, producing such celebrated graduates as Ricky Ponting, Glenn McGrath, Adam Gilchrist, Damien Martyn and one still-more-celebrated class clown in Shane Warne. Yet even then the academy was on borrowed time, having always had more admirers abroad than at home.

For some years, the state associations had grown reluctant to allow their best young cricketers out of their sights for prolonged residencies. With Australian cricket in rude financial health, those associations had invested heavily in their own development programmes. They were galled by the thought of other states profiting from their talent – as happened, for instance, when Queensland, who couldn't offer

Shane Watson a Sheffield Shield spot, lost him to Tasmania, who could. Schemes to bind players to their states of origin were then rendered inoperable by the first Cricket Australia pay deal with its players, which viewed such arrangements as restraint of trade.

So when Rod Marsh was recruited to open England's academy in August 2001, it was even as the concept was perishing in Australia. In its stead arose the Centre of Excellence at Allan Border Field in Albion, Brisbane, whose clientele was not to be emergent cricket talent but older players with pre-existing first-class experience undertaking shorter stints. It opened in January 2004 under the oversight of current national coach Tim Nielsen.

Yet while the Centre of Excellence has kept the states happy, one can't help wondering now whether it has something to do with Australian players tending to mature later, or, in Mitchell Johnson's case, barely at all; and also whether the diffusion of the national focus in junior development has further exposed cricket to the depredations of the football codes, especially Australian rules. Eighteen-year-old Alex Keath, who recently represented Victoria against England, is a rare counterexample to a disturbing trend: champion cricketers drawn away in their teens by the Australian Football League's far-reaching national draft.

Face it: were you a star schoolboy athlete, which would you find more enticing? A year at a national cricket academy run by a legendary cricketer or involvement in a state development programme full of professional coaches heavy with qualifications – or, as a third alternative, an AFL club subsidising your parents and paying your school fees solely for the opportunity to bid for your services further down the track.

You might by now have detected another of those Australia–England role reversals so vexing locals this summer. Parochial self-interest undermining national priorities? Wasn't that meant to be England's problem, not Australia's? Yet interstate rivalries have always abounded here, reinforced by Cricket Australia's antique governance structure, where the voting arrangements have barely changed since 1905. The federal cricket bureaucracy now has a great many mouths to feed. Over the last two years, CA has had to disgorge to the states A$96 million in dividends, a third more than its total surpluses from continuing operations. These rivalries may be further entrenched by the enriching of the Big Bash League, which will give states access to income streams outside those traditionally funnelled through Cricket Australia from international fixtures.

CA's strategists forecast that domestic T20 will in time provide up to half Australian cricket's revenues. Good news for some; but it doesn't sound like an organisation preparing for a reverberating renewal of collective purpose, ready to sacrifice everything in order that the country's cricket team regain global supremacy.

Australian cricket's other relationship ripe for scrutiny if the Ashes remain in England is with India, with whom CA is a joint-venture partner in the instantly forgettable Champions League, played in September 2010, and against whom soon after Australia played a two-Test series in order that India could burnish its number one Test ranking.

Observers looked askance at CA's decision to compel Doug Bollinger and Mike Hussey to represent their IPL franchise in the Champions League rather than prepare for the Border–Gavaskar Trophy with the national squad. The Test series then probably cost Nathan Hauritz his Test place, while Bollinger and Simon Katich also sustained injuries and have since joined him on the sidelines.

To be fair, Australia remains only 0–1 down in an Ashes series sensitively poised, neither side having great strength in depth; England is not yet a good enough side to dominate indefinitely. But a loss to England tends to provoke deeper self-examination in this country than to, say, India or South Africa. Thus there is a growing sense that it might not only be on the field that Australia is becoming a mid-ranking Test country.

15 DECEMBER 2010
THIRD TEST

Thought Bubbles

When South Africa played Australia in Perth two years ago, coach Mickey Arthur taped to their dressing-room wall a small poster of Ricky Ponting. Around it were drawn thought bubbles of the kind customary in comic strips, each containing a potential worry or distraction of the Australian captain, about his team's form or his own. One of them was the prospect of Australia losing their first home series for sixteen years: at Perth, then Melbourne, the Proteas turned this from phantom to fact.

It was a neat trick, actually devised by team psychologist Jeremy Snape, who argued that teams visiting Australia were inclined to obsess over their own frailties, forgetting that their foes were also flesh and blood. And if you imagine reprising it now, you soon start running short of bubbles, for Ponting and his team have spent their week since the Second Test plunged in self-examination, having in that match been as clearly outclassed by England as perhaps on any occasion in the last generation. Trouble proverbially comes in threes, and so it has for Ponting: batting, bowling and fielding.

Needing to win two of the three remaining Tests, the Australians have arrived in Perth with the prospect of perhaps as many as five alterations to their Adelaide line-up. Criticised for their trust in continuity, Andrew Hilditch and his fellow selectors now find themselves lambasted for faith in change. In particular, their promotion as specialist spinner of 26-year-old Michael Beer has been a gift to headline writers, speculating that Hilditch must surely have examined him through Beer goggles – et cetera, et cetera. The truth is actually worse: Hilditch has not seen him bowl at all.

Were the next Test on Melbourne's easy-paced drop-in pitch, in fact, Australia would almost certainly be planning for the Ashes of 2013 already. But WACA curator Cameron Sutherland's surface of Harvey River clay with 'a fair bit of grass on top' may have arrived in the nick of time to redress the imbalance between the teams, adding that little bit of environmental uncertainty to an evaluation of their relative strengths.

England's record at the WACA is dismal as could be: they have won only one of eleven Tests here, and exceeded 300 in an innings only once in the last twenty years. And although it sounds counterintuitive to suggest that England will miss a cricketer whose wickets so far have cost 80 runs each and whose only innings lasted one delivery, Stuart Broad's absence will remove a crucial underpinning. He was England's quickest and most aggressive bowler in the two Tests, hitting Ricky Ponting's helmet in Brisbane and persuading Michael Clarke to don a chest guard in Adelaide, while his century-making potential at number eight lent a depth to the English order that Australia could not match.

A fill-in composed of Chris Tremlett's bowling and Tim Bresnan's batting would fit the bill adequately, but it doesn't work that way: Australia must wish similarly for a combination of Doug Bollinger's bowling with Mitchell Johnson's fitness. Tremlett bowls the tighter lines, obtains the greater bounce and reverse swing, but he is a more natural replacement for Steve Finn; Bresnan has the more recent international experience, is generally considered the sounder temperament, and looks a natural to push into the fabled Fremantle Doctor, the cooling afternoon breeze that blows in off the sea. If England *do* pick Tremlett, it suggests they are very confident indeed.

Not that they wouldn't have reason to be. Since Peter Siddle took six for 54 on the rubber's first day, Australia have been outplayed by growing degrees: having taken a hat-trick on his twenty-sixth birthday, Siddle is yet to claim a wicket in his twenty-seventh year. Only Michael Hussey and Brad Haddin have made good with the bat, repeating their Gabba partnership in a minor key at Adelaide Oval. Shane Watson, Michael Clarke and the captain himself have much to prove with the bat; Ben Hilfenhaus has ample room for improvement with the ball.

As for the newbie, Michael is very much a boutique Beer, as it were. This time twelve months ago, the tenth bowler to assume Shane Warne's mantle in less than four years was trundling away for the great man's old club of St Kilda, kept out of the state side by Bryce McGain and Jon Holland. In winter, Beer quit his Melbourne job with Puma, dragged his left-arm orthodox kitbag across the Nullarbor Plain, and winkled out five Englishmen at the WACA Ground in October's tour match while conceding 207 runs – which by recent standards of Australian slow bowling qualifies him as a veritable destroyer. Mickey Arthur, now coach of Western Australia, rates him highly, Beer's height (6ft 1) conducing to bounce, his outgoing temperament suggesting resilience. Shane Warne lifted his gaze from Liz Hurley's cleavage long enough to bless the promotion. Too few have actually seen Beer bowl to differ.

Too many saw Mitchell Johnson bowl at Brisbane to believe that Australia would dare pick him again, but the pre-match vibe is that they just might. His record in Perth is impressive: on the right sort of pitch, with a calm domestic environment, an auspicious horoscope and a favourable alignment of the planets, he might yet cause surprises. At the moment, all the same, Johnson is like the American economy: patchy and frail despite repeated stimulus schemes and short-term fixes. If chosen, the first few overs may tell.

Certain to play are the New South Welshmen Steve Smith and Phil Hughes, who have succeeded the underperforming Marcus North and the overtaxed Simon Katich. Both are exciting cricketers who performed passably for Australia A three weeks ago; Hughes is still, perhaps, a little too exciting for his own and the next man in's good. Both would have hoped to play in this series. Neither would have expected their opportunities to arise so soon.

Otherwise, even Australian rhetoric, at which they used to excel, is not what it was. Usually a forum of robust self-assertion, Ponting's most recent column in *The Australian* was a diffident one. Of Adelaide he commented: 'If we had held our chances here and there and been able to sustain pressure for slightly longer periods, I think things could have been different.' Of Perth he added: 'We've got to make sure we believe in each other and what we are doing is right. If we do that I honestly believe a win is just around the corner for us.'

'If', 'could', 'think', 'believe', 'around the corner' – assuming these speech balloons correlated to thought bubbles, Ponting is channelling the same self-delusion and wishful thinking that for so long characterised English cricket. He will need to clear his conglomerated mind this week if he is to steer Australia back into the series.

16 DECEMBER 2010
Day 1

Close of play: England 1st innings 29–0
(AJ Strauss 12*, AN Cook 17*, 12 overs)

The most-discussed twenty-two yards of turf in Australia and the country's most-debated home line-up in years today both promised more than they delivered in the Third Test at Perth: on both counts, Australia was the loser.

Loaded to the gunwales with pace bowling in the expectation of a pitch in the old WACA tradition, Australia were sent in and scuttled by an England team that made up for what the pitch did not actually provide by disciplined line and smart catching.

As in the Second Test, Australia's middle and lower order did its best. Having accumulated 243 through its last seven wickets at Adelaide, the team found 232 among its last six here. The trouble was that the starting point was barely improved. Two for three at Adelaide was 36 for four here. At the close of the first day in Adelaide, England were 244 in arrears with all their wickets intact; here the difference is 239. Good teams can recover from such early misadventures; this is not a good team, or at least is not playing like one at present.

'The finest, most fragile area of grass known to sports,' says Joseph O'Neill of cricket pitches in his acclaimed novel *Netherland*. 'For all its apparent artificiality,' he notes, 'cricket is a game in nature.' Studying this pitch and the reactions to it in the prelude to the Third Test has, indeed, been a little like watching a wildlife documentary.

Phil Hughes summed up initial responses when he asked if curator Cam Sutherland would be giving it another cut; West Australian coach Mickey Arthur countered that visitors should not approach it through green-tinted spectacles. From day to day, according to watering, weather, fancy and folklore, the surface seemed to be greening and yellowing before onlookers' eyes.

It certainly had some eye-catching qualities. Although the pitch is the same as was used for the Test against the West Indies last year, the grass is of a finer quality than usual. But recent heatwave conditions have baked it hard, and the promise of bounce was hard to resist. The additional consideration was that, with their high clay content, pitches here are inclined to crack, sometimes dramatically, like crazy paving. During a 194-over fiasco here in 1993, the cracks were so wide that batsmen seemed to disappear down them; a pitch earlier this season in a state Second XI game looked like the junction of tectonic plates. Yet they caused no concern whatever when South Africa successfully overhauled 414 in the fourth innings two years ago.

Both teams invested accordingly. Australia became the Team With No Beer by excluding their specialist left-arm spinner; England picked Chris Tremlett ahead of Tim Bresnan for his additional 8 inches of height and 5mph of speed, then committed themselves by inserting their opponents. It paid off quickly.

The last ball of Anderson's first over glanced Watson's thigh pad on the way to fine leg, only for Prior to take a levitating left-handed catch – a snare that deserved a wicket and almost got one when the appeal was upheld by Doctrove, until the referral was upheld by Aleem Dar. The last ball of Tremlett's first over then brooked no argument, seaming back through Hughes's all-too-permeable defence to clip the top of off.

In Anderson's third over, Strauss at first slip could not quite hang in the air long enough to control a slash from Watson (2) that slapped into his upstretched left hand. But Anderson had to wait only four further deliveries for a wicket when Collingwood at third slip flew high to his right to catch Ponting's hard-handed edge. Again Australia's captain played a ball the length of which suggested he could comfortably have left.

Anderson we knew of. Tremlett? Judging by his physique, he has been charged by God to bowl fast. No wonder his erstwhile county captain Shane Warne once said he had the potential to be 'the number one bowler in the world'. He looks like he could have stepped out of an electronic game: 6ft 7in tall, sculpted jaw, prominent cheekbones, broad shoulders tapering to a minimal waist.

Obstacles to his progress have been temperamental: he purportedly makes Bambi look like Jon Bon Jovi. In hindsight, his haymaker to break Anderson's rib at England's pre-tour boot camp was poor preparation but a good omen. Tremlett might have bowled a couple of feet fuller at times, but his spell of 6–1–17–2 could otherwise hardly have been improved. His prize wicket of Clarke, again skittish, again fending away from his body, was Prior's 100th Test catch.

After an hour, Australia were 33 for three. They eked fifty from 133 deliveries, 110 of them scoreless. Hussey raised a cheer when he hooked Finn for six, as fine as Roy Fredericks did Dennis Lillee thirty-five years ago, but this was a solitary flare rather than Fredericks-style pyrotechnics. Finn trapped Watson with a surprise yorker, and England had penetrated to Australia's all-rounders in an hour and a half.

Was it the pitch? The toss? The occasion? The bowling was keen, the catching sure. The batting was simply poor, below Test class, as though Australia had spent so long fantasising of slapping down their bowling full house that they'd given no thought to England's three of a kind. It got worse too. One day, Smith could make a handy Test number six – but not, quite, yet. Pushed back by Tremlett's short ball, he was unprepared for the fuller follow-up. Shortly after lunch, Australia were even more poorly placed than they had been at the corresponding stage at Adelaide Oval.

For the third consecutive Test, Hussey and Haddin provided the choicest Australian batting. Having looked on his last legs just six weeks ago, Hussey could play for another six years on his present form. Haddin greeted the arrival of Swann at 2 p.m. by lifting him over mid-off for four and mid-on for six. With a slash over gully from Finn, one of three boundaries in a ragged over, Hussey raised his own half-century in 98 balls.

Just when the partnership had percolated for 62 runs from 79 deliveries, Swann turned one past a startled Hussey prod and, acting on the rumour of an edge, successfully sought a referral over the head of the impassive Doctrove, whose decisions these days look increasingly like merely bases for on-going negotiation. Johnson used the sweep to good advantage against Swann, a six leaving his bat with a resonant 'clop' in addition to eight boundaries. Only stattos were disappointed by Johnson's runs, their being the first by a number eight batsman in this series. The good it could have done him was seen in his overs before the close, where he shaped a couple of balls away from England's openers, as he hadn't in Brisbane.

But watching Johnson, Siddle and Hilfenhaus add 67 for the last two wickets from 97 deliveries, harnessing the pace and handling the bounce quite easily, one wondered how Australia had gone so badly astray in the morning. And there were few alarms as Strauss and Cook guided England through the final fifty minutes, Cook even registering a fifth six in sixty-two Tests, with a wind-assisted up-and-under over third man. Without their own assistance from the elements, Australia are going to have to work this Test out themselves.

16 DECEMBER 2010
THE WACA

Perthabad

Perth is the city farthest from any other city in the world; its cricket ground is, proverbially, the one whose conditions are among the most different from those of other Test venues. This was meant to be the Test where Australia's local knowledge would count most, and England would be made to feel less like visitors and more like aliens.

Like so much else about this series, in which the gap between 'plan' and 'execution' is widening to Great Australian Bight proportions, little time had elapsed today before the roles of predator and prey had been reversed, it being Ricky Ponting's team that looked like it had never travelled west of Adelaide, Andrew Strauss's that seemed uncommonly comfortable.

The prelude to this match had actually been ever-so-slightly odd, with the Australians incanting a mantra of enjoyment. Ricky Ponting spoke glowingly of the renewed energy in his camp lent by the youth of Phil Hughes and Steve Smith. The latter announced that he had been appointed team jester: 'I've been told that I've got to come into the side and be fun. For me, it's about having energy in the field and making sure I'm having fun and making sure everyone else around is having fun, whether it be telling a joke or some-thing like that.'

'Have fun!!' coach Tim Nielsen enjoined his charges from his Cricket Australia blog. It sounded like a scout troop on a camp where it's rained for a week, everyone has diarrhoea and there is nothing to eat but canned baked beans, but the Akela keeps insisting on another chorus of 'On Top of Old Smokey'. One–nil down in an Ashes series is not a fun scenario; the WACA is not a fun ground, resembling, as it does, an overgrown Portakabin, with official ordinances that proscribe 'hard foam eskies', 'vuvuzelas' and 'racial vilifi-cation' in that order.

Not that there was any hint of the last. On the contrary: with the St George Crosses merging into the red and white of the Vodafone livery, the WACA seemed an almost unrelieved expanse of Englishness, with only the occasional yellow outcrop to interrupt the view. As Australia crumbled, the only fun was among visiting spectators.

Then there were the selections. For years, Perth's residual reputation for pace and the green sheen on its pitches has led to its being described as a kind of honeytrap for excitable young pacemen, whom it is said to entice to wild and woolly extremes. In fact, it has become, like every first-class pitch around Australia, good for batting, simply harder and a little glossier than most.

Today it was not a kid tearaway letting enthusiasm get the better of him, but Australia's wise selectors, who chose a team with no fewer than five fast-medium bowlers, relying for its slow bowling on a 21-year-old who has paid 45 runs for each of his first-class wickets. If this match stretches into a fourth and fifth day, that attack may start growing a mite monotonous.

Finally, on a pitch that then did little more than a Test pitch should on an average first morning, Australia's top order proceeded to make a simply disciplined attack look entirely lethal. It was Bob Simpson, a West Australia Sheffield Shield star in the late 1950s, who is usually credited with the philosophy of batsmanship at the WACA: you protect the stumps, play with either a completely vertical or horizontal bat, and leave on length. Such is the clay in the pitch and the carry to the keeper that most balls can be safely let go; it is the fuller delivery that causes problems.

This surface is classically hard – so hard that when Brad Haddin stabbed a ball of full length into the ground from Finn after lunch, it bounced over Bell's head at point and still had the impetus to make it to the boundary. But it required nothing to survive that wasn't within the powers of the average Test batsmen – leading one to the uncomfortable conclusion that Australia's, at least at the moment, are falling below that median.

Hughes may be the first opening batsman to arrive in Test cricket without a front-foot defensive stroke, the absence of which in England last year made his batting look like a combination of a sharkskin suit with a Hawaiian shirt. He has tightened his technique a tad since, but not as much as he should have. To a ball from Tremlett that needed a straight, dead bat, he was playing ambitiously to leg. It was an aggressive shot; it may even have been a fun shot; it wasn't the shot of a Test match opener.

Perth was where Ponting made his Test debut fifteen years ago, being unlucky to fall four short of what, had the referral system been in place, would have been a hundred. He was consoled at the time that there would be more hundreds, and there have been thirty-nine, but not one in Perth, where he has passed fifty only thrice since. It was here a year ago, in fact, that he experienced the memento mori of being clocked agonisingly on the arm by Kemar Roach as he essayed his pet pull, an episode he has admitted made him think: 'How on earth did I do that?' The question Ponting will have asked himself on failing today was: '*Why* on earth did I do that?' To the fifth ball of Anderson's third over, the bowler's stock away swinger, Ponting's stroke was a long way from compulsory; it was hard-handed, groping for the ball. It wasn't clear whether Ponting's look of dejection was a response to Collingwood's super-fine catch or his own misbegotten shot.

Again this summer, Clarke cut an anxious figure for a batsman with a Test average six months ago of 52, his only scoring shot a speculative cut just wide of gully's left hand. Again, like his captain, he seemed overeager to lay bat on ball, offering a crooked defensive bat to a ball requiring no more than a regulation leave.

Watson was happy to leave, as is his wont: he scored from only nine of his forty deliveries faced, and would have offered a shot at few more. He was caught, instead, flat-footed, by the surprise fuller delivery. Between Tests, Finn swapped his schoolboy cowlick for something a little more streamlined and spiky; although expensive today and down a little on pace, he shows parallel signs of maturing as a bowler.

From this point, the innings represented only a negotiation on the scale of the debacle. Although the lower echelons fought hard, wickets fell at intervals congenial to England, and when Australia's bowlers had a dozen overs at Strauss and Cook late in the day they were fast, aggressive and *too short* – England's captain and vice-captain left with aplomb. They already appeared comfortable, settled, grooved. It was Ponting who vanished into the shadows of the players' pavilion looking like a stranger in town.

17 December 2010

Day 2

Close of play: Australia 2nd innings 119–3
(SR Watson 61*, MEK Hussey 24*, 33 overs)

Were Mitchell Johnson a racehorse, they would never stop swabbing him. Were he a Pakistani, his performances would be under more or less constant scrutiny. So exhilarating one day; so execrable the next. Two weeks ago, he looked to be in more pieces than Humpty Dumpty. Yet Australia have succeeded where all the king's horses and all the king's men failed, for today he bounced his country back into the Ashes of 2010–11 in two explosive spells.

In nine overs before lunch, Johnson unseated four batsmen for 20 runs; in eight after the interval, he winkled out another two for 14. You need to read both the runs *and* the wickets too. Johnson is by reputation penetrative *and* profligate – these analyses were in the Glenn McGrath or Curtly Ambrose category, taking everything, leaving nothing.

Three of the victims – Cook, Trott and Pietersen – had brought 962 series runs into the game; the fourth, Collingwood, was the player on whom England has often relied in the past to rally resistance, famously denying Australia victory at Cardiff last year. Australia's decision to field four pacemen plus Watson in this game is still to be vindicated, but mainly because so far one has almost been enough; their lead at the close was a round 200, which in a low-scoring game verges on decisive.

Logic suggests that there should be no correlation between Johnson's batting and bowling, but Johnson is not a cricketer in thrall to logic. It is not necessarily that when he fires with the bat he succeeds with the ball, but that at his worst he achieves a kind of total anonymity. He came into the Test after six noughts in his previous dozen innings, his only score of note, a 47 at Mohali, preceding his only spell of effect in that time, a five for 64.

His rousing 62 yesterday, then, might just have been the blue touchpaper needed. In his two overs last night, he generated some suggestive shape away from the left-handers, which continued today into the right-handers, at ever-improving speeds. Many thousands of man-hours of coaching, and thus Cricket Australia dollars, have been ploughed into that shape – the investors should have been gleeful.

The day began with Australia in listless search of wickets. In the third over of the day, Andrew Strauss (16) drove flat-footed at Harris. At first slip, Shane Watson reeled back like a movie stuntman shot at the OK Corral and somehow managed not to touch the ball at all; Haddin watched transfixed as it ran away to the third-man boundary. This wasn't simply a miss; it was a mockery. In Harris's next over, Strauss tucked away three leg-side boundaries – a hook in the air, a pull along the carpet and a flick off the toes – and the chagrined bowler gave way at the Prindiville Stand End to Johnson.

His effect was immediate, drawing Cook into an airy drive that Hussey came forward to pouch in the gully – a crucial wicket given the breadth of Cook's bat in the first two Tests. Better was to come. After pushing Trott back with a well-directed bouncer, Johnson caught him on the crease, then beat Pietersen for pace as he shambled across his stumps, the referral system failing to exonerate him.

When Harris soon after got a ball to hold its line to Strauss, committed to defence, it was abruptly the turn of Australian fielders to be clustering round their bowlers, forming a well-wishing retinue as they retired for a fine-leg breather. Johnson's bouncer to Collingwood was perhaps the ball of the day, the batsman struggling to stretch his frame in order to get in harm's way, then to extract himself from same. He might have been thinking about the same ball when he was trapped lbw, hopelessly late on the downswing, his pads emitting the thud of a rug on a clothesline being struck by a carpet beater.

Thereafter, England were in retreat – it was just a matter of how organised they could make it. On the scene of his best Test score in Australia, and also the odd grade game during his season eight years ago at University of Western Australia, Bell again looked as good as any batsman in the series. As in Brisbane, though, he perished when he sought to make hay in the company of the tail – it must surely be time for him to graduate to number five or even four.

Prior played on unluckily, Swann nicked daintily, and England missed the ballast of Broad at number eight as the tail were swept away. Johnson finished with six for 38, gesturing, apparently, in the time-honoured tradition, in the direction of the press box at the Members' End atop the Lillee–Marsh Stand. Unbeknown to Johnson, his media detractors are this year square of the wicket – it was his only loss of direction all day.

In snapping at Australia's heels, England inflicted some lucky bites. Amid an otherwise inconsistent spell, Finn had Hughes caught at second slip, and Ponting given out on referral caught down the leg side, as at the Gabba, although the evidence was what you would call circumstantial rather than empirical, an observable deflection rather than a noisy nick. When Clarke played on after four rather frenzied boundaries, the last hour loomed as pivotal: Australia claimed it conclusively, Hussey's energy inspiring similar industry from Watson as they moved to a fifty partnership from 65 deliveries.

There remains a lot of cricket in this game, and some of it is bound to involve batting. Six batsmen have so far made half-centuries, suggesting that it is possible to get in and enjoy the conditions, which are fascinatingly unique: when Prior stabbed Hilfenhaus into the pitch after lunch today, the ball bounced over the bowler's head and picked up pace en route to the boundary – a phenomenon of the hardness of the wicket block and the slight convexity of the outfield. The way Hussey collared Swann late in the day suggests that Australia see him as their biggest threat; there is no ambiguity, at least now, about whom is England's.

17 DECEMBER 2010
MITCHELL JOHNSON

Swings and Roundabouts

There is a lovely story about Keith Miller playing for New South Wales in the mid-1950s and basking in the afterglow of taking seven for 12 to bowl South Australia out for 26. 'Mr Miller,' asked a reporter. 'Can you tell us why you took seven for 12 today?'

Miller paused to reflect. 'There are three reasons I took seven for 12 today, son,' he said at last. 'First, I bowled bloody well. Second . . .' He paused again. 'Second . . .' He shook his head: 'Awww, ya can forget about the other two.'

Would that Mitchell Johnson could approach bowling with such ease and insouciance: Australian cricket's number one management challenge would then be a regular world-beater. On the other hand, one would then be deprived of the almost numinous air that surrounds him when everything combines in his favour. As Australia veered back into the Ashes of 2010–11, the difference was Johnson, who afterwards answered questions in that coy, shy country-kid kind of way of his.

Rather a lot were about sledging. Both teams have been more visibly garrulous in this match, in England's case somewhat pointlessly. But it was Johnson's bowling that really did the talking, and it is of disproportionate significance to his team. That intensity, that athleticism, that elastic snap of his elongated arm swing and explosive turn of speed – they stand out proud in an attack of solid triers.

Over the past couple of years, swing has been Johnson's faithful frenemy. When he developed it in South Africa last year, he looked like he could take on the world; when it deserted him in England, he seemed bereft. It is easy to forget that in his formative years, he seldom saw the new ball for Queensland, where it was shared among the likes of Andy Bichel, Michael Kasprowicz and Ashley Noffke.

Instead, Johnson became a cricketer of angles: an angled approach, an angled arm, an angled delivery across the right-hander and into the left-hander. These angles are both benefit and curse, making him unpredictable, but also unreliable, and requiring constant maintenance, which in the middle of a Test series must be like changing a tyre on a moving car.

If anything was different here to the Johnson of Brisbane, it was that after a week with bowling coach Troy Cooley and conditioning coach Stuart Karppinen, Johnson appeared to be running in both slower and straighter – for him, almost hugging the stumps. His arm came through perhaps a tad higher, and his swing into the right-hander returned – even though with characteristic modesty he later admitted he hadn't actually tried to swing it. Happy the man who swings it when he doesn't mean to.

The other effect was on Johnson's control, the impact points on his pitch map fitting snugly into a corridor on the stumps and outside off, rather than, as in Brisbane, resembling the result of a particularly wild game of paintball.

He probed defences more or less constantly, when he did not punch his way straight through them.

But who really knows which technical advice did the trick, or whether it did at all? Certainly no Australian bowler is so used to having his ears dinned, by experts and non-experts alike. Some mornings this summer he must have woken and questioned everything. Was his front arm in the right position as he poured his cereal? Was his wrist behind the knife as he buttered his toast? The other day, a newspaper ran an interview with the Toowoomba plumber for whom Johnson briefly worked in 2004 while sidelined by injury. Not unkindly, the plumber suggested that Johnson's hips weren't coming through straight. Maybe this is a technique used in plumbing to avoid undue bum crack.

Perhaps it was the sight of Perth, where Johnson has prospered before; perhaps it was his first-innings runs; perhaps it was the helpful easterly breeze; perhaps it was getting the better of minor skirmishes with Kevin Pietersen and Jimmy Anderson. Johnson is assuredly a confidence cricketer. His problem as far as fans are concerned is that this tends to turn those around him into confidence tricksters, as they go through contortions trying to cover for him when he is bad.

After his none for 170 in Brisbane, for example, there was a chorus of Australian denials that he had underperformed. 'He didn't have his best game,' said coach Tim Nielsen. 'He didn't bowl as well as he would have liked.' Greg Chappell said that he and his fellow selectors recognised he was 'not in the peak of form'.

At Adelaide, Johnson was wheeled into a press conference to discuss his omission from the XI accompanied almost by a funeral dirge, only to then remain in the squad. Just before this Test, the story had changed again, Greg Chappell insisting that Johnson had not actually been dropped at all but rested after the Gabba – resting, it seemed, in the same way as a Norwegian Blue parrot is apt to rest. Where Johnson is concerned, Australian cricket surmounts its reputed aversion to cant.

On days like today, you are compelled to admit that there may be method to such handling of Johnson, because he is the bowler in Australian ranks with the greatest potential to turn matches. His pace is such that batsmen are loath to commit to the front foot against him, and for a bowler with such a tendency to spray it around, he takes a high proportion of unassisted wickets: almost 30 per cent.

Three lbws and a bowled today reflected both bowling accuracy and batting diffidence. Pushed so far back by sharp bouncers, Trott and Collingwood had nowhere to go when the ball jackknifed back; creeping so far across, Pietersen placed his eyes dangerously outside the line. Once out of position against a bowler of Johnson's velocities, prayer is a batsman's only recourse. The trio didn't have one between them when their pads were struck.

All the same, it is another indication of the changed nature of Australian cricket that it depends to such a degree on a bowler of humours so variable. If his country is to fight its way back nearer the top of international cricket, Johnson will not only need to bowl as bloody well as Miller, but also to make it an act as simple.

Day 3

Close of play: England 2nd innings 81–5 (JM Anderson 0*, 27 overs)

Just before 6 p.m. tonight, Ricky Ponting hurried towards the players' pavilion, head down, wringing his left hand, in the company of an Australia trainer. Two nights ago, with Australia under the cosh, the sight would have been cause for further dismay. Great – now the captain's cactus. That'd be right . . .

As it is, the situation would have taken the edge from the pain. Ponting had actually just made a bit of a meal of a straightforward chance to second slip by Jonathan Trott off Mitchell Johnson, but in parrying it upwards provided a second chance for Brad Haddin to take. And between them, they had made sure that the Ashes of 2010–11 would go to Melbourne pegged level.

The last doubt was removed in the following over, the day's last, when Paul Collingwood was pouched at second slip by Ponting's stand-in Steve Smith off Ryan Harris. At the close, Australia were five wickets from victory, England 310 runs away. As his team headed in, Ponting emerged from the shadows to meet them, stretching his good hand out to shake those of his team-mates, who have carried Australia, and perhaps also his captaincy, back from the brink of oblivion.

Reducing England to 81 for five was well ahead of Australia's expectations when they began bowling the day's last twenty-seven overs after tea. If not quite as exciting as expected, Cameron Sutherland's pitch has been a gift to cricket: the carry is still excellent, with no evidence of variable bounce, and the pace is quick, although not so quick that Watson and Hussey haven't been able to pull off the front foot with impunity. Aggressive fast bowling and sharp catching did the trick: the game now won't last long enough for Australia to feel the lack of a specialist slow bowler.

It was also a triumph for cumulative pressure. A quite full, very quiet house, refreshed by a pleasant breeze, hung on each ball through the first hour, when Watson and Hussey showed as few signs of budging as at one stage did the sightscreen in front of the Lillee–Marsh Stand. They can put a man on the moon . . .

Strauss's thinking was a little static too, involving a 7–2 field with sweepers on both sides to Watson, thinking to slow his progress, on the suspicion, not unfounded, that his innings would peter out of its own accord. But perhaps because Watson was not called upon to bowl his usual allotment of overs in England's first innings, he was more active and alert than usual, the presence of the responsive and nimble Hussey encouraging him to take singles, mixing twenty-six of them among his eleven fours. It also had the effect of taking lbw out of play – quite a concession to a batsman England had already dismissed five times in like manner, and would finally dismiss a sixth.

Hussey raised the 150 with a sizzling square drive from Anderson, then pulled Tremlett exuberantly in the air in front of square leg. With all Australia's morning forebodings allayed, and Billy Cooper ecumenically trumpeting 'Waltzing Matilda', Watson charged through the 80s with a celebratory cover drive and off drive from consecutive Finn deliveries.

Fortunately for England, Watson soon after planted his front foot against Tremlett, and was given out by Ray Erasmus. Watson solemnly sought the intervention of the referral system, only to be baffled by the verdict – like someone whose cash card has been swallowed by an ATM, he trailed away feeling himself a helpless victim of a previously trusted technology. The replay clarified with a cruel candour: Watson's bat had snicked his back pad just before the ball had hit his front pad. One wonders if cricketers will one day miss their illusions.

It was a decidedly mixed day for the referral system. Smith (1) had more luck, joining the queue of batsmen to challenge Billy Doctrove in this match when a ball from Finn emerged from between bat and pad in transit to Strauss at first slip. Showing some presence of mind, Smith referred promptly, with a small shake of the head, whereupon the replay revealed that the delivery had both missed the bat and would also have cleared the stumps. Hussey was then given out lbw to the session's last ball from Tremlett by Erasmus, then given in after a referral, the ball clearing the stumps – bounce here taketh away as well as giveth.

Perhaps the oddest moment of the day was when Anderson appealed for lbw against Smith (28), referred when Erasmus demurred, and was repudiated on the basis that even though the ball was hitting leg stump, it wasn't *hitting it enough* – a third as opposed to a half. The decision thereby devolved to Erasmus again, who unsurprisingly stood by his initial judgement.

Smith survived to prosper, with a little luck, albeit well deserved, helping Hussey add a busy 75 at four runs an over. He has the face of a sitcom mischief-maker, built to break into a snicker, and a similar playfulness to Greg Ritchie, whom Alan Ross once said you expected any minute on the field to start munching a Mars Bar. He hasn't bowled a ball in the game but already looks a better bet than Marcus North and Xavier Doherty put together.

When Tremlett removed Smith and Haddin in short order, and Johnson drove Collingwood tamely to short cover, England found themselves in better cheer than for a day. Collingwood celebrated with a bouncer wide that would have been a half-volley had it been bowled from the other end, Finn with a bouncer from the opposite end that Harris turned into a wicket with a needless hoick.

Hussey by this time had a chanceless and tireless thirteenth hundred, a second against England on his home ground. He was helped by some indifferent tactics, Strauss cajoling his bowlers into a predictable diet of short-pitched deliveries, which Hussey never wearied of hooking and pulling. His light feet also nullified Swann, England's match-winner at Adelaide, who came on at 1.30 p.m. and bowled only five exploratory and expensive overs. At 284 for eight, Swann also dropped Siddle (0) at short cover, an awkward chance to his right, but one that by England's recent standards was eminently catchable: Australia's lead was then 365, an awkward size but by recent Perth benchmarks gettable.

It added subtly to the pressure when England began their chase of 391 to win circumspectly, and with a heart flutter, Cook having to scamper back after setting off prematurely for a single, bowler Johnson's kick not quite as accurate as in Wellington in March when he caught Tim McIntosh short of his ground. Not that it mattered overmuch, Cook falling in the next over when Harris bent one back into him which would have hit leg stump had it not been impeded by the batsman's back pad. Having escaped Johnson yesterday, Strauss was not so lucky today, caught between wind and water, playing and not, as the ball held its line on off stump.

Had England gone into the close with two wickets down, they might just have slept optimistically. Pietersen was certainly of that mind, resisting sternly and strokelessly for almost forty minutes and only three singles, only to perish to a wretched shot, defending with the face of the bat towards cover as he walked forward – a cardinal sin at the WACA. It was Hilfenhaus's first Test wicket for 471 deliveries, since his dismissal of Strauss in the first over of the series, although by the close this was mainly a curiosity.

Collingwood kicked the ground angrily as he trailed off, not surprisingly as the ball before he had had a chance to get off strike but been turned back by night watchman Anderson – when you're not hot in this series, you are very cold indeed. Just ask Ricky Ponting.

18 DECEMBER 2010
HUSSEY, WATSON, SMITH

Past, Present, Future

A balmy day, a happy crowd, an England collapse, an imminent victory: it might almost have been an afternoon out of Australian cricket's salad days. Tomorrow is Ricky Ponting's birthday and, while his finger might be sore, they really will all have come at once.

As a victory, it won't be a classic. Australia will finish as they started, a team in transition. But the transition will at least look like it is to somewhere rather than involving further steps into the unknown. And while the bowling will have clinched it, it will have been the much-maligned batting that set it up, having in doing so provided a glimpse of Australian batsmanship past, present and future.

It is not unkind to see 35-year-old Hussey, stoutest and stickiest of Ponting's old band of brothers, in the past tense. He is a representative of Australian cricket's abiding values, having added a cubit to his span by an ethic of unrelenting self-improvement.

Hussey started his career about 25km north of the WACA, at the Perth first-grade club of Wanneroo, where his father Ted is still secretary. At the Roos, he was a contemporary of Damien Martyn, so intimidatingly gifted as a teenager that he would call laconically after each shot – 'one', 'two' or 'three'; fours came too easily to bother.

Regarding himself as nowhere near so talented, Hussey decided that the road to success ran through a valley of vigour and rigour. He has since made servants of net bowlers the world over, among the most willing being Monty Panesar at Northants – so much time did they spend in the nets together that restricted access conditions were finally imposed on them.

The other peculiarity of Hussey's technique is that he is a right-handed left-hander – that is, he does everything except bat the other way round. It's a legacy of 1980s backyard games with his similarly right-handed brother David: one of them had to be Allan Border, and Michael volunteered. Into the same category fall David Gower, Stephen Fleming and Matt Hayden, all powerful through the covers, as well as with the traditional left-hander's on-side partiality. Hussey never thrashes forward of the wicket on the off side: he caresses square and punches straight, a strong top hand always in control, with the minimum of backlift and a truncated follow-through. These were profitable shots at the WACA today, where the boundaries down the ground are shortest.

Hussey's signature this summer, of course, has been his pull shot, which he has played fearlessly, especially in Brisbane. England challenged it today, throwing down the gauntlet of Perth's challenging bounce, but Hussey as a native son made the shot look as safe and conventional as a forward defensive.

When a good batsman trusts himself, he does not think twice – it is thinking twice, in fact, that is inclined to cost you. On 92, Hussey, by now in the tail's company, faced Tremlett, refreshed by having just bowled Haddin, and reinforced by three men on the fence. Hussey was ready, pulling from in front of his face, weight on the front foot to keep the ball to ground, controlling it so precisely that it bisected two of the boundary riders; three balls later, he repeated the shot, this time forward of square, to reach a hundred. Hard work, homespun style, heady strokeplay: this innings was Hussey in excelsis.

Twenty-nine-year-old Shane Watson is Australian cricket present, part of its current make-do-and-mend modus operandi, devised to fill the all-rounder role of Freddie Flintoff, finally coming to rest in the opener's niche left last year by Philip Hughes. He oozes power, his check-drives to mid-off and mid-on fairly fly, and he lets the ball go with a decisive flourish – a good attribute in Perth, as witnessed on the first day.

Watson has always been a textbook cricketer, even if for the first five years of his career the textbook was *Grey's Anatomy*. That proneness to injury has since been counter-acted by a Brisbane physiotherapist, Victor Popov, who weened Watson off weight-bearing exercise by introducing him to Tabata training: a regime of light weights at high speed to consolidate core strength, plus Pilates to enhance flexibility.

But while the musculature has improved, Watson's batting has rather marked time, perhaps because Ponting's reliance on him for relieving overs, perhaps because his innings seem to decelerate as the ball ages and run-scoring gaps are plugged. Often while opening with Simon Katich, he would streak away with early boundaries, only to be caught up by his dogged partner later – their strike rates ended up virtually identical.

Watson was blessed today on both counts. England's first innings was brief enough that he did not have to bowl, while Hussey's buzzing energy kept the singles ticking where sometimes they peter out. This was his best innings of the summer, and at times radiated real authority, although it was also not too surprising when he fell five short of his hundred: he has passed fifty fifteen times in Tests, and only twice pushed on to hundreds. Watson is in transition as assuredly as his team.

Steve Smith is Australian cricket's future. There is already a sense of imminent eventfulness about his presence at the crease, and today he did not disappoint. He almost ran himself out backing Hussey up too far, bowler Tremlett's throw just missing the non-striker's stumps. A top-edged hook from Finn then landed between the advancing Tremlett and Bell, and an upper cut as he limboed beneath a Tremlett bouncer cleared a gasping cordon. A pull shot from the next ball, however, showed off the 21-year-old's precocity. England must have hoped to stride through at this point; he impeded them like chewing gum on the soles of their shoes.

Smith looks a little like the boy at an Aussie club who smashes it round in the juniors so often on Saturday morning that they finally promote him to the seniors in the afternoon, where he does more than plug a gap, and soon makes himself at home; in the boy-among-men role in this team, he recalls the sight of his captain on this ground fifteen years ago. He duplicated his captain's dismissal in this innings too, succumbing to a leg-side strangle when Tremlett came round the wicket.

What becomes of Smith is complicated by his leg-break bowling. Shane Warne has already commented that time spent on his batting will come at a cost to the development of his wrist-spinning skills. There are, after all, only twenty-four hours in a day. But just now, Smith looks like he wants to use all of them. He cannot get enough of cricket – and on days like today, who can blame him?

19 DECEMBER 2010

Day 4

Close of play: England 2nd innings 123 (37 overs)

If it were done when it is done, 'twere well it were done quickly, and all it took today were ten overs for Australia to eradicate the last five England wickets and tie the Ashes of 2010–11 up at 1–1. On the first day, the sum of 268 runs, being Australia's total, looked paltry. Today, the sum of 267 runs, being Australia's victory margin, appeared over-whelming.

There was little drama about the final rites, even an air of conviviality. Shortly after 11 a.m., the strains of 'The Last Post' wafted over the WACA, courtesy of Billy Cooper. What else? A minute or two later, Cooper was at it again. This time it was 'I Do Like to Be Beside the Seaside'. As it died, Steve Finn edged to second slip: time for the beach. Say what you like about the Barmy Army, they have a talent for making the best of things – it probably comes of practice.

There was even a sense of right order restored. As Australia lorded it over England, Shane Warne was being reported to have deluged a blonde with obscene text messages, that disorienting brunette interlude apparently an aberration – just like the good old days. There was only one absence this concluding morning, that of Ricky Ponting, marking his thirty-sixth birthday by nursing a fractured little finger on his left hand, sustained late the night before. It was vice-captain Michael Clarke who enjoyed the luxury of deploying four slips, gully, point and short leg, and a bowling attack able to exploit them.

Ian Bell played some shots of quality, rather too good for someone reduced to batting number seven in this second innings by the ineffectual use of the night watchman, before falling lbw – arguably the first time he has been genuinely defeated by a bowler in the series, having twice fallen while hitting out in the company of the tail. Otherwise, the day was largely for the benefit of man-of-the-match Mitchell Johnson and man-of-any-other-match Ryan Harris, nine for 82 and 106 respectively, the former bowling the potentially irritating Swann all over the place, the undersung latter claiming a Test-best six for 47. Ponting saluted both afterwards, making a good fist of keeping his sense of vindication quiet. Rumour has it that he pressed strongly for Johnson's inclusion, and that the selectors gave in on condition he include a fourth quick bowler in case of another Mitchell meltdown. Having worked against Australia all summer, accidents may now be working in their favour.

'It's transformed him and it's transformed the way he's seen in this series,' said Ponting afterwards, seated alongside Johnson. 'Now is not the time to panic,' said Strauss, inviting the question of when is. On the subject of his finger, Ponting pronounced himself satisfied that it would prove no impediment to his playing in Melbourne, which makes complete sense. He is cut from the same cloth as Allan Border, who so frequently played with broken and chipped fingers that you almost swore he punched walls on purpose. At one-all in the Ashes series, too, he is in the same boat as Macbeth, 'vaulting ambition' ready to 'o'erleap itself'.

19 DECEMBER 2010
RYAN HARRIS

One Crowded Hour

On the flight from Adelaide to Melbourne after the Second Test, reporters were surprised to find Ryan Harris among the passengers. No, he explained, he was not flying home to Brisbane, nor even in transit to Perth for the next game: he had an appointment to see his surgeon, the same surgeon he consults after virtually every game, who takes the measure of the steadily eroding cartilage in his right knee and, if he's satisfied, clears him to play again.

If there is one consolation for England in Harris's nine for 106 against them at the WACA, it is that in an Australian cricket age without a name, he is destined for one crowded hour of glorious life. On days of heavy toil, he experiences the sensations in his leg that athletes colloquially, graphically but matter-of-factly call 'bone-on-bone'. Surgery could repair the structure, but would also cost him up to eighteen months recovery time, and at thirty-one that is simply too long.

So, Harris makes the best of it. When the knee swells, as it did after he took nine for 140 for Queensland against Ricky Ponting's Tasmanians in the Sheffield Shield five weeks ago, there is nothing for it but to rest the joint and decant the excess fluid. But fifteen years ago, Harris would not have been playing at the equivalent stage of his life, because Australian cricket would not have been wealthy enough to sustain him medically and logistically. He is a cricketer lucky in his era. He will not play fifty Tests, but he may play twenty, and that is twenty more than this affable, self-deprecating bowler expected until very recently.

Ponting, moreover, is a stark raving fan. Harris swings the ball away at speed: 150 Tests have taught the captain that bowlers with such a profile win Tests. In an attack so dependent on the shit-or-bust Mitchell Johnson, Harris's old-fashioned hit-the-deck ways are also a set-and-forget reassurance. While his nickname Ryano is hardly original, it does recall Darren Gough's cheery self-description: 'You know why they call me Rhino? Because I'm as strong as an ox.'

As Ponting mingled on the field among his victorious team this morning, he somehow reached Harris last, but it was with Harris he remained longest, patting his back all the way off – with his right hand at least, his left little finger being a tad tender for too much congratulary work. It transpired that this is something Ponting has to do quite a lot with Harris, whom he confided later is one of those perfectionist bowlers who thinks he 'has never bowled a good ball'.

It is hard to reconcile this predisposition with the broad-shouldered, gravelly-voiced, sun-goldened figure on whose head the baggy green reposes rather more naturally than, for example, Johnson, where it might as well be a bandana to go with his body ink. But it makes a certain sense. If you knew your time was short, you would want every ball to be the best of which you were capable; if every delivery was exacting a measurable physical toll, you would not wish to waste a calorie of effort. Twenty wickets from four Tests at less than 20 should comfort Harris, just as twenty wickets for Australia in this match will have comforted Australia's selectors.

The forty-wicket Test match is a rare enough event as to suggest a complete domination of ball over bat these days. In fact, it was a little more complex. Three bowlers (Harris, Johnson, Tremlett) claimed twenty-six wickets at 13 between them, the other specialist bowlers thirteen wickets at 40. From side-on, where most of the press have been congregated, it has looked throughout as though the WACA's famous siren song proved too strong for some bowlers to resist, Steve Finn and James Anderson in particular pitching consistently a yard or two short, excited by the bounce and the tentative Australian batting on the first morning.

Australia took nine unassisted English wickets, five lbws and four bowleds; of England's six, two lbws and four bowleds, two of the latter were dragged on to the stumps. Australia's batsmen played the pull shot repeatedly; England's hardly had the opportunity at all. Strauss exonerated his bowlers from criticism after the match today – one can't help feeling that this was too much an accentuation of the positive.

Harris's second innings lbw victims, by contrast, were plumb, the batsmen playing back but the ball hitting the stumps halfway up. Alastair Cook did not even bother to refer his decision yesterday; Ian Bell only did so for form's sake today. Collingwood, too, succumbed to a full delivery that he had moved too far back to do anything but nick. England's batsmen may not have been psyched out by Australia's bowlers, but Australia's bowlers had certainly weighed up England's likely response to the unfamiliar environs.

As for Harris, it was time to accept congratulations, one of the first arriving in the form of a text from his surgeon, who counselled him to look forward to the Boxing Day Test. Harris should: he took six for 68 for Queensland against Victoria there three weeks ago. The salient fact, however, is simply that he will be there. In one crowded hour, every minute counts.

THIRD TEST   Western Australia Cricket Association Ground, Perth
16–19 December 2010
Toss England   **Australia** won by 267 runs

AUSTRALIA 1st innings			R	M	B	4	6	SR
SR Watson	lbw	b Finn	13	72	40	1	0	32.50
PJ Hughes		b Tremlett	2	10	6	0	0	33.33
*RT Ponting	c Collingwood	b Anderson	12	11	10	3	0	120.00
MJ Clarke	c †Prior	b Tremlett	4	13	10	1	0	40.00
MEK Hussey	c †Prior	b Swann	61	139	104	9	1	58.65
SPD Smith	c Strauss	b Tremlett	7	46	37	0	0	18.91
†BJ Haddin	c Swann	b Anderson	53	119	80	6	1	66.25
MG Johnson	c Anderson	b Finn	62	117	93	8	1	66.66
RJ Harris		b Anderson	3	8	5	0	0	60.00
PM Siddle		not out	35	69	59	3	0	59.32
BW Hilfenhaus	c Cook	b Swann	13	25	12	3	0	108.33
EXTRAS		(lb 3)	3					
TOTAL	(all out; 76 overs; 322 mins)		268	(3.52 runs per over)				

FoW | 1-2 | (Hughes, 1.6 ov), | 2-17 | (Ponting, 4.5 ov),
| 3-28 | (Clarke, 7.6 ov), | 4-36 | (Watson, 16.1 ov),
| 5-69 | (Smith, 27.3 ov), | 6-137 | (Hussey, 40.4 ov),
| 7-189 | (Haddin, 57.3 ov), | 8-201 | (Harris, 59.5 ov),
| 9-233 | (Johnson, 70.3 ov), | 10-268 | (Hilfenhaus, 75.6 ov)

BOWLING	O	M	R	W	ECON
JM Anderson	20	3	61	3	3.05
CT Tremlett	23	3	63	3	2.73
ST Finn	15	1	86	2	5.73
PD Collingwood	2	0	3	0	1.50
GP Swann	16	0	52	2	3.25

ENGLAND 1st innings			R	M	B	4	6	SR
*AJ Strauss	c †Haddin	b Harris	52	125	102	8	0	50.98
AN Cook	c Hussey	b Johnson	32	96	63	3	1	50.79
IJL Trott	lbw	b Johnson	4	7	8	1	0	50.00
KP Pietersen	lbw	b Johnson	0	2	3	0	0	0.00
PD Collingwood	lbw	b Johnson	5	25	17	0	0	29.41
IR Bell	c Ponting	b Harris	53	133	90	6	0	58.88
†MJ Prior		b Siddle	12	62	42	1	0	28.57
GP Swann	c †Haddin	b Harris	11	45	31	1	0	35.48
CT Tremlett		b Johnson	2	21	14	0	0	14.28
JM Anderson	c Watson	b Johnson	0	7	6	0	0	0.00
ST Finn		not out	1	2	1	0	0	100.00
EXTRAS	(b 8, lb 4, w 1, nb 2)		15					
TOTAL	(all out; 62.3 overs; 267 mins)		187	(2.99 runs per over)				

FoW
1-78	(Cook, 24.1 ov),	2-82		(Trott, 26.3 ov),
3-82	(Pietersen, 26.6 ov),	4-94		(Strauss, 31.3 ov),
5-98	(Collingwood, 32.3 ov),	6-145		(Prior, 46.4 ov),
7-181	(Swann, 57.1 ov),	8-186		(Bell, 61.1 ov),
9-186	(Tremlett, 62.1 ov),	10-187		(Anderson, 62.3 ov)

BOWLING	O	M	R	W	ECON	
BW Hilfenhaus	21	6	53	0	2.52	(1nb)
RJ Harris	15	4	59	3	3.93	(1w)
PM Siddle	9	2	25	1	2.77	(1nb)
MG Johnson	17.3	5	38	6	2.17	

AUSTRALIA 2nd innings			R	M	B	4	6	SR
SR Watson	lbw	b Tremlett	95	221	174	11	0	54.59
PJ Hughes	c Collingwood	b Finn	12	51	31	1	0	38.70
*RT Ponting	c †Prior	b Finn	1	17	9	0	0	11.11
MJ Clarke		b Tremlett	20	21	18	4	0	111.11
MEK Hussey	c Swann	b Tremlett	116	296	172	15	0	67.44
SPD Smith	c †Prior	b Tremlett	36	83	62	2	0	58.06
†BJ Haddin		b Tremlett	7	17	10	0	1	70.00
MG Johnson	c Bell	b Collingwood	1	5	4	0	0	25.00
RJ Harris	c Bell	b Finn	1	14	7	0	0	14.28
PM Siddle	c Collingwood	b Anderson	8	33	26	1	0	30.76
BW Hilfenhaus		not out	0	8	5	0	0	0.00
EXTRAS	(lb 6, w 4, nb 2)		12					
TOTAL	(all out; 86 overs; 390 mins)		309	(3.59 runs per over)				

FoW	1-31	(Hughes, 12.2 ov),	2-34	(Ponting, 16.1 ov),
	3-64	(Clarke, 20.4 ov),	4-177	(Watson, 50.2 ov),
	5-252	(Smith, 68.4 ov),	6-271	(Haddin, 72.3 ov),
	7-276	(Johnson, 73.3 ov),	8-284	(Harris, 76.2 ov),
	9-308	(Siddle, 84.1 ov),	10-309	(Hussey, 85.6 ov)

BOWLING	O	M	R	W	ECON	
JM Anderson	26	7	65	1	2.50	(1w)
CT Tremlett	24	4	87	5	3.62	(1nb, 2w)
ST Finn	21	4	97	3	4.61	(1nb)
GP Swann	9	0	51	0	5.66	
PD Collingwood	6	3	3	1	0.50	(1w)

ENGLAND 2nd innings			R	M	B	4	6	SR
*AJ Strauss	c Ponting	b Johnson	15	39	35	3	0	42.85
AN Cook	lbw	b Harris	13	23	16	1	0	81.25
IJL Trott	c †Haddin	b Johnson	31	85	61	3	0	50.81
KP Pietersen	c Watson	b Hilfenhaus	3	36	23	0	0	13.04
PD Collingwood	c Smith	b Harris	11	38	27	1	0	40.74
JM Anderson		b Harris	3	22	14	0	0	21.42
IR Bell	lbw	b Harris	16	32	23	3	0	69.56
†MJ Prior	c Hussey	b Harris	10	19	9	0	1	111.11
GP Swann		b Johnson	9	8	5	1	0	180.00
CT Tremlett		not out	1	12	3	0	0	33.33
ST Finn	c Smith	b Harris	2	6	7	0	0	28.57
EXTRAS	(lb 8, nb 1)		9					
TOTAL	(all out; 37 overs; 167 mins)		123	(3.32 runs per over)				

FoW	1-23	(Cook, 6.1 ov),	2-37	(Strauss, 9.5 ov),
	3-55	(Pietersen, 18.1 ov),	4-81	(Trott, 25.5 ov),
	5-81	(Collingwood, 26.6 ov),	6-94	(Anderson, 30.5 ov),
	7-111	(Bell, 34.1 ov),	8-114	(Prior, 34.4 ov),
	9-120	(Swann, 35.4 ov),	10-123	(Finn, 36.6 ov)

BOWLING	O	M	R	W	ECON	
BW Hilfenhaus	10	4	16	1	1.60	
RJ Harris	11	1	47	6	4.27	
MG Johnson	12	3	44	3	3.66	
PM Siddle	4	1	8	0	2.00	(1nb)

Part V

Fourth Test

Melbourne Cricket Ground
26–29 December 2010
England won by an innings and 157 runs

G Whiz

A little over a month ago, England would probably have settled for arriving at Boxing Day at one-all; a little over a week ago, Australia would certainly have been content with the same. Welcome to the Ashes of 2010–11, in which expectations are in a state of constant revision, and to the Fourth Test, where the balanced scenario may flush out a record Test crowd tomorrow on Boxing Day.

The last time cricket's oldest rivals met here four years ago, Australia had already regained the Ashes, and were incinerating England for the sake of it. Under mackerel skies, the Australian stars were Matthew Hayden, Andrew Symonds, Stuart Clark and Shane Warne, who claimed his 700th Test wicket. None form part of this team; only three of that XI do, and captain Ricky Ponting will be playing with a sore left pinky.

This summer's cricket has been more like 2009 redux: a series in which the rivals have taken turns royally stuffing one another, because neither is quite good enough to dominate throughout, and in which they have seemed incapable of parrying the other's attacking thrusts. Both teams this season have at times been reduced to near helplessness, Australia by Cook, Trott and Pietersen, England by Johnson, Hussey and Haddin; it has looked like a clash of first against tenth rather than fourth against fifth, albeit with the upper hand alternating.

For the Fourth Test, Australia may even repeat their gamble of last year, when after their conclusive victory at Headingley they took an unchanged side into the Oval, sans a specialist spinner – with, on that occasion, disastrous consequences, as its pacemen were ineffectual on a dry pitch that turned sharply on the last couple of days. 'The four quicks complemented each other well in Perth and they all played the role I wanted them to play,' Ponting mused aloud yesterday. 'So if they can do a similar job here, the England batsmen will find it difficult.'

But inside the giant crucible of the MCG, winds swirl; there will be no stiff easterly to help Johnson's inswing. Balls arriving throat high at Perth, too, tend from the same length to arrive at waist height in Melbourne, as the MCG's curator Cameron Hodgkins warned yesterday: 'I would think on the WACA's worst day they would still be faster and bouncier than anything we normally turn out. We're quite slow on the first day normally and it probably causes the most difficulty for batsmen who want to get on with it, so patience is normally a fairly key ingredient here.'

After his success in arguing for Johnson at Perth, it is likely that Ponting will get what he wants, balance or no. Yet if we have learned anything in these Ashes, it is that conditions count in cricket as perhaps in no other sport. Three Tests played with near-identical personnel could hardly have been more different. On Brisbane's slow pitch, stubborn batsmen became almost immovable; on Adelaide's flat wicket, swing and finally spin prevailed; on Perth's bouncy tarmac, pace obtained its reward, although it was bowlers of fuller lengths who did best as batsmen were pushed back on their stumps. Batting might be hardest of all in Melbourne on the first day, and the captain winning the toss will be tempted to insert.

For their part, England are also making noises of resistance to change. Strauss insisted yesterday that Ian Bell would remain grooved at number six, even as the batsman himself was brooding on a record without an Ashes hundred for sixteen appearances: 'I'm happy with the way I'm playing but I want an Ashes hundred, and a few of them to be honest.' He won't get them in the company of the tail, and England's tail in Perth especially, which didn't so much wag as writhe in agony.

The other possibility is 21-year-old Steve Finn making way for the older, steadier Tim Bresnan, on the grounds that Finn is too costly, conceding 4.3 an over. It seems like a retrograde step, but teams often make them after a defeat, albeit that it always seems to be bowlers rather than batsmen who are first under the bus. The Australians have attacked Finn this summer, perceiving him as the weakest of England's four bowling links, but his fourteen wickets at 33 are one of the reasons that England in consecutive Tests have taken twenty Australian wickets, something they were expected to struggle to do.

All is set for another new-fashioned arm-wrestle, of tiny differences that may or may not grow large. For England in Perth, the second day dismissal that ramified was Alastair

Cook's. England were cruising at 78 for none. Cook had played, for him, expansively, enjoying the bounce. Johnson had bowled 282 deliveries in the series with barely an appeal, let alone a wicket; indeed, he had hardly beaten the bat.

Johnson's 283rd ball did not so much swing as slide away from the left-hander. It was the kind of ball Cook had been safely letting go all summer, but he was a batsman in hot form, England were on top, and Johnson was a negligible quantity. England's vice-captain looked to drive on the up through cover point – the shot of a winner, keen to put away a weakened opponent.

When the thick edge was smoothly taken by Hussey at gully, the predominant Australian emotion was relief rather than relish, marking the end of something rather than the start of something else. Yet for the next half-hour, Johnson was like a fox in a hen run, making a bloody, feathery mess of a middle order hitherto cock of the roost. Without that nanosecond's relaxation by Cook, Johnson would have continued bowling to left-handers, generally good leavers of the ball. As it was, Johnson's bowling exploded like a perfect storm: a succession of right-handers, a helpful wind, a bowler suddenly confident to stretch for a few extra clicks, and a referral system hovering over every lbw.

It is hard to see England relaxing again in the same way. They are the better led, the better drilled and the more even team. Australia have relied on individuals rising above themselves, hitting long-lost straps, rekindling long-doused fires. Duncan Fletcher used to talk about cricketers 'coming to the party'. England's has been a pretty good-humoured one in which nobody has been sick in the punchbowl. Australia's has depended for its good cheer on someone every so often putting a lampshade on their head.

Whatever happens from here, the fortunes of the series have provided (cricket) season's greetings to Cricket Australia. Their slogan all summer has been 'History Will Be Made': there is, on Boxing Day, just the chance it might, with the fifty-year-old Test record attendance of 90,800 set at the same ground under threat. For once in a journalistic lifetime, the expression 'standing room only' will be more than a cliché: the Melbourne Cricket Club have released standing-room tickets, of which 5,000 in total are available. The attendance of members will affect how many of the arena's 95,000 seats are filled. If the record does not fall, the rest of the crowd's practice of booing the members when the Mexican wave reaches their enclosure will be well and truly justified.

26 DECEMBER 2010

Day 1

Close of play: England 1st innings 157–0
(AJ Strauss 64*, AN Cook 80*, 47 overs)

It was a record day at the MCG, as expected. The mega crowd did not actually eventuate, 84,245 leaving the fifty-year-old world attendance record intact. The records instead were of ruin: from the lowest Australian first innings at home in almost sixty years, to its lowest in the Ashes at the MCG ever.

As a long day waned, having been prolonged by a rain break, England were 59 runs ahead with all their wickets in hand, Australia having capitulated for 98 in 42.5 overs – ten more runs than they scraped together against Pakistan five months ago, although that was at Headingley while their countrymen were thinking football-shaped thoughts rather than on the biggest day of the local summer. With an unchanged XI and a ring of confidence, Australia allegedly came into this Fourth Test with that sought-after 21st-century quality of 'momentum' – just as England did in Perth, in fact. The way things are going, pretty soon we'll be talking about the curse of momentum.

As batting conditions go, these went. It was cool, overcast, with a little moisture in the pitch as well as the air. In the middle of the day, the bowlers were refreshed by a ninety-minute weather hiatus; an outfield rendered slow by football forgave errors of line and length; grass lush from rain preserved the ball's shine.

Both captains wished to bowl. Only one could. Strauss was blessed – and burdened, because inserting the opposition attracts disproportionate condemnation when it goes wrong. Under such circumstances, a captain wants everything to stick, and Watson vexed him by being dropped twice before he had scored, by Collingwood low to his left at third slip, by Pietersen at head height in the gully. Although neither was straightforward, both fell into the category of chances England have become accustomed to taking. There would have been some sweaty palms in the visiting cordon until Tremlett's lift caught Watson unawares in the fourth over.

It was a nervous, even slightly messy first hour. Hughes and Ponting, 5ft 7 and 5ft 10 respectively, were repeatedly tucked up by the bounce; both inside-edged close to the stumps. England's direction was also poor, Prior too often sent skedaddling down the leg side. In one such instance, Prior cost his team a referral for an Anderson delivery that clearly glanced Hughes's shirt. His reputation for optimism now precedes him; you would not ask him for a tip on the stockmarket or the races.

Having emerged to a pleasing ovation, and from back-to-back *Herald Sun* happy-snap front pages, Ponting played the first resounding shots of the day, when he twice pulled short deliveries from Anderson that arrived at a hospitable waist height. But in the next over, Hughes drove expansively with an open blade, a culpable shot, providing Tim Bresnan with a first Ashes wicket.

Ponting fell immediately after drinks when Tremlett, relieving Anderson from the Southern Stand End, found just about the perfect length for this pitch. Australia's captain departed with a reproachful glance at the pitch, and perhaps a rueful rumination on his luck at the toss: in Ashes Tests, he has now lost more than twice as many as he has won. To the home team's 37 for three there was a cloying familiarity, the team's starts in this series having ranged from the calamitous to the merely mediocre: 100 for three in Brisbane, 2 for three and 64 for three in Adelaide, 36 for four and 64 for three in Perth. Hitherto they have relied on Hussey to set them straight; today they did so once too often. Just as the weather closed in, Anderson drew from him a reluctant, firm-footed jab, and an edge that, to English ears, would have reverberated as pleasingly as the peal of a church bell.

Clarke tided Australia over the rain, but he is not the player who last year almost could not stop himself scoring runs; with the exception of his second innings at Adelaide, he has been batting non-start all summer long. He played one firm drive, several harried prods, and his crouch, pronounced in Brisbane, seemed lower than ever, like he was trying to peer underneath a lorry.

The bowling was consistently dangerous. Tremlett, quicker than in Perth, made Stuart Broad's injury look like England's greatest stroke of good fortune this summer. Normally inscrutable, he allowed himself one sardonic smile when he beat Hughes's outside edge, and what bordered on glee when he had Siddle caught behind. Anderson, less talkative and more accurate than in Perth, puzzled the Australians again with his use of the crease, which exaggerates the need to play him. Bresnan, who replaced Finn, filled in the gaps, and dismissed the dangerous Haddin; Prior took six catches without having to dive or even stretch for any of them. With Australia 91 for nine, the stump-cam showed the back of Harris's bat, which read appropriately 'CHAOS'. Funnily enough, he showed as good a defensive technique as anyone, looking comfortable on the back foot, and playing one tasty square cut. When your most composed batsman has a Test average of 6.4, you know you are in trouble.

As the innings ended, both Harris and Hilfenhaus ran for the boundary, either eager to partake of the bowling conditions themselves, or trying to minimise their embarrassment. In the intermission, however, the clouds parted, and the ground, Strauss and Cook were bathed in sunshine; the sideways movement pretty well vanished. England's openers tucked in eagerly, cutting and pulling with ease, enjoying the trampoline bounce which makes short balls here sit up and beg for punishment. Only Hilfenhaus found the consistency necessary for the circumstances, wringing an affirmative lbw verdict against Alastair Cook (30) from Tony Hill, only to have it countermanded on referral to Ray Erasmus after the replay revealed a thick inside edge.

Australia's avenging angel at the WACA, Mitchell Johnson, was here distinctly earthbound, his first three overs without pace, accuracy or threat. Most importantly, they hung as shapelessly as Mama Cass's kaftan. In the second of his two spells from the Members' End, 3–0–17–0 and 4–0–25–0, Johnson also sent four byes past Haddin's outstretched right gauntlet that would have brought a gulp of recognition to the throat of anyone who watched him in Brisbane. Standing at mid-off for the sake of his finger, Ponting looked unusually friendless and forlorn. The crowd had already started to thin, the lower terraces left roomy by early, disillusioned departures. The way his team-mates had deserted him earlier, the captain might have yearned to follow them. As it was, the happiest Melburnians today were probably those who, like many members, did not turn up at all.

26 DECEMBER 2010
MIKE HUSSEY

One Out, All Out

'He's Out', read the headlines in English newspapers at news of the fall of Bradman. It was tempting to imagine something similar as Michael Hussey disappeared from view into the basement catacombs of the MCG's Ponsford Stand to leave Australia 58 for four shortly before lunch in this Fourth Test.

All summer long, Hussey has been the thin green and gold line, a one-man resistance movement, a reminder of better days. In the first three Tests, he compiled more runs than any batsman in the five Tests of last year's Ashes. When he was caught at the wicket today, it seemed insufficiently momentous to say that he had merely been dismissed. It felt like the Fall of the House of Hussey. *Monsieur Cricket: C'est Fini.*

In fact, if you're to pick Hussey up cheaply anywhere, Melbourne is where you will do it, perhaps because he prefers pace on the ball, perhaps because he can be a tentative starter and quicker bowlers deck it round here. His MCG average is now less than 30, compared to 75 at the other Australian Test grounds.

This was also the reward for thoughtful, patient, probing bowling. Hussey left half the balls bowled to him today, but England did not grow bored and stray on to the stumps, conceding him easy on-side runs; nor did they bombard him pointlessly, feeding his pull shot, as at Brisbane and Perth.

Instead, they counted on a disciplined line, a mostly full length and the influence of the arithmetic mean: sooner or later, the hottest streak must end.

James Anderson had time to bowl only one further delivery, which snaked past Steve Smith's furtive prod, before rain moved in. Time to reflect; for Australia, time to worry. This *had* to happen. *Now* what would they do? It was already almost too late. Smith at number six is a promising cricketer, but as neither batsman nor bowler is he someone to be relied on in Test cricket. If Smith is the answer, you are caused to reflect, what is the question? As Australia's only slow bowler here and in Perth, he has delivered half a dozen patchy overs.

It looked, in the end, a little like a team that thought it could carry the day with a positive attitude, a spring in its step and a bit of baggy-green dreaming. But this was not such an occasion, nor is this a venue at which to rely on fancy and faith. In Melbourne's broadsheet daily, *The Age*, Dean Jones devoted a Christmas Eve column to the subject of batting on the first day at the MCG, stressing the importance of circumspection: he entreated Australian batsmen not to drive, to be wary of the pitch's residual tackiness, to preserve wickets early in order to benefit afterwards. As Smith, Phil Hughes, Michael Clarke, Brad Haddin and Peter Siddle were all dismissed on the front foot, going hard at the moving ball, it was indicative of poor reading habits as well as poor batting.

The example was set early. The contest of opening batsman and bowler is cricket's Socratic dialogue, inquiry and response, proposition and rebuttal. The first cricketer to make a name for himself on Twitter, Hughes seems to see the game in terms of attitude, aggression and a good time rather than a long time. In Tremlett's first over, he slashed square and larruped the ball through the covers. England's bowlers promptly tightened their lines to keep him under control, whereupon he became like a boy threatening to hold his breath until he burst; his open-faced drive on the up to be caught in the gully even as the drinks retinue were waiting by their Gatorwagon was the shot not of a Test opener, which he is meant to be, but of a batsman averaging less than 20 this season, which he is.

Once Ponting had fetched the closest thing to an unplayable delivery all day, it was notable just how minimal was the sense of event about the coming of the rest of the batsmen. Back in the day, the Australian order deployed like the cast of one of those old-fashioned, big-budget star vehicles of the 1960s and 1970s: *The Battle of Britain*, perhaps, or *A Bridge Too Far*. It felt like there was no end to the batting. When Steve Waugh and Adam Gilchrist were at numbers six and seven, it almost seemed to get better as it went on.

Not only does this Australian order have no such star quality, it exudes vulnerability. As an observer, you don't struggle to imagine its weaknesses: Watson's block about hundreds, Hughes's block about blocking, Clarke's back, Ponting's age, Haddin's impetuosity. We saw today the batting in its true light, that Hussey has been guiding Australia across a narrow bridge of struggling competitiveness while a chasm of abject failure has yawned beneath. Had he not failed here, the team would simply have been overwhelmed a little later – but it was always going to happen.

Day 2

Close of play: England 1st innings 444–5
(IJL Trott 141*, MJ Prior 75*, 136 overs)

It was the sound of one man snapping. The man was Ricky Ponting. You might lose it too, were you in his position: being stuffed out of sight in the biggest series of your life. But what you must not do, under any circumstances, is lose it with an umpire.

Two days ago, Ricky Ponting was on the front pages of newspapers playing with his beautiful two-year-old daughter, a portrait of contentment. Tomorrow those same front pages will be blazoned with pictures of him browbeating umpire Aleem Dar over a decision in which a) the umpire was right; b) the fielding side was far from unanimous anyway; and c) the cost turned out to be minimal. Worse than a crime, as Talleyrand said, it was a mistake.

This is how it happened. From the last ball of Harris's sixteenth over, the fourth with the second new ball, Kevin Pietersen's forward lunge was cleanly bisected, the ball carrying to Haddin. The keeper raised an arm in appeal, albeit rather quizzically. Harris did not join him; Pietersen looked bemused.

When Dar shook his head minimally, as is his wont, Ponting advanced from mid-off gesturing in favour of a referral. Peter Siddle then crossed from mid-wicket, and a lengthy contretemps ensued, with increasingly frantic gesticulation from Australia's captain, amid apparent grunts of support from the Victorian. Although the review by third umpire Ray Erasmus upheld Dar's decision, the remonstration went on . . . and on, and on, the umpire looking an increasingly persecuted minority, the Australians distinctly boorish hosts.

The bone of contention was that during the big screen's Hot Spot replay, Siddle had spied a faint white dot near the bottom of the bat – confusing, but nowhere near the trajectory of the ball, and certainly no justification for carrying on an appeal so long that it almost made it to The Hague. The scene carried on amid booing and catcalling from the crowd of 67,149, but as Ponting also exchanged words with Dar's colleague Tony Hill and Pietersen, the general air was of silent disbelief – surely the best Australian batsman of his generation and Australia's winningest captain had not come to this.

In one respect, the Australians deserved commendation: they harnessed their indignation well. Siddle, swung into the attack from the Southern Stand End, had Pietersen lbw minutes later as the batsman moved too far across his crease; he then took two smart catches at fine leg. But not even Cricket Australia's PR team could spin this, Siddle rendering the post-match press conference farcical by declining to answer even the gentlest and most basic questions about the incident. This was an ICC matter, journalists were told as Siddle sat down. No comment. Smirk. No comment. Smirk. Look at me, Mum: I'm saying 'no comment'. There was an old saying in the Soviet Union: 'We pretend to work and they pretend to pay us.' At times like these, press conferences achieve comparable futility: they pretend to talk and we pretend to listen.

The incident overshadowed the day, although as far as Australia's Ashes fortunes are concerned not quite enough. At stumps, England were 346 ahead with five second-innings wickets in hand, with Jonathan Trott embedded at the crease on 141, having put on 158 with Matt Prior at a breezy four an over. A general audit of the day was not unflattering to Australia: England added 287 for the loss of five wickets on a day they might have dominated. Having lost the first day by so far, however, the hosts had needed to come rather more than a merely respectable second.

Siddle did most to keep his team in touch, starting the day with a sharp and hostile spell attacking the stumps from the Members' End, having Cook taken at slip by Watson when he failed to negotiate a little extra bounce, and Strauss caught in the gully by a leaping Hussey when one steepled as England's captain tried to drop his wrists. Siddle even got the odd delivery to swing despite the day's bracing cold. Thirty-one runs accrued in the first hour, ten in one over – it was the first period in which Australia had had any presence in the match at all.

England re-established through Pietersen and Trott. Pietersen punched his first boundary from Siddle down the ground, then flipped the next through mid-wicket where a taller, nimbler figure than Clarke might have conjured a catch. From there, his strokes unfurled steadily. When Steve Smith came on at the Members' End to bowl his leg-spin without an outfield fifteen minutes before lunch, Pietersen lit on half-volleys as delightedly as a pedestrian spying a two-pound coin on the pavement, smashing over mid-on then mid-off.

Pietersen and Trott share a country of origin, but, as their careful compilation of 92 in 186 balls showed, not much else. The mercurial Pietersen can bat a little absently, as though in the act of doing something else, the way he performs his preparatory squats as the bowler approaches, and walks forward on the drive; when he's out he tucks his bat under his arm as daintily as an umbrella or a rolled-up newspaper. Mind you, he is in better order than a year ago, when a damaged Achilles tendon had reduced his footwork to an arthritic shuffle. Now he pushes out decisively – even a half-stride from Pietersen is further than most players come forward – and his height equips him to deal with the vagaries of bounce and late movement.

The equable Trott is a cricketer of substantial and visible effort. The sinew bulges in his forearm as he takes his stance, indicative of the rigid top-hand control. He holds his pose after each defensive stroke, inwardly measuring it off against some Platonic ideal, while his attacking shots have a deliberate air, as though chosen judiciously from a range of possibilities. Between balls, of course, he sets to marking his guard, over and over, deeper and deeper, like a hairdresser obsessing over the neatness of a part or a dry-cleaner fretting over a trouser crease.

Siddle again bowled well after lunch and was underneath when Collingwood and Bell failed to keep down hook shots from Johnson. To use football parlance, appropriate given the venue, he qualified hereabouts as a ball magnet. England would have been under greater pressure had Trott (49), coming back for a third on Ponting's arm, not just regained his ground as Hilfenhaus broke the non-striker's stumps. He underwent a penitent stage, dwelling over his next 20 runs, before restoring his momentum with a well-timed on drive and a conspicuously well-controlled hook. Prior (5), meanwhile, enjoyed an unusual stroke of fortune, walking for a palpable nick to the keeper, then staying when Dar detected a not-so-palpable no-ball and called on Erasmus for verification.

It was, literally and figuratively, a false hope. Trott played with undeviating vigilance, Prior with growing freedom, even abandon, taking heavy toll of Smith. As Ponting permutated what ended up as seven bowlers for the rest of the day to no effect, Prior went to a third fifty in nine Ashes Tests, Trott to a third hundred in five.

To his credit, Ponting applauded Trott's milestone spontaneously and lingeringly. Also to his credit, he apologised and pleaded guilty at the evening hearing before ICC referee Ranjan Madugalle, who docked him 40 per cent of his match fee ($5,400) for breaching article 2.1.3 (h) of the code of conduct, which relates to 'arguing or entering into a prolonged discussion with the umpire about his decision'. The court of public opinion may not be so straightforwardly placated.

27 DECEMBER 2010
RICKY PONTING

White-Coat Fever

Every man has his weakness. With Shane Warne, it's blondes. With Ian Chappell, it's Ian Botham – and vice versa. With

Ricky Ponting, it's umpires. Other players suffer white-line fever; he has white-coat fever. Few cricketers, and certainly no current international captain, has a poorer reputation: in the presence of officialdom that has somehow crossed him, he is never knowingly outstropped.

So when the red mist descended today and Ponting challenged the authority of Aleem Dar, it was not without a backdrop or context. Australia's leader is a very great cricketer indeed; he also has a tendency to treat umpires not as respected representatives of the Laws of Cricket, but like malfunctioning appliances.

There were a thousand pities to it, but among the deepest was that the incident was so needless. The match did not hinge on whether Kevin Pietersen had edged Ryan Harris to Brad Haddin; it was at best a speculative appeal, in which the bowler for one had hardly joined, and ended up costing Australia next to nothing. Ponting's anger was a day late. His plight is the fault of Australia's batsmen, who made belated Christmas presents of their wickets on Boxing Day.

So it evoked the pressure under which Ponting has played this series, a great player in hard times, the last survivor of a dynasty, a final vestige of former greatness. But it was also not out of character. In fact, if anything was going to push Ponting's buttons, it was a decision with which he did not agree, and an official in the wrong place at the wrong time. Call it displaced anger.

With certain umpires, even good ones, Ponting has developed unpleasant histories. The capable Mark Benson, who first incurred his ire during the DLF Cup in August 2006 for having the courage to reverse a decision, retired last summer after a Test at Adelaide where Ponting rounded on him for rejecting a caught-behind appeal against Shivnarine Chanderpaul, a decision upheld by the technology.

Aleem Dar, the ICC's umpire of the year, first suffered the sharp edge of Ponting's tongue in April 2006, when Australia's captain harangued him in Chittagong over a decision involving Aftab Ahmed. He experienced it again in England's second innings at Brisbane, as Ponting audibly condemned a decision not to grant his claim of a low catch from Alastair Cook as 'piss-weak umpiring', even though Dar was merely the messenger delivering an off-field verdict.

And these are old, old stories. In his own diary of the 2005 Ashes, Ponting documents such episodes as growling at Billy Bowden for not giving Simon Jones out lbw at Edgbaston ('What was wrong with that?') and chewing out Steve Bucknor for giving Damien Martyn out lbw at Old Trafford ('That was a diabolical decision. He smashed that.'). In *his* account of that series, Ponting's *bête noire* Duncan Fletcher accused Australia's captain of a policy of conscious intimidation: 'Whenever a decision went against Australia during the series, did you notice how Ponting would invariably walk straight up to the umpire and challenge his decision using overbearing body language?' A policy probably dignifies it; it is, more accurately, a habit. But bad habits poison. When Ponting was fined after upbraiding umpire Norman Malcolm for failing to give Patrick Browne out at Grenada in June 2008, he responded to chidings from Cricket Australia dismissively: 'I don't think I'm ever going to be able to just stay mute, shrug my shoulders and accept bad mistakes as part of the game. That's not me.' He wasn't kidding.

Ponting doesn't bear sole responsibility for today's events. In his attitude to umpires, he has been regrettably indulged. Told he had made a grammatical error, the Holy Roman Emperor Sigismund is said to have replied: 'I am King of the Romans and above all grammar.' Authority has failed to disabuse Ponting of his parallel conviction where umpires are concerned. Had the ICC and/or Cricket Australia taken firmer action against Ponting earlier in his career, there might have been no incident today.

One additional factor should be taken into consideration: the dynamic at Perth, where Australia came off the better for a Test visibly shorter of beg-pardons than others in recent years, and where nostalgic local observers felt their sap rise at the sight of an Aussie team going lip-for-lip with an opposition again. The chief executive of the Australian Cricketers' Association, Paul Marsh, went so far as to suggest that the home team had been victims of political correctness – that since Australia's ugly Sydney Test with India three years ago, and the public odium in which the team languished afterwards, Ponting's team had lost their combative edge. 'I think there's no doubt the team's performance has been affected,' Marsh said. 'Hard aggressive cricket is in the Australian team's DNA and unfortunately the players started second-guessing their natural instincts in the heat of battle for fear of reprisal from Cricket Australia or a public backlash from the vocal minority.'

It would not be a surprise if such sentiments found a receptive ear or two in the Australian side, not least with the captain whom in January 2008 bore the brunt of the criticism, sententious op-eds, resignation demands, calls for the revival of public flogging, etc. To be fair, such remarks actually played pretty well in the media too, which enjoys stories emphasising that Test is a four-letter word. But behind vocal minorities sometimes lurk silent majorities, of the kind now deliberating on the legacy of this great cricketer. Their verdict in this matter will be as significant as the ICC's.

28 DECEMBER 2010

Day 3

Close of play: Australia 2nd innings 169–6
(BJ Haddin 11*, MG Johnson 6*, 66 overs)

For a ground so huge, the MCG empties with remarkable speed. Within five minutes of stumps tonight, the third-day crowd for the Fourth Test of 68,733 had virtually cleared out, leaving the arena to the human bollards of the security staff. While how many will return tomorrow can only be guessed at, one thing is all but guaranteed: they will be either English or masochists.

At the close, Australia were 246 runs from making England bat again, with four wickets remaining. They collapsed today as Hemingway once said a man goes broke: slowly, then all at once, losing five wickets for 59 runs in thirty overs after tea, being already a man down after an injury to Ryan Harris. The

Ashes are so close for Andrew Strauss that the smoke is in Ricky Ponting's eyes.

It will be a deserved victory. Coach Andy Flower described Adelaide as a 'perfect Test'. Yet his team has here almost improved on perfection, murdering Australia on the first day, and burying them the next two. They could retain the Ashes at Sydney by turning up for the toss and spending the next week at the beach.

There was no hint of later hecticness when play resumed, and Jonathan Trott continued on his own unassuming way. One straight drive from Hilfenhaus summed up Trott's whole game: simple, compact, unostentatious, effective. There remains a suspicion of vulnerability when the pace is on, but this has never been a pitch to test that conjecture. When he's in the mood, he just stays and stays and stays, his objective of long-term settlement somehow expressed in the repeated furrowing of his guard, where he might be intending to plant a row of beans.

England's last five wickets were rounded up for 69, bringing on an early lunch, more or less inevitable after Prior and Bresnan fell in the first three-quarters of an hour. Amid this good Australian news, however, was sprinkled bad. Harris limped off in his fourth over, looking as though he had stepped on a starfish in a rock pool; it transpired he was feeling the effect of a stress fracture in his left ankle, which will make him an unlucky casualty of this series. Just nine days ago, the great-hearted Harris was celebrating his successful campaign against a knee injury; now he begins a new battle.

Despite the total on which England was converging, progress was anything but monotonous. The pitch continued to offer the bowlers just a little, the ball beating the bat every few overs; the bounce endangered Swann's helmet more than once. When Siddle bowled Anderson to claim his sixth wicket for 75, England had stretched their lead to 415 with less than half the Test match over. It also meant that more than half the batsmen in the match had been dismissed in single figures: indicative of conditions in which early survival called for some luck.

In their second dig, Australia veritably raced to 50 in ten overs, half the time it took them on the first day, thanks to a combination of attacking fields and overeager bowling. The bat was not beaten until Bresnan came on after forty minutes, bent his back and went past Watson's surprised outside edge. Good teams create opportunities under these circumstances, and England conjured one brilliantly. In Swann's second over, Hughes was caught on his heels by Watson's late call for a single to cover; Watson's lumbering gait sometimes seems to mislead partners about his intentions.

Trott, unwearied by the 46 singles, 20 twos and 7 threes he had run in more than seven hours, moved smartly to scoop and deliver, and for the second time this summer broke an Australian opening stand. The key, though, was Prior's swiftness in meeting the throw and directing it on to the stumps – as Hilfenhaus did not yesterday, when Trott was diving for the crease to beat Ponting's return. When bad cricket meets good cricket, the result is not always foregone, and here was a matter of perhaps nine inches – but that was enough.

In the early stages of Australia's innings, Tremlett bowled finely without reward, in that way of his where there might almost not be a batsman at the other end. He walks back, runs in, lets go, follows through – and the cycle repeats, irrespective of outcome, except on the occasion of a wicket, when a shy smile is revealed. After Prior and Strauss entered into earnest discussion about calling for a review when Hughes (12) possibly grazed one down the leg side, they looked up to find Tremlett, back turned, already taking those slow, measured steps to the end of his run.

As the session progressed, it became hard, austere, patient cricket from both batsmen and bowlers, Watson guarding one of those starts he is inclined to waste, Ponting preserving the vital spark of his captaincy. In theory at this stage, Australia could still regain the Ashes. In theory, though, the referral system is also a good idea; it is in practice that it messes with one's head.

Two decisions were epistemological case studies. Ponting (2) was hit just above the knee-roll when the ball jagged back from Anderson and he was given not out by Tony Hill. On replay, the ball could be seen to be just trimming the bails. Had Hill given it and Ponting called for a referral, he would have been out, as there weren't sufficient grounds for overturning the decision; as Hill did not, it would have been not out in the event of a Strauss referral.

Shortly after tea, by contrast, Watson (52) padded up as Bresnan swerved the ball back, and Hill upheld the appeal. When Watson sought a review, the replay showed the ball to be barely grazing the top of the stumps, but he was sent on his way, again because of insufficient evidence for a change of mind. Watson, who in his *own* mind has never been dismissed lbw, vanished from the ground still sunk in thought – not, for him, a natural state.

With the ramparts breached, England plunged into the Australian citadel. Bresnan reaped the rewards for persistence, unexpected pace and expected reverse swing, enabled by an abrasive square. He obtained movement into Ponting to bowl him off an inside edge, then movement away from a fretful Hussey that drew a fatal check-drive to short cover.

The latest chapter in *Clarke Agonistes* was then hard to watch. As Swann obtained a pleasing drift, Australia's vice-captain made a painfully poor start, missed at 2 by Prior as he was drawn out of his ground. Concreted into his crease thereafter, his strokeplay grew similarly circumscribed: given one low full toss on the pads, which a year ago would have been four, Clarke could do no more than drill to mid-on. It was almost a relief when Swann floated one across his vision from round the wicket and he pushed too hard, being smartly taken by Strauss at second slip.

After an early mishook which fell just short of a diving Tremlett at fine leg, Steve Smith played some crisp and original shots, one back cut for four with the bat at forty-five degrees tucked under his chin. But with three overs of the day remaining, he dragged Anderson on while attempting an impertinent pull, rendering the game all over bar the shouting – although of that, if you are an English fan, there may be quite a lot tomorrow.

28 DECEMBER 2010
RICKY PONTING

36 and All That

Ricky Ponting began the Fourth Test on the brink of a unique achievement: with victory in Melbourne, he would enter a club of one comprising those who have played in a hundred Test wins. He will end the game with a unique non-achievement, as thrice a losing Ashes skipper, beaten here about as badly as a Test captain can be: outplayed, out-generaled, out twice for little, even out-earned, having forfeited 40 per cent of his match fee to the ICC exchequer.

As matters stand, in fact, Ponting's chances of another shot at his milestone are complicated by his new millstone. To lose the Ashes twice might be thought misfortune; thrice looks like carelessness. But more than that, having been deserted by luck at the toss and by his sang-froid with the umpires, he finally and irrefutably lost his batting today.

Since Brisbane, Australia's batting coach Justin Langer has maintained a nonstop, low-level patter about how well the captain is hitting them – brilliant, better than ever, ready for action. Well, yes, one might say: in the nets, he gets to face his own bowlers. In the middle, Langer can hardly have missed his old confrère's lack of balance. Anxious to cover off stump, Ponting has been jumping into, and outside of, the line of the ball; moving so far across, in fact, as to expose his leg stump, down which side he has twice nicked fatally. His downswing, never the acme of straightness, has grown as crooked as a barrel of fish-hooks. A door need only be slightly off its hinges in order to stop closing properly; likewise a defensive technique.

The heart told you to expect a big fuck-off hundred this afternoon; the head anticipated something gutsy and cussed that might go on a while but would prove to no avail. And this has been an Ashes series played very much in the head, in the meticulousness of England's preparation, and the illusions of Australia's response.

Ponting arrived today, of course, to find the MCG still subtly reverberating from the uproar of his contretemps with Aleem Dar. Among the commentariat, in the blogocracy and Twittersphere, enabled by numberless clicks on YouTube, the ICC's decision to fine Ponting an amount equivalent to a couple of his well-dressed wife's ritzy handbags was being debated.

The captain confined himself to old media, getting his 'side of the story' out on ABC radio and Channel Nine, although not exactly doing himself that many favours. While apologis-ing and expressing his appreciation of the umpires, he also indulged in some special pleading. 'I had a chance to look at it again last night,' Ponting insisted. 'I still, in my heart and in my mind, believe that he inside-edged that ball. I think if you look at the replay properly, in the way that it needs to be looked at, I think everyone will understand that Hot Spot mark wasn't a long way away from where the ball passed the bat . . . but that's irrelevant now. The decision was made and I've got to get on with it now.'

These were strangely obdurate propositions. 'If you look at the replay properly'? 'The way it needs to be looked at'? 'Everyone will understand'? Says who? And given that, as Ponting acquiesced, this excuse for an argument was 'irrelevant', why bother trying to make it? The answer is that Ponting is a proud, stubborn man. It has been a great quality. One sees it in the washed-out, worn-out, saggy baggy green that he would no sooner part with than the *Légion d'honneur*; one senses it in his ever wirier frame, toughened and tautened by a training regime that would daunt a man a decade his junior. But the stubbornness has now shaded into intransigence. He has been reduced on occasions this season to a kind of doublethink. Before this Test, for example, he ventured: 'I actually look at our lack of runs as a positive going forward. We just can't keep performing this badly.' Eh?

Worse, 36-year-old Ponting has slipped into denial about his own game. He is averaging 28 in his last ten Tests. His failures and those of his vice-captain Michael Clarke have effectively ringbarked the Australian batting in each Test of this series, leaving decay to set in. At the start of the summer, Australia's selectors offered Ponting the chance to drop down the order to number four. He dismissed it. The selectors haven't gotten much right this series, but as he eked out 20 over 102 painful minutes today, Ponting was demonstrating their foresight.

Every batsman is vulnerable during their first twenty balls. It's when they bat for 73 deliveries, as Ponting did today, and still look like they've just come in, that they are truly struggling. In the first innings, Ponting fetched a good delivery; in this second, he scarcely managed an authentic stroke before dragging Bresnan on. The nick on to the stumps, moreover, is one of batting's ugliest dismissals, making a mess of everything: bat, stumps, feet, mind. Ponting fell in such a fashion three times during last year's Ashes, including in the climactic Test at the Oval – it was somehow fitting today.

It is not a backhanded compliment to say that the best part of Ponting's captaincy has been his batting. After all, batting successfully as a captain is a challenge that has defeated some great players: look at the vicissitudes of Mark Taylor's form, the sharp declines of Richie Richardson and Mahela Jayawardene. Ponting is not a hugely original tactician; nor, in later years, has he had the *materiel* at his disposal that gained Steve Waugh his great reputation. But his shadow has always been lengthened by his ability to inspire, empower, resist and rally with the bat, and his loss of that capacity diminishes him disproportionately.

It seems impertinent to be talking of successors while such a great cricketer is still in harness, like arguing about the apportionment of an estate over a still-warm body. But as the slight frame of Australia's captain withdrew into the shadows of the Ponsford Stand today, there was the possibility we were witnessing another milestone: Ponting's last Test at the MCG.

29 DECEMBER 2010

Day 4

Close of play: Australia 2nd innings 258 (85.4 overs)

With the clock approaching noon today, England retained the Ashes with victory by an innings and 157 runs in the Fourth Test at the MCG. The situation in Australian cricket, meanwhile, approached high noon, with the possibility of some bloodshed.

England's win gave them a 2–1 lead in the series to take into next week's Fifth Test at Sydney, which it is highly likely will be played against a quite different Australian team. In his post-match remarks, Ricky Ponting, still nursing his wounded finger, was circumspect about his prospects of even playing. 'Hopefully', which along with 'to be honest' and 'execute our skill set' is among the most popular press conference idioms of the tour, was scattered through his comments with rather more force and pregnancy than usual.

On this day sixteen years ago, a crowd turned up to watch the last rites of an MCG Ashes Test and were rewarded for their faith by a Shane Warne hat-trick which Channel 9 are still replaying – at least a score of times in this game alone. There were no such dramatics today, just a little belated Australian spunk.

With the eleventh ball of the day, the deserving Chris Tremlett found his way to Johnson's stumps via pad and bat; Tremlett also had Haddin (33) dropped at the wicket as the ball died on the fourth-day pitch. There were enough

Australians in to cheer boundaries by the home team, but more miscellaneous roars of Barmy Army self-amusement indicative of the day's holiday feel.

This seemed to infect England too, whose cricket grew a little demob-happy. Swann had Siddle (21) dropped at slip by Collingwood, the ball having taken a slight deflection from Prior's glove, and Haddin reached a half-century off 86 balls by bisecting them also. For the Australians, with nothing much to play for, the scenario was quite freeing, and their best partnership of the match flourished, 86 from 99 balls.

Haddin, who seems to have the peachiest bat in the Australian dressing room and the nerve to use it, hit Anderson and Swann back over their heads as though from a stationary tee, the latter into the crowd where a spectator caught it one-handed – arguably the best Australian fielding of the match.

Siddle also hit effectively, showing a penchant for the slog sweep, until Swann threw it up wider of off stump and tempted him to drive down the ground, where Pietersen took the catch. Third top scorer in both innings, taker of six wickets and two catches, the Victorian has nothing to reproach himself for in this Test – which places him in a very small Australian club.

When Haddin signalled Australian surrender by making no effort to seek the strike, Hilfenhaus completed a pair by nicking Bresnan to Prior. Australia's keeper dropped dolefully to his haunches as England flocked into a heaving huddle, joined in their ecstasy by the obligatory cameramen, who arrived hotfoot from the Ponsford Stand fence while the last appeal was still echoing around the ground.

To the same cameras at the presentation, Ponting anticipated an afternoon of quiet deliberation with the selectors, even if the way Australia's selectors have been going this summer, this sounded more like a threat than a promise. He is not a quitter. His broken finger was X-rayed again this morning as a precaution. There was no need to look inside his head: its attention and focus will be undivided.

Forty years ago, Bill Lawry was sacked as Australian captain under similar circumstances. The difference then was that a vice-captain, Ian Chappell, had been groomed at length, and was ready to oversee the necessary generational change. A greater problem for Australia than even Ponting's form is that his deputy, Michael Clarke, has gone from fours and sixes a year ago to sixes and sevens today. He has even stopped tweeting, a tic of his that had become as ingrained as a stammer. It would not come as a surprise if Clarke gave way at the SCG to 24-year-old Usman Khawaja, his fellow old boy of Westfield Sports High School, who was on stand-by for this Test had Ponting's finger not passed medical inspection. Khawaja will have big shoes to fill, although they are smaller than they were – likewise for others who succeed to this Australian team.

29 DECEMBER 2010
ENGLAND'S PREPARATION

A Hindsight View of Foresight

All summer, while watching this Ashes unfold, one has been semi-consciously ticking off mental notes of corresponding dates four years ago. The Gabba Test was shadowed by the memory of Harmison's first-ball wide, the Adelaide Test by Shane Warne's last-day coup, the Perth Test by Gilchrist's riotous hundred. Today in Melbourne, a state of total topsy-turvitude was reached. England retained the Ashes on the fourth anniversary of nothing at all, Andrew Flintoff's team having lost the previous Ashes Test here in three days.

Four years ago, England arrived in Melbourne having already surrendered the Ashes, and amid salaams of praise for the retiring Shane Warne and Glenn McGrath. Their role in the series had contracted to that performed by the Washington Generals in games with the Harlem Globetrotters: human obstacles around whom trick shots were to be executed. Their defeat was similarly foreordained. Andrew Strauss recalled it today as 'the lowest point of my career and a lot of guys felt similarly'.

Four years ago, it was Australia setting the off-field standard too. There was John Buchanan's boot camp. There was Ricky Ponting's drive to win the DLF Cup in Malaysia and the Champions Trophy in India, in order to instil winning habits. There were the roles found for bowling coach Troy

Cooley and fielding coach Mike Young, Australia having envied England's backroom staff in 2005.

Flash forward, and the roles have been exactly swapped. The boot camp was on the other foot, as it were, Andy Flower cobbling together his own. England chose a batting coach experienced in Australia, Graham Gooch, and a bowling coach from Australia, David Saker – these offices had been held four years earlier by Matthew Maynard and Kevin Shine, neither of them steeped in conditions down under.

In 2006, Duncan Fletcher was content with one drawn first-class game before the First Test. 'My philosophy was always that I did not want players tiring themselves out before the series started,' he argued in *Behind the Shades*. 'I preferred them slightly underdone as opposed to overdone.' Arriving at the Gabba raw, England left it cooked. Landing this time two weeks earlier, a month before the First Test, England played full-dress sides in three full-scale matches, two of which they won.

A certain scepticism is advisable where such comparisons are concerned. Preparation is often a phenomenon glimpsed in hindsight. Wellington didn't ask for the 'playing fields of Eton' to be prepared *in case of* a Battle of Waterloo; he sensed their significance afterwards. A boot camp, three first-class games and the coaching services of Vince Lombardi would not have prevented Flintoff's team losing 5–0.

But what has been important about the preparation of this England team has been the sense it has instilled and conveyed of common purpose. In particular, you could not get a cigarette paper between Andrews Flower and Strauss – they seem capable of finishing one another's sentences. In the November edition of *Wisden Cricketer*, they were asked to delineate their leadership philosophies: their answers could have been transposed without difficulty, especially those stressing the need for players' self-reliance and self-direction.

The team both carries their stamp, and does not. Perhaps only Javed Miandad in history has mastered the reverse sweep more completely than Flower, but none of England's batsmen have relied on the stroke this summer. Although Strauss is an avowed non-reader of media lest he encounter anything 'too complimentary or too critical', he seems comfortable with all Graeme Swann's video japes, and even to enjoy them. Where Australian players talk always of their 'plan', their English counterparts are prepared to exercise judgement themselves. When Alastair Cook batted for two days in Brisbane, you can be pretty sure he did not prepare for it by PowerPoint.

In instituting Flower's tough physical regime, too, Strauss enjoys a great advantage. Where bowler Flintoff towards the end of his career was barely capable of playing let alone training, batsman Strauss can tackle all the off-the-field work. Had Flintoff undertaken one of the 'pressurisation' routines in which England's players now practise while also exhausting themselves through boxing, sit-ups, press-ups et al. in order to learn to play tired, his recovery session might have put *l'affaire Fredalo* in the shade.

The most visible manifestation of England's esprit de corps, thanks to Richard Halsall and his bowling machines, has been in the field. Not since Mike Brearley's team of 1978–79 has an England side so eclipsed Australia in catching, throwing, intercepting and retrieving. Part of this was in specific contemplation of the flat pitches of Australia, on which twenty wickets can be elusive, and where thrift in the field is paramount. But it has also contributed to what might be called – hesitantly, because the word was last year used to death – England's 'aura'. Slick fielding doesn't just exploit doubt; it induces it.

The MCG's surface area often sorts visiting teams out. Thanks to the Australian rules football played here, the outfield is slow, so everything must be chased, and big, requiring powerful throwing arms. Yet it was noticeable throughout this game how superior England's outcricket was. Where Australia's returns from the deep were arriving on the bounce and landing at Haddin's feet, England's kept rocketing over the stumps. As at Adelaide, Jonathan Trott broke the Australian opening partnership with a quicksilver pick-up and flick-in.

Above all, perhaps, English preparation has conquered Australia's local knowledge. It has traditionally been far harder for English players to come to Australia than vice versa, because of our variety of cricket microclimates: if anything, the venues this season have been more various than for some time, after criticism of their growing uniformity.

Yet it has been Australia who have looked more often like the visiting team. In Melbourne, for instance, England had Tim Bresnan to take advantage of the abrasive square and bowl reverse swing; Australia had nobody. What a difference, then, four years can make. Such a difference, in fact, that the visitors can at last cease brooding on the events of four years ago.

30 DECEMBER 2010
AUSTRALIA'S MALAISE

A Bad Day at the Office

After all the presentation ceremonies and sprinkler dances concluded at the MCG on Wednesday, the show had to go on. The Ashes might have been decided and the ground might have been largely empty, but on trooped hundreds of lookalike tinies for their lunchtime display of Milo in2Cricket.

Such scenes normally have an appealing gaiety. But in the aftermath of the towelling inflicted on the home side, there was an undertone of desperation. These are the hearts and minds Cricket Australia will have to win in order to compete in future, with England, and with rival sports. Quick, sign them before the AFL does!

The Ashes provokes soul-searching as no other cricket event. Two summers ago, Australia were soundly beaten by South Africa. Nobody then was plunged into self-doubt or self-recrimination. We were 'rebuilding'. We were 'in transition'. We had lost a generation of fine cricketers. Patience was required.

But England is Australia's eternal benchmark – as Australia is England's. Nobody in either country is any the less exercised by England's retention of the Ashes for the fact that the series has pitted fourth in the world against fifth according to the International Cricket Council rankings. 'Do anything you like,' was Ian Chappell's famous advice when Allan Border became Australian captain in the mid-1980s.

'Just don't lose to the poms.' Australian cricket has failed in its prime directive.

Nor will the euphemisms about transition suffice any longer. England have had to rebuild too. The First Tests of 2005 and 2010 had three players in common on both sides: Ricky Ponting, Michael Clarke and Simon Katich for Australia; Andrew Strauss, Ian Bell and Kevin Pietersen for England.

From England's much-maligned county system has since emerged an opening batsman with fifteen Test hundreds while he was still twenty-five, Alastair Cook, and the world's best slow bowler, Graeme Swann. In the same period, Australia's widely envied domestic competition and expensive Centre of Excellence have produced heavily hyped colts like Phil Hughes and David Warner, and psychiatric case studies in Mitchell Johnson and Shaun Tait.

Hughes holds down a position as a Test opener after a summer containing one half-century in thirteen first-class innings. Warner has one half-century to show for his season of flitting between games for Australia, New South Wales and New Zealand's Northern Districts. His big day out in Perth aside, Johnson's wickets in his last three series have cost 60 each. Tait looks like spending the rest of his career bowling spells no longer than four overs.

Here is a conundrum. In the last decade, Australian cricketers have become the best paid in the world, even interstate players earning six-figure salaries as a matter of course. It has become possible for an Australian cricketer to make a tidy income on the basis of quite ordinary performances.

Worse, players are surrounded now by a complicated superstructure of overlapping programmes, checks and balances, regulating their workloads, monitoring their progress, making their decisions. Johnson is an outcome of this culture, a cricketer of great raw talent who now seems incapable of doing anything for himself, a Frankenstein's monster put together from a thousand different modifications and adjustments.

It is no wonder that when they talk today, Australian cricketers sound like mid-level bureaucrats, evading accountability, doing as they are told. Everyone has 'plans'. Everyone has 'skill sets'. Nobody seems to do anything individually. When Shane Watson bowled poorly in Brisbane, for example, he explained that it was because 'all of us as a bowling group weren't able to consistently execute to build the pressure that was needed'.

Of course, every cricketer tends to sound like a drone in press conferences. If the Australians this summer have sounded like bureaucrats, the Englishmen have sounded like politicians, earnestly avoiding the saying of anything at all. Behind the scenes, however, there is a strong sense of England doing what Australia used to be renowned for: grooming strong-willed, self-directed cricketers.

The worrying observable reality for Australia is that the three most impressive Australians this summer, Michael Hussey, Brad Haddin and Ryan Harris, are all in their thirties, all the products of an earlier, hungrier culture. This raises disturbing questions about the effectiveness both of the Centre of Excellence, the Australian cricket incubator in operation since January 2004, and of Tim Nielsen, who ran it in its first three years before succeeding John Buchanan as national coach – not to mention the judgement of those at Cricket Australia who before the Ashes extended Nielsen's contract for three years.

Judges as sound as Steve Waugh and Peter Roebuck have expressed concern about the accent in Australian senior coaching on shorter forms of the game. 'You have to have the basics and good foundation that you know will hold up under pressure and right now I don't think some (players) have done the hard work,' said Waugh last week. 'They are opening their front leg up and playing a lot of shots front-on to the bowler. I think in a tough situation you have to be side-on, leave the ball and play with soft hands, and they are not really doing it.'

Inauspicious, too, is that Australian cricket actually seems in the process of weakening rather than strengthening its centre, while quietly giving five-day cricket up for lost. Although the total crowd for the Boxing Day Test reached a quarter of a million, CA's public affairs manager Peter Young insists on describing Test matches as 'a bit like reading Shakespeare or listening to Beethoven' – a sentiment straight from his marketing department that manages to be both pretentious *and* condescending.

Enormous resources and manpower are being dedicated at present to the expansion of Australia's interstate domestic Twenty20 competition, which will from next year become the Big Bash League, involving some of the features of the multi-billion-dollar Indian Premier League: franchise teams, private ownership and hopefully big television bucks to boot.

Cricket Australia presents it as a bold response to its generational malaise, to engage parents and ten-year-olds that market research suggests are latching instead on to the various football codes, and to develop 'new markets' – an expression administrators now use as heavily as cricketers use 'skill sets'. But because the Big Bash League can never seriously rival the IPL, the risk is that Cricket Australia is simply rolling out a 'me-too' product in a format that will be passé in ten years. And that they are doing so because the federal structure of Australian cricket encourages the state associations to act chiefly in their own interests, in order to perpetuate the sizeable secretariats they have come to employ.

What sort of cricketers, furthermore, will a T20-centric system produce? Don't bet on there being an Australian Alastair Cook or Graeme Swann any time soon, or even another Simon Katich, let alone a Ricky Ponting. When Australia's captain was ushered a little closer to the exit on Thursday, he was not just a declining Australian captain but an anachronism – a tough, brave, single-minded, self-motivated, record-breaking Test batsman with no time for T20 and its artificialities. The cricket of the future, it seems, will be less like the game he grew up on, and more like the pursuit played on the MCG outfield after the Ashes were sewn up.

FOURTH TEST   Melbourne Cricket Ground 26–29 December 2010
Toss   England   **England** won by an innings and 157 runs

AUSTRALIA 1st innings			R	M	B	4	6	SR
SR Watson	c Pietersen	b Tremlett	5	14	12	0	0	41.66
PJ Hughes	c Pietersen	b Bresnan	16	59	32	2	0	50.00
***RT Ponting**	c Swann	b Tremlett	10	52	38	2	0	26.31
MJ Clarke	c †Prior	b Anderson	20	89	54	2	0	37.03
MEK Hussey	c †Prior	b Anderson	8	44	41	1	0	19.51
SPD Smith	c †Prior	b Anderson	6	18	15	0	0	40.00
†BJ Haddin	c Strauss	b Bresnan	5	23	16	1	0	31.25
MG Johnson	c †Prior	b Anderson	0	8	4	0	0	0.00
RJ Harris		not out	10	39	23	2	0	43.47
PM Siddle	c †Prior	b Tremlett	11	25	15	1	0	73.33
BW Hilfenhaus	c †Prior	b Tremlett	0	10	8	0	0	0.00
EXTRAS		(lb 2, nb 5)	7					
TOTAL	(all out; 42.5 overs; 195 mins)		98	(2.28 runs per over)				

FoW	1-15	(Watson, 3.2 ov),	2-37	(Hughes, 13.1 ov),
	3-37	(Ponting, 14.2 ov),	4-58	(Hussey, 25.2 ov),
	5-66	(Smith, 29.3 ov),	6-77	(Clarke, 33.4 ov),
	7-77	(Haddin, 34.5 ov),	8-77	(Johnson, 35.2 ov),
	9-92	(Siddle, 40.3 ov),	10-98	(Hilfenhaus, 42.5 ov)

BOWLING	O	M	R	W	ECON	
JM Anderson	16	4	44	4	2.75	
CT Tremlett	11.5	5	26	4	2.19	(1nb)
TT Bresnan	13	6	25	2	1.92	
GP Swann	2	1	1	0	0.50	

ENGLAND 1st innings			R	M	B	4	6	SR
*AJ Strauss	c Hussey	b Siddle	69	232	167	5	0	41.31
AN Cook	c Watson	b Siddle	82	212	152	11	0	53.94
IJL Trott		not out	168	486	345	13	0	48.69
KP Pietersen	lbw	b Siddle	51	127	89	7	0	57.30
PD Collingwood	c Siddle	b Johnson	8	27	15	1	0	53.33
IR Bell	c Siddle	b Johnson	1	19	13	0	0	7.69
†MJ Prior	c Ponting	b Siddle	85	201	119	11	0	71.42
TT Bresnan	c †Haddin	b Siddle	4	22	17	0	0	23.52
GP Swann	c †Haddin	b Hilfenhaus	22	51	28	3	0	78.57
CT Tremlett		b Hilfenhaus	4	8	7	0	0	57.14
JM Anderson		b Siddle	1	5	6	0	0	16.66
EXTRAS	(b 10, lb 2, w 3, nb 3)		18					
TOTAL	(all out; 159.1 overs; 700 mins)		513	(3.22 runs per over)				

FoW	1-159	(Cook, 51.1 ov),	2-170	(Strauss, 55.3 ov),
	3-262	(Pietersen, 86.3 ov),	4-281	(Collingwood, 91.3 ov),
	5-286	(Bell, 95.3 ov),	6-459	(Prior, 141.1 ov),
	7-465	(Bresnan, 145.4 ov),	8-508	(Swann, 156.3 ov),
	9-512	(Tremlett, 158.1 ov),	10-513	(Anderson, 159.1 ov)

BOWLING	O	M	R	W	ECON	
BW Hilfenhaus	37	13	83	2	2.24	(1w)
RJ Harris	28.4	9	91	0	3.17	
MG Johnson	29	2	134	2	4.62	(2nb, 2w)
PM Siddle	33.1	10	75	6	2.26	(1nb)
SR Watson	10	1	34	0	3.40	
SPD Smith	18	3	71	0	3.94	
MJ Clarke	3.2	0	13	0	3.90	

AUSTRALIA 2nd innings			R	M	B	4	6	SR
SR Watson	lbw	b Bresnan	54	136	102	6	0	52.94
PJ Hughes	run out (Trott/†Prior)		23	49	30	2	0	76.66
*RT Ponting		b Bresnan	20	101	73	2	0	27.39
MJ Clarke	c Strauss	b Swann	13	81	66	0	0	19.69
MEK Hussey	c Bell	b Bresnan	0	9	7	0	0	0.00
SPD Smith		b Anderson	38	91	67	6	0	56.71
†BJ Haddin		not out	55	135	93	4	1	59.13
MG Johnson		b Tremlett	6	23	22	0	0	27.27
PM Siddle	c Pietersen	b Swann	40	70	50	4	1	80.00
BW Hilfenhaus	c †Prior	b Bresnan	0	5	4	0	0	0.00
RJ Harris		absent hurt	-					
EXTRAS	(b 1, lb 6, w 2)		9					
TOTAL	(all out; 85.4 overs; 354 mins)		258	(3.01 runs per over)				

FoW
1-53	(Hughes, 11.3 ov),	2-99	(Watson, 31.6 ov),
3-102	(Ponting, 35.4 ov),	4-104	(Hussey, 37.5 ov),
5-134	(Clarke, 52.5 ov),	6-158	(Smith, 61.5 ov),
7-172	(Johnson, 67.5 ov),	8-258	(Siddle, 84.2 ov),
9-258	(Hilfenhaus, 85.4 ov)		

BOWLING	O	M	R	W	ECON	
JM Anderson	20	1	71	1	3.55	(1w)
CT Tremlett	17	3	71	1	4.17	
GP Swann	27	11	59	2	2.18	
TT Bresnan	21.4	8	50	4	2.30	(1w)

Part VI

Fifth Test

Sydney Cricket Ground
3–7 January 2011
England won by an innings and 83 runs

In with the New

The email distributed in early afternoon by Cricket Australia slightly boggled the mind. There would be a press conference at the Sydney Cricket Ground at 5.30 p.m. Present would be chief executive James Sutherland 'and two Australian cricketers'. Australia's team for the Fifth Test had not yet been announced: could it be that they were scrounging to gather an XI?

As it turned out, TBA and A.N. Other were Michael Clarke and Usman Khawaja, replacements for Ricky Ponting as captain and as batsman. And funnily enough, although Clarke has played sixty-eight Tests and Khawaja none, more questions surrounded the former than the latter.

Clarke is twenty-nine. He has made 4,697 Test runs at 46.97, with fourteen hundreds. Although he still wears the nickname he was given as a prodigy, Pup, he has been captain-in-waiting to Ponting for two years. But he is Australian cricket's Dr Fell, whom the fans do not like, why they cannot tell.

It may be his self-conscious metrosexual airs and graces. It may be his habit of appearing on billboards advertising this, that and himself. It may be the tattoos, of which Clarke has ten, including one on his right shoulder that celebrates his bikini-model ex Lara Bingle. But this I know, to sum it up: they do not like him, that man Pup. The same day of his appointment as Australia's forty-third captain, a tabloid in Clarke's Sydney home town had reported the results of a poll giving him a 15 per cent approval rating.

Of course, this is cricket, not *Australia's Got Talent*. And Cricket Australia have really invested too much in Clarke for them to back out now. Given that Ponting is still deemed the man in possession, and Clarke is depicting himself as a locum, more unrest would be sown by the latter's non-appointment.

Clarke has the confidence, having looked born to the job since his debut six years ago. Clarke has the experience, having led Australia in thirty-six short-form internationals. And whatever the ink on his arms and torso, he has kept his nose clean: since their very public bust-up in March, he has treated La Bingle as just another bit of body art.

What Clarke does not have is the necessary form, with just 322 runs at 21.46 in his last eight Tests since accepting a promotion to number four, or the fitness, suffering as he does from a long-term disc problem. His decision to persevere in all three formats of the game has made a rod for a back that does not need it. Bowlers have been hemming him in on the back foot: he does not pull with any fluidity, and has as a result been playing at deliveries wider and wider in search of scoring opportunities. Pace and bounce have worried him. He batted at Adelaide Oval wearing a chest guard, which seemed as incongruous on him as flares and a feather boa.

While Clarke led Australia to the final of the World Twenty20 earlier this year, his strike rate in the format is a slowcoach 103 per hundred balls. He shows, moreover, no deep love of the format, eschewing the Indian Premier League, perhaps because of the likelihood that his valuation there would not match his self-estimation.

Then there is the perennial conjecture about Clarke's status in his own dressing room. Will the team pull for him as they did for Punter? Given the Australians' recent record, this hardly seems relevant. If all that pulling for Punter has failed to prevent the team sustaining two innings defeats, then it's arguably time for push to come to shove. Those who purport to have the skinny on the team dynamic usually turn out to be working on second-hand or external impressions. What is said of Clarke is that he is a nervous waiter, and that he has a propensity for showering because of a tendency to perspire; apparently he also likes to clean his teeth. Sounds like a dental role model in the making at least.

Clarke is known to have had an altercation with Simon Katich after a Test at the SCG two years ago, Clarke's eagerness to get away after the game to meet Bingle irking the traditionalist Katich. But people keeping harking back to that *cherchez la femme* story because there has been so little to go on since. In fact, Clarke probably suits the team chosen for Sydney as well as he has for a while, containing as it does Phil Hughes, with whom Clarke shares a coach in Neil d'Costa, and Steve Smith, with whom Clarke shares regular mutually admiring tweets. The elevation of New South Wales's captain Haddin as Clarke's as well as his team's backstop will be a reassurance too. They have shared thirteen Test partnerships at an average of 82.5.

While it has long been expected that Clarke would captain Australia, what was not expected was he would take over under these circumstances: one anticipated deep deliberation, orderly succession and elaborate ceremony, as was the case with Mark Taylor, Steve Waugh and Ponting, rather than a hurried email not even stating his name. He has in a sense been given two messages: both that the job is his, and also that it is his to lose.

2 JANUARY 2011
FIFTH TEST

The Living Dead

New Year's Resolutions? For 2011, Australian cricket has a few. They want to retain the World Cup. They hanker to beat India here, which will be tough, and to see off Sri Lanka there, which won't be much easier. The most important resolution is one with which they began 2010 and which they are now in no position to renew: regain the Ashes. But they can make a start on it.

A little and a lot ride on the Sydney Test. The result cannot affect custody of the urn, as the Barmy Army will ensure nobody forgets over the next five days. Yet Michael Clarke's appointment as Ricky Ponting's proxy has added spice to the contest. The 29-year-old batsman comes into the job as to an ancient but decaying ancestral seat, occupying a great mansion in which all the family silver has been melted down – in a state, moreover, of what a youthful heir would describe as 'temporary embarassment' while trying to cadge a fiver from the footman. Two half-centuries in his last fifteen Test innings is a performance record as embarrassing to recount as it has been to watch.

At least things can hardly get worse. If Australia survive the Test match without anyone slipping over in the shower or scalding themselves at the tea urn, they will feel a sense of quiet vindication. Nor can Clarke complain about his charges, six of whom will be fellow New South Welshmen playing on their home ground.

Australia will nominally be weaker than in Melbourne, even if Ponting has not been his inspirational self at number three this summer. Ryan Harris, with the thrust of a muscle car but the chassis of a tenth-hand VW combi, is a grave loss. Although Bollinger took three wickets in each innings of the recent Sheffield Shield match, they were from Queensland's dysfunctional order, and the memory of his performance at Adelaide Oval, breathless for all the wrong reasons, remains fresh.

The elevation of Usman Khawaja, however, is a progressive step, and not simply because he is the first Australian Muslim cricketer and a multicultural posterchild in the making. He is one of those batsmen whose quality stands out even in the nets – strong off the back foot, prolific through point, composed against the short stuff – and should arguably have been phased in during Australia's benighted northern campaign in July and August.

What's more, Khawaja has earned his place by weight of runs: 2,068 of them at 51.7 with six hundreds from 27 first-class games. It is difficult to examine the statistics of some of the others mooted for national selection, like Callum Ferguson (first-class average of 35 with four hundreds from 47 games) and Shaun Marsh (first-class average of 36.3 and five hundreds from 56 games), without beginning to wonder if national honours haven't become rather cheap in this day and age.

Khawaja sets his captain an interesting poser. He bats number three for his state, having opened for much of his career, and is thus a like-for-like swap with Ponting. It makes sense, in fact, to separate the left-handers in Australia's top order. But an Australian batsman has not debuted at first-wicket down for eighteen years, and Clarke might feel the pressure, especially given the perception of him as rather too rapt in his personal performances, to shield Khawaja. There are risks to either approach. Uneasy is the head that wears the number one helmet.

Having spent a few days on furlough, England will want their wits about them here. They have not played at the SCG on this tour. Their Sydney record is not the worst: they took a dead Test off Australia here in 2003, had the better of draws in 1991 and 1995. It is also, nonetheless, where they lost the only big game of their 1986–87 pageant of success, and a repeat here would travesty the difference between the sides, making for the first two–all that has ever felt like a four–nil.

Andrew Strauss's climatic luck, at least, looks to be persisting. The English have been blessed this summer by unseasonally mild weather, sparing their four-man attack the heavy labour in heat that might have exhausted it sooner, and providing periods of cloud cover for the delectation of James Anderson. Rain is forecast for Sydney on all five days, and it is only a year since Australia capitulated on the first day to Pakistan in conditions conducive to swing and seam after a delayed start. England will fancy themselves in similar circumstances. For Australia, 2011 might have to get worse before it gets better.

3 JANUARY 2011

Day 1

Close of play: Australia 1st innings 134–4 (MEK Hussey 12*, 59 overs)

Weather maps were studied as avidly as pitch maps at the Sydney Cricket Ground today, as rain loomed and finally fell in copious quantities at 5 p.m., by which stage Australia were glad of it. They made a useful start to this Fifth Test and ushered in a promising debutant, but England kept them on a tight leash: twice they choked and gagged as wickets fell on the brink of interruptions.

It was always going to be one of those days, and stand-in skipper Michael Clarke took the initiative of batting when Andrew Strauss called incorrectly in what England's Tim Bresnan called 'very English conditions'. Clarke's enthusiasm was palpable: he arrived at the toss nine minutes early, and pored over England's team sheet as though he wanted to catch a spelling error. The visitors were happy to go along with it: Strauss would also have offered Australia first innings.

Still, there was more to the atmosphere than cumulus. There were also two Australian debutants, welcomed to the fold with a restoration of the ritual that had fallen into disuse under Ricky Ponting, with two past masters doing the honours. Mark Taylor presented a baggy green to Usman Khawaja and none other than Shane Warne anointed Michael Beer. So, no pressure there, then . . .

Australia's openers also took up the cudgels with some conviction. Watson got moving with a lazy overthrow, Hughes with a feisty punch down the ground in Chris Tremlett's second over. But generally this was a morning for patience and self-denial. The default position was bat to the sky, front pad thrust out – a pose which would have been handy in Melbourne, and here had an edge of atonement to it. A superior short leg to the *faute de mieux* Alastair Cook might have caught Watson (6) off Tremlett; otherwise, the bowlers fell somewhat short, of length and expectations.

When Anderson came off after five overs with a pedantic warning from Billy Bowden for running on the wicket, Hughes hit his replacement Bresnan through mid-off and cover for consecutive boundaries to round the hour out cheerfully, at 31 for nought. Swann came on just before noon from the Randwick End, and Hughes cut his second ball for four to raise the fifty partnership in a painstaking 123 balls.

Hughes came into Test cricket with a back foot that edged towards square leg, locking himself up and limiting his access to the ball. He has reduced this, very gradually, to a twitch of his left foot, but still comes forward reluctantly, as though being asked to volunteer for a dangerous mission in occupied territory, and is apt to jab at the ball away from his body – as today. With lunch looming, England blocked the game up, bowling twenty-eight deliveries without conceding a run off the bat, whereupon a short delivery from Tremlett drew from Hughes a fatal defensive spasm.

This stuck Khawaja with an anxious wait through lunch, part of which he apparently filled by napping for twenty minutes. Certainly he betrayed no nerves as he tucked Tremlett's loosener away for two, then nailed a pull shot that crossed the square leg boundary before most had an opportunity to look around. In Tremlett's next over, he clipped crisply to the same boundary. The camera located his parents Tariq and Fozia in the crowd, his mother's hands clasped as though in prayer, although he hardly looked in need of that sort of help. For those who had not seen him previously, he cut a strikingly serene figure; for those who had, it was confirmation of their high opinions.

Just when Australia might have been considering theirs a good day's work, Watson lunged at Bresnan to squander another start: this time a rather anonymous 45 in just over three hours, and 127 balls. At the moment he is like the self-improving reader who makes an annual promise to get through *War and Peace,* only to lose track of all the Rostovs and give up at about page 100 each time. The light, too, was now so poor as to make Clarke's pink bat grip look luminous, and when rain sent the players from the field for the second time, only the ground's impressive drainage kept the break as short as an hour and a half.

After resumption at 4.05 p.m., the crowd of 43,561 was

lucky to see another hour's play – Australia were not. Clarke wafted to gully, and Khawaja top-edged a sweep at Swann, when he was just a ball away from a tidy overnight not-out. It made for a faintly bedraggled scoreline after the earlier possibilities, even if batting does not look like it will ever be easy here – always assuming there will be all that much of it. The ground presented an unpromising sight in the gloaming, and there will be more weather-map watching tomorrow.

3 JANUARY 2011
USMAN KHAWAJA

Our Man Usman

Over the years, making your debut for Australia has been a pretty cushy deal. Nice cap. Nice little earner. Above all, lots of protection, like having your own personal posse of bodyguards. The arrival of Usman Khawaja today told you something of changed times locally even before he had faced a ball.

Test batsmen seldom play their debut innings at number three. Don Bradman, Ian Chappell, David Boon, Ricky Ponting: all achieved greatness in the role rather than having greatness thrust upon them. The last Australian to be baptised in a Test match at first-wicket-down is the current batting coach, Justin Langer, who in the absence of a queue to face Curtly Ambrose and Courtney Walsh almost twenty years ago stepped cheerfully forward. But the baggy green was stuck faster to Langer's head than Doug Bollinger's rug to his, and most teams prefer bedding young players down a little more gently. The partner Khawaja joined after lunch today, Shane Watson, began his maiden Test innings here six years ago with the score 471 for five.

Khawaja was, of course, joining a team already beaten soundly in this series, and whose out-of-form proxy captain Michael Clarke was in no real position to act as bulwark, even if he was so disposed. On the contrary, the 24-year-old was there partly to act as protection for his team's most experienced player – a peculiar turnabout in responsibilities.

Not that any of this obviously fazed the preternaturally composed Khawaja, whether it was appearing in the stead of Ricky Ponting, being presented with his cap by Mark Taylor, or being watched by his hero Steve Waugh. He wore his pads to the national anthem, oblivious to any message this might convey about lack of faith in his openers, and through the first session, where the camera found him once or twice, giving a convincing impression of relaxation. It followed him into the middle immediately after lunch, when he whirled his second ball through square leg for four – a pull shot as good as any played by the player he has replaced.

How a batsman meets his first few balls in Test cricket is seldom indicative of all that much. David Gower famously pulled his first ball for four; Marcus Trescothick waited three-quarters of an hour to get off the mark. This was rousing stuff nonetheless: what used to be thought of as characteristically Australian batting, treating each ball on its merits, and its demerits. Thereafter, he performed as instructed, approaching the innings as he would any on his home ground. Khawaja has good soft hands, pleasingly simple footwork, the appearance of time to play his shots as a result, and an impressively unflustered air at the crease. He didn't score a run in front of point, and on a quicker pitch than this might have been squared up more often, but he looks to have the nous to adapt.

As impressive as his enterprise was how he dealt with inactivity. When after a few overs Strauss and Anderson met to intrigue at the end of the bowler's run, Khawaja withdrew a few steps towards square leg and waited patiently while they machinated, then was ready in his stance by the time Strauss had jogged back to slip. Fifteen from his first eight balls, he located only a single from his next twenty deliveries, and only two singles in the twenty before tea, but never seemed agitated. 'I had a ball out there,' he said afterwards – it looked like it.

In mental approach, if not in style, his cricket bears the stamp of his mentor with New South Wales and also Randwick Petersham Cricket Club, Simon Katich, and recalls that straightforward principle of batting once enunciated by Graeme Pollock. Irrespective of the quality of the attack, Pollock argued, a batsman could expect at least four or five bad balls an hour without needing to force the issue. Hit each of these for four, and two sessions was all you should need to be approaching a hundred. It's a philosophy unconsciously imbibed by Pollock's quondam countryman Jonathan Trott, and conspicuously lacking among Australians this summer. Among those most out of touch with this principle of Test match batting, in fact, is Australia's newest captain, whose overeagerness this summer has gradually become overanxiety. To see Strauss post two gullies as soon as he came in this afternoon, and watch him cut firmly but straight to the finer of them, was to feel tangled in a tape loop.

Khawaja continued after tea with a front-foot pull and a square drive from Bresnan that made batting look simple, and dealt coolly with balls that, in seaming past the outside edge, reminded us it wasn't. But just when he should have been hunkering down, he tried for the first time to manufacture a shot, a sweep against Swann's spin before he had quite judged the bounce or deviation. And that put him in the same category as many an Australian batsman this summer: a waster. Since Brisbane, only Hussey has contributed a century to the local cause. Khawaja's was the eighteenth score of 35 or more in that time not prolonged to three figures. If it seems harsh to hold Khawaja in his first Test to account for such an error of judgement, that is the fate of players joining weak teams: they experience pressure to perform at once.

In addition to being a distinctly handy player, Khawaja is, of course, a Muslim – the first of that faith to play cricket for Australia. This seems as unimportant to him as it seems important to many others, and the novelty is showing signs of wearing off quite quickly: in the media area, Australian journalists already refer to him familiarly as Uzzi, in the same nickname tradition that gave us Hughesy, Smithy, Warnie etc. They have been teasing their visitors all summer with the proposition that South Africa's best batsman plays for England; how long before Pakistan's best batsman is said to play for Australia?

Khawaja marks a new Australia, however, in a more conventional cricket sense, by being a young player with an already man-size task. One would prefer not to burden him with great expectations. But it may not be that easy.

4 JANUARY 2011

Day 2

Close of play: England 1st innings 167–3
(AN Cook 61*, JM Anderson 1*, 48 overs)

'Come on Aussies show your spirit' read a deathless tweet flashed on the Sydney Cricket Groud replay screen this morning to show how in touch Cricket Australia is with the ways of young folk. Another reference to Johnnie Walker, perhaps. Under their new captain, nonetheless, Australia did exhibit some extra spunk, in a well-contested second day of the Fifth Test.

After England's domination of their first hours in the field and with the bat, one would hardly have rated Australia's chances of coming third in this match. Yet were it not for the no-ball that prolonged Alastair Cook's crucial innings, they might well be slightly ahead: as it is, England remain 113 runs in arrears with seven wickets remaining. Again, a replay shaped events. Cricket is fast becoming two games: one in real time, the other in slow motion.

The day's opening stanzas were summed up in the *moue* of appreciation formed by Michael Hussey as a ball from Tim

Bresnan pitched leg and missed off stump by two feet. Probing bowling in helpful overhead conditions was matched by sublime fielding, and there was a whiff of demoralisation when a flat-footed Haddin flailed at Anderson in the day's fourth over.

Hussey and Steve Smith joined forces without ever appearing a happy or complementary partnership – just two batsmen thrown together, doing their best but somehow out of kilter, Hussey dour to the point of inertia, Smith fighting against his kid-on-red-cordial excitability, Hussey fussing around his crease as if in need of a dustpan and broom, Smith waving his bat around like a feather duster. They seemed to have just come out the other side when a nagging spell of medium pace from Collingwood parted them.

With the memory of his second-innings dismissal in Melbourne fresh, Hussey fell into a lulling routine of crisp drives to short and extra cover. But just when a comfortable détente seemed to have been achieved, Collingwood zipped one back to bowl him off a mix of inner edge and outer thigh. It was almost as though Hussey had so drilled himself not to be dismissed in one fashion that he overlooked all other possibilities: he had the minor consolation of joining a useful list of batsmen defeated by Collingwood's pawky variations, Tendulkar, Dravid, Ganguly and Sangakkara among them.

The new ball was taken with immediate effect, Collingwood now at third slip when Smith wasted an hour and a half's application with a wild drive at Anderson, who dismissed Siddle in his next over. But forty minutes before lunch, England got a little ahead of themselves. Pietersen could be seen essaying phantom shots at mid-off, while Strauss pushed the field back to give singles to both Johnson and Hilfenhaus in order to maximise the latter's strike.

When Hilfenhaus played and missed long enough to get a sighter, Australia's ninth wicket added 76 from 89 balls in sixty-four minutes of uncomplicated clumping either side of the intermission. Hilfenhaus, having incurred an inert pair in Melbourne, strolled into a six off Bresnan that landed among laughing members. From the next two balls, Johnson swept Swann for four and six into the terraces in front of the Brewongle Stand, and after a parodic block raised his 63-ball half-century with a single to square leg. Australia's 280 was beyond their overnight expectations, and well beyond those that would have been nurtured after their batsmen's early eclipse.

When England commenced their reply, Michael Clarke entrusted Hilfenhaus and Johnson with the new ball – not a bad shaft of captaincy, as it was hardly what England would have expected. Australia's new captain also had his first experience of what is known to befall best-laid plans, when Hilfenhaus and Johnson opened with several overs of weary dross.

Strauss has perhaps never played with greater freedom in Australia. He hooked Hilfenhaus twice for four, then massively into the members for six, a shot the more impressive for its almost nonexistent backlift and bravura follow-through. When he drove Siddle down the ground and through cover for four, England's captain flashed his partner a smile as broad as after retaining the Ashes.

Under the circumstances, the Australians did well to regroup. Hilfenhaus resumed after tea from round the wicket and swung one in that held its line to hit Strauss's off stump, and Johnson coaxed Trott into playing on a delivery as nondescript as many of his successful deliveries: for all the dreck he has served up, he is Australia's highest wicket taker this series.

Had a thick inside edge from Pietersen (8) gone onto the stumps, or had he on 26 connected with a glorious off drive whose breeze could be felt in the Noble Stand, England's chase might have faltered. As it was, the crucial reprieve was given by Michael Beer's fourteenth delivery in Test cricket. At 137 for two, Cook (46) forgot himself so completely as to shovel down the ground, where mid-on Hilfenhaus caught the ball amid much rejoicing, only for umpire Billy Bowden to call for a foot-fault referral which revealed the bowler to be pirouetting beyond the front line.

You can tell how gruelling a series this has been from the fact that lines such as 'bitter Beer', 'frothing Beer' and 'flat Beer' immediately sprang to mind, then 'welcome Beer', 'well-earned Beer' and 'Beer o'clock' when he took a nicely judged catch at deep fine leg to catch Pietersen's top edge from Johnson just before nightfall. But Cook, having quietly left 5,000 Test runs behind him, remained encamped at stumps, bending low over his defensive bat, and leaving night watchman Anderson to face the greater proportion of the day's last few overs, intent on the morrow. If the third day fluctuates as the second, and the weather continues staying away, this could be a better game than it initially promised.

4 JANUARY 2011
AUSTRALIA'S BOWLING

Disturbances in Sydney

Among the many prohibitions blazoned all over the rule-ridden Sydney Cricket Ground is one above eyelevel on the glass of the media area which reads: 'Any disturbance affecting the enjoyment of spectators should be reported to SCG staff.' In the hour before tea today, the phone in the administrative office should have been ringing off the hook.

Out in the middle, with an Ashes Test on the line, Australia's attack was bowling as badly as it has all summer – halfway down the pitch, despite its slowness, and without pace or shape. The fielding was flat. The effort was directionless. Captain Michael Clarke bore the expression of a second-hand-car buyer on the point of realising that the most reliable component of his newly acquired automobile was the ashtray.

For much of the summer, critics have homed in on Australia's batting as the root of all their misfortunes. The bowlers by comparison have gotten off fairly lightly. In fact, while they have had their moments, these have seldom been in combination: Siddle succeeded at Brisbane and Melbourne, Johnson and Harris at Perth, and Hilfenhaus . . . well, nowhere really. Now they had all taken the day off. At tea, England were 73 for nought in sixteen overs, an unheard-of rate of progress for Strauss and Cook, this summer or any.

How do teams bowl as badly as this? It cannot have been as though the bowlers were unfamiliar with the conditions. Johnson and Hilfenhaus had earlier made merry with the bat for an hour, and thereby acquired a thorough acquaintance of the wicket.

Nor can the Australians have been unprepared. Between innings, there was the now familiar sight of the team about to bowl going through token preliminaries. Tim Nielsen and Justin Langer led a slips catching drill. Bowlers ran round cones and heaved medicine balls. Orange fielding mats were deployed, isotonic drinks consumed, and a last few rousing injunctions issued to 'execute skill sets'.

And then . . . everyone bowled rubbish, on a pitch without the lift to bang the ball in, and in environs that, thanks to the arena shape the ground has developed so as best to host Australian football, now lack the ground-level breezes that used to abet swing. The third ball of Hilfenhaus's fourth over disappeared over square leg for a contemptuous six, while Johnson's sixth over was his worst since Brisbane – that it cost only seven runs was a tribute to some agile wicketkeeping by Haddin, who to Australia's quickest bowler must sometimes be tempted to take up his stance at short fine leg. Meanwhile, in the equipment driveway beneath the Bradman Stand, the best bowler at the ground was rolling his arm over to the star of, among other things, *Nick Fury: Agent of S. H. I. E. L. D.* and *Shaka Zulu: The Citadel*. Shane Warne to David Hasselhoff: this is the stuff of which Big Bash dreams are made.

In fact, just as the game was disappearing, the Australians did remarkably well to retard England's progress in the extended session after tea. Siddle ran in hard, Hilfenhaus bowled a patient spell from round the wicket, and Johnson claimed a couple of his trademark lightning wickets – he never strikes twice in the same place. The fielding also improved, Usman Khawaja, one of three fielders chasing back to third man, diving headlong to save a boundary. And Clarke captained thoughtfully, chivvying his men along, setting some imaginative fields that took advantage of the slow outfield, and backing his intuitions.

The choice of Johnson to share the new ball with Hilfenhaus was a sound one, even though it didn't come off, while the introduction of Beer just as the run rate was decelerating was nicely timed, and very nearly brought Australia a seminal wicket. As it was, Beer's bowling of Australia's nineteenth no-ball of the series cost his team a breakthrough for the second time, one that might prove even more crucial than the reprieve that Johnson granted Matt Prior in Melbourne.

England, who have trespassed not half as often, and who bowled only one no-ball in each of the Tests at the Gabba and Adelaide Oval, have here perhaps stolen another small march on Australia. Their practice sessions are informally umpired, compelling bowlers to pay attention to their front-foot transgressions. Australians in training, as Johnson conceded after play, are not so zealous. 'I still bowl half a foot over in the nets but I don't know how we're going to fix that.' Again with the 'we': what is it with this team's aversity to individual responsibility?

The recent empowering of umpires to check on the fairness of deliveries even after wickets fall has made no-balls a subtly more culpable offence. A game of inches is turning into a game of centimetres before our eyes – or, to be more exact, before the inhuman eye of the replay. It was enough to cause a 'disturbance affecting the enjoyment of spectators' – if they were Australian, anyway. The roar that followed, however, was a reminder that no error accrues without bestowing benefit elsewhere.

5 JANUARY 2011

Day 3

Close of play: England 1st innings 488–7
(MJ Prior 54*, TT Bresnan 0*, 141 overs)

A running gag in the popular video diaries posted by Graeme Swann on the England Cricket Board website is the resemblance of Alastair Cook to Sheriff Woody from *Toy Story*. Skinny? Check. Well groomed? Check. String coming out of his back. Well . . . Anyway, the likeness is deepening: Cook keeps starring in sequels.

Today, too, may have been a rare case of the sequel outdoing the original. Having taken his first guard an hour before tea yesterday, Cook more than batted the clock around, finally falling after tea for 189 in 488 minutes and 342 deliveries, an innings containing 55 singles, 26 twos, 16 fours and judicious leaves outside the off stump beyond number. Cook's Brisbane original was to keep the series alive; this follow-up has killed it, and England's opponents, stone dead. Cook's sixth-wicket partnership of 154 from 282 balls with Ian Bell ensured that only one team can win this Fifth Test, and that the series result will fairly reflect the disparity between the teams.

When at last Cook was caught in the gully, Watson celebrated by hollering at the heavens, as old-time actors used to shout into the Sydney breakers to improve their vocal projection. It was meant to evoke triumph; it savoured simply of desperation. England a hundred in the lead, Australia being carved up like a Christmas turkey, and he's roaring? Hmmm . . . perhaps he had just executed his skill set. By the time dim light ended the day at 5.30 p.m., England's lead had more than doubled, and Watson probably had no puff left.

The day dawned overcast, too, though not perhaps quite so overcast as Australia would have wished. Anderson punched a cover drive for four from Hilfenhaus, then after twenty minutes played down the wrong line at Siddle. England were still a hundred runs in the red, further breaches could have hurt, and, again, little things meant a lot. In Watson's first over and the last ball before drinks, Cook (87) nicked just short of Clarke at second slip. A run shy of his third century for the series, he also turned Beer to Hughes at short leg where he was exonerated by electronic examination – to be fair to the Australians, neither the fielder nor Haddin looked convinced the catch had carried.

With a flick through mid-wicket and a jogged single in Beer's next over, Cook cantered to three figures, and statisticians enjoyed a beanfeast. He had, for example, now emulated David Gower, John Edrich and Chris Broad, all top-order left-handers coincidentally, in achieving a Test hundred at four Australian venues.

Particularly sharp eyes noted that he passed 1,000 first-class runs for the tour, a delightfully old-fashioned record for a delightfully old-fashioned cricketer. Above all, perhaps, stattos will have to look hard for a more epic form turn-around. In his first eight innings of last summer in England, Cook eked out 106 runs at an average of 13; in nine innings since, he has made 886 runs at 111.

Forty-five minutes from lunch, Beer finally obtained his maiden Test wicket, fifty-five deliveries after it first felt within his grasp, when Collingwood holed out down the ground and Hilfenhaus took the catch – this time legitimately. Beer, who goes through his repertoire as mechanically as a cuckoo clock, has failed to convince anyone here that he is a superior spinner to Nathan Hauritz, who continues languishing in internal exile. But at least he was now on the board.

In his beginning, Beer probably also marked an end for Collingwood: the 34-year-old's foray down the wicket was premeditated; the shot was essayed two metres short of the pitch of the ball; it was a raging against the dying of the light. Collingwood has been a brave, defiant cricketer. Four years ago, he was the one Englishman who consistently gave as good as he got verbally, his coach Duncan Fletcher complaining that team-mates had left Collingwood to 'take on the whole Australian team'. That role has been made redundant. With 119 in his last ten Test innings, he has become a memento of a kind that a good team, as England deserve to be considered, should be capable of leaving behind.

As Bell settled in smoothly with Cook, in fact, Australia's effort began to fray. Having bowled only the first three overs of the morning from the Paddington End, Johnson started his second spell from the Randwick End with a ball that barely landed on the cut strip. The *frisson* he caused at Perth is a distant memory. When he might at a pinch have run Cook (129) out fielding off his own bowling and throwing blind at the non-striker's end, a droll press-box colleague commented that he got closer to the stumps when throwing than bowling. The joke lingered. His arm now looks more suited to throwing a Frisbee, or a plate at a Greek wedding, than to bowling a cricket ball, and the Barmy Army regard him simply as a pretext for their favourite song: 'He bowls to the left/He bowls to the right/That Mitchell Johnson/His bowling is shite.'

Bell took advantage by finally producing the innings of which he has seemed capable all summer, but for the frailties of England's tail, and his role in ministering to it. From a personal point of view, Bell's was a critical knock. Failure here would have taken the gloss off all his contributions so far: in a year or two, most people would have forgotten that he has looked, day-in, day-out, England's most fluent and attractive batsman. He again looked a treat, driving like a Rolls-Royce, and cutting like a sushi chef. But it was intent that oozed out of him, as well as style. So much intent that he featured in an interlude as peculiar as any in this series – and there have been some peculiar ones.

When the fourth ball of Watson's seventeenth over passed between Bell's bat and pad, the game dissolved into a now-regrettably familiar tableau. Aleem Dar gave Bell (70) out. Bell walked down the wicket and consulted Prior. Time passed – long enough to wonder how a batsman can not know if he has hit the ball. Finally, Bell requested a referral. Oh well, here we go again . . .

The fielders waited. The umpires waited. The batsmen had a drink. The replays rolled, and the Hot Spot revealed . . . nothing. There was surely an irony here, given the weight Ricky Ponting attached to the Hot Spot in Melbourne: he that lives by the Hot Spot shall die by it also. Then, just as Bell was resuming his innings, the television turned as a *deus ex machina* to the snickometer, which revealed . . . a sound. Make of that what you will – many journalists at stumps clearly intended to. In the interim, please enjoy the law of unforeseen consequences: a good umpire in Dar made what was almost certainly a correct decision, only to be undermined by a system intended to improve accuracy in umpiring.

As it was, Bell *officially* survived only one chance, a hot caught-and-bowled dropped by Steve Smith, whom Clarke finally remembered was playing in time for him to bowl the 102nd over. Just before 5 p.m., Bell punched the same bowler through cover and gave a skip of delight in completing his first Ashes hundred. That skip became a trampling as Prior, who compiled a brassy 100-minute fifty, helped him add 107 at almost four and a half runs an over. By day's end, the cricket had acquired a dimension not unknown where sequels are concerned: the feeling that one has seen this story before.

5 JANUARY 2011
ALASTAIR COOK

Strokes of Genius

Before Australia's second innings in Melbourne, Shane Watson was asked what would be his approach to his team's huge first-innings arrears. Without a second thought, Watson revealed his 'plan': he would bat for two and a half days. Never mind that his limit in this series has been about two and a half hours. Later that afternoon, another start was duly wasted.

Nobody has asked Alastair Cook for his 'plan' this summer. He says 'obviously' a lot in press conferences, but so does everybody else, and in his case it's almost apologetic. The way he plays, batting *is* obvious, containing no obscurities or hidden subtleties. He is like a skilled expositor with a gift for making complicated ideas sound simple. 'I don't really know what else to say,' he confessed to a television questioner at day's end. His batting this summer has already spoken volumes.

Of today's 189, it suffices to comment that it broke Australia's spirit, glimpses of which Michael Clarke's team had shown on the second day. It felt like a part of the single continuous innings Cook has played all summer, during which he has batted as though involved in the painting of the Sydney Harbour Bridge, no sooner finishing at one end than starting at the other.

The SCG in the morning was an uncommonly cheerful sight, awash in pink in aid of the McGrath Foundation and its good works in the raising of funds for breast cancer research. Even the statue of Steve Waugh unveiled before play was adorned in a fuschia neckerchief, so that Australia's great champion resembled a Mardi Gras cowboy. For a moment it appeared that Cook would be expected to recommence batting in a pink helmet. In fact, Cook even eschewed the popular pink grip, settling instead for being in the pink of form – and if you were hitting the ball like Cook at the moment, you'd be careful about altering what you had for breakfast every morning lest somehow it interfere with your luck.

Four years ago on this ground, Cook recalled that comment of Douglas Jardine's about batting against Bill O'Reilly: 'I cut out every shot that got me out and found that I didn't have a shot left.' It was hard to see how he would ever score a run, and precious few of them did he obtain. Now his leaving is part of a bigger, wider, more complete game. 'Knowing where your off stump is' is one of those cricket expressions that sounds perennially mysterious to the uninitiated. After all, doesn't it just sit there alongside the other two?

Cook the expositor unravels its meaning: by letting balls go that compel no stroke, he draws bowlers into his pads, coaxes them to pitch the ball further up for driving, and generally tires them, little by little, minute by minute. He makes the non-stroke into a kind of stroke, silence into a sort of statement.

Cook has also turned the press box into a fastness of anorakism. All day could be heard whispered exchanges:

'most runs since'; 'most by a left-hander since'; 'between Sutcliffe and Hammond'; 'just like Gavaskar'; 'level with Lara'. Behind every hard-bitten cricket hack lurks a boy with pencil, a scorebook and a *Wisden* or two.

The most flavoursome record of all was the one concerning the length of time that Cook has batted this summer. Read it and reel: with potentially an innings still to go, he has been at the crease for thirty-six hours and eleven minutes, breaking a record of delicious obscurity set forty years ago by John Edrich.

Tennis has its records of epic five-setters, but only cricket keeps such close tabs on durations, and on hours of occupation, because in order to score one must first survive. In its way, Cook's batting harkens to the origins of cricket, when the roughness of pitches first compelled batsmen to work out ways to defend themselves, and its place in nature, when the format was set by the passage of the day.

In recent times, Twenty20 has chewed away at that essence of batting, utterly skewing the dynamics of risk and reward. The abbreviated game marches to the drumbeat of the strike rate, which makes a celebrity of Keiron Pollard, and a slowcoach of Michael Clarke. But while the strike rate sounds somehow more scientific, it's a reductive precision, for it pretends that batsmen are only active when actually facing the bowling. In fact, you don't cease to be part of the game at the non-striker's end; you aren't absolved from responsibility, excused from concentration or invulnerable to dismissal. In addition to the 242 scoreless deliveries of Cook's innings, he was a faithful back-up through 351 as a partner. On the measure of a strike rate, these did not exist. Minutes, by contrast, are immediately suggestive. On the rule of thumb that there are 360 in a day's play, you can tell at a glance that Cook has been at the crease for roughly six entire days in this series – almost a third of the total play. In his own self-effacing way, he has utterly hogged the centre.

Fifteen years ago, *The Times*' chief cricket correspondent saved a Test match for England against South Africa. Mike Atherton faced 492 balls, although what did this imply other than a lot? Far more evocative is it to recall that he endured for 643 minutes. The image of Atherton's innings that most people recall is not of any shot or even milestone, but the one of him looking up from his haunches and giving his partner Jack Russell a smile – weary, wary but game. Cook, then, has done still more than be the fulcrum of England's exertions in this Ashes series. He has given us a little instruction in cricket – by his deeds, of course, rather than his words.

6 JANUARY 2011

Day 4

Close of play: Australia 2nd innings 213–7
(SPD Smith 24*, PM Siddle 17*, 67 overs)

The final day's play in the Ashes of 2010–11 will commence at 10.03 a.m. The reason: a complex recalculation based on residual time lost to rain on the first day which it would be pointless to explain. The same was very nearly true of play on the fourth day of this Fifth Test, where England outclassed Australia in ways it feels tedious and repetitive to enumerate.

At the close, Australia were set to lose three Tests in a series by an innings for the first time since . . . well, ever. In the day's first half, their listless attack was relieved of 156 runs in 36.5 overs by England's last three wickets; in the second, they lost seven batsmen in 44 overs either side of tea. Steve Smith and Peter Siddle negotiated an extra half-hour that Andrew Strauss requested, but Australia remain 151 runs short of making their opponents bat again, and England stand on the brink of a 3–1 victory.

Today's should actually have been the best batting conditions of the match – almost of the series. The SCG pitch had flattened right out, the sky was nearly cloudless, the outfield had quickened, both attacks were weary from five weeks' hard graft, and a crowd of 35,622 was in high humour. England certainly revelled. Having taken toll of some tired Australian bowling late on the third day, Matt Prior positively scampered to the fastest English hundred of the series in 109 balls – the fastest by an Englishman against Australia, in fact, for nearly thirty years.

'Crikey,' said an Australian colleague behind me after tea yesterday. 'I've looked up and Prior's forty already. How did that happen?' This is Prior's chief faculty, for surprising opponents with instant aggression, sucking bowlers into his off-stump slot by hanging slightly back, then veritably pelting between wickets. Not even Pietersen in this England line-up scores more quickly than Prior's 62.92 per hundred balls.

Of all England's cricketers this summer, Prior has probably

occasioned the fewest words – no bad thing, given that wicketkeepers become most obtrusive by their errors. He has taken twenty-two catches with scarcely a murmur of praise or blame, the best haul in forty years.

Over the years, Australia has not been a happy hunting ground for English glovemen. Alec Stewart never managed a full series here. Geraint Jones and Jack Russell lost places mid-series, Jack Richards and Steve Rhodes post-series. Not since Alan Knott's two tours, furthermore, has a visiting keeper consistently made Ashes runs in Australia. Four years ago, Jones and Chris Read scraped together 98 runs in ten innings.

Prior, by contrast, is that rare English player who looks born for Australian climes, in his keeping and batting enjoying the bounce, the carry and the minimal sideways movement. As he has assimilated these conditions this summer, he has proved more and more effective, helped by some opposition bowling and captaincy that might be politely described as thought-free. As is usually the case, fully 96 of his 118 runs were scored on the off side, including a six down the ground and all eleven of his boundaries. Clarke finally set an off-side sweeper when the quicker bowlers operated, but the simpler expedient of bowling straight and attacking the stumps was somehow thought either too obvious or too subtle. Prior took particular toll of the third new ball, which neither swung nor seamed for the Australian quicks, instead leaving the bat with a crack.

Thanks to some sensible defence and bottom-handed hoicking from Bresnan, England's eighth pair added 102, as its seventh pair had added 107, its sixth pair 154 and ... well, you get the picture. England's last pair, Graeme Swann and Chris Tremlett, then purloined another 35 in seven overs to add irritation to insult to injury, and extend England's lead to 364.

As he has been inclined to do all summer, Watson set off as though planning to erase this deficit by stumps on his own, driving, cutting and pulling seven boundaries in forty balls. Hughes all but disappeared from view, only to re-emerge when both batsmen ended up at the non-striker's end having turned an easy two into their second run-out in three starts. Watson, of course, turns up at run-outs like Lara Bingle turns up at openings, but here he could at least share the blame: both batsmen cantered the first casually; both were ball-watching; neither appeared to call decisively. Perhaps still brooding, Hughes fenced at Bresnan six runs later.

Captain Clarke and Usman Khawaja endured through to tea, and the latter had just begun asserting himself, with a reverberating pull shot from Anderson, when he followed one from the same bowler that swung away like a Roberto Carlos free kick. Clarke, who recovered something like freedom in his foot movement against Swann, had struck six affirming fours when he too misread Anderson's trajectories.

Had Bell caught Haddin (7) diving to his right at short cover and reduced Australia to 139 for five, there might have been no reason to return tomorrow. As it was, England shortened their work when Pietersen caught Hussey in the gully. With shadows lengthening across the ground, the man with the longest shadow of all bowled his quickest spell of the match from the Randwick End, Tremlett beating Haddin's pull and Johnson's prod for pace with consecutive deliveries;

Siddle just ensured that his would be the only hat-trick of the series by digging out a yorker.

About half an hour after play, the ground was finally swept by a drenching rain, the results of which were left glistening on the covers beneath its floodlights. So it turns out that there *was* one new development today: Australia, it seems, can no longer even do rain properly.

6 JANUARY 2011
SHANE WATSON

When Success Is Failure

Shane Watson will end this Ashes series with an average of nearly 50. In a team as thoroughly beaten as Australia, such a statistical achievement would normally attract such adjectives as 'honourable', 'laudable', maybe even 'valiant'. Regard this as an exhibit in the case against interpreting a series from the average tables.

Even before he concluded his Test summer today with a run-out of comical awfulness, Australia's Allan Border Medallist had been an underachiever. On seven occasions he has batted for more than 100 minutes; only once has he gone beyond three hours. Even leaving aside the argument that, thanks to flat wickets and fat bats, 50 is the new 40, Watson has achieved a conversion rate uglier than that between sterling and the Australian dollar.

His bowling, a useful adjunct for Ricky Ponting over the

last eighteen months, has also faded. Although he has probably bowled a little better than his three wickets at 74 would suggest, you would be hard pressed to bowl worse. His fielding, too, has remained clumsy, and he occupies first slip with as much animation as a waxworks dummy. For all that, a big innings today, as it has for Ian Bell and Matt Prior, might have put an attractive gloss on Watson's season. And the way it did not eventuate arguably explains quite a lot about the Ashes of 2010–11.

The chemistry of some opening combinations produces spontaneous energy; in the case of Shane Watson and Phil Hughes, it is more like gradual decomposition. They cut a curious sight simply in walking out. Where Cook and Strauss walk side by side, parting after a final glove-touch, Watson and Hughes could be playing different sports. While Watson approaches the crease at a deliberate plod, Hughes runs out like an Australian rules footballer plunging through his team's crepe-paper banner.

Nor do they exude permanence and cohesion in the middle. They have the potential advantage of being a left-hander and a right-hander, but neither the alertness nor the fleetness of foot to take advantage of it. Watson is a ponderous runner, and an apparently quiet caller, who had been involved in six Test run-outs before today. He is now in harness with a lazy runner in Hughes. To call them 'partners', in fact, is more a polite convention than a description; at the moment, they are simply two men who, for convenience's sake, happen to put the pads on at the same time. If they were in relationship therapy, the counsellor would tell them that they are 'bad for each other'.

Today's mishap would have made club cricketers blush. Hughes turned Swann to mid-wicket, and both batsmen set off, albeit at no great rate. Michael Hussey, for example, would never have taken the first run so gently; he would have had his head down checking his partner's cues for interest in a second, in doing so increasing the pressure on the fielder. So slowly did Watson and Hughes chug, it was like Sky had gone to the slow-motion replay early.

To the reason for this lack of urgency, one needed to cast one's mind back ten days, to when a hasty call from Watson and a tardy response from Hughes nipped their partnership in the bud. You imagined them between times discussing the importance of not being run out with the same emphasis as Basil Fawlty gave to not mentioning the war. The result was similar, although as funny only if you were English.

Hughes, ball watching, turned and came back without pausing – without obviously calling either. Watson responded to Hughes's advance, set off for a second run, then turned to watching the ball too. In doing so, he missed that Hughes had pulled up, apparently transfixed by Pietersen's fielding. Soon enough, the pair were transfixed by one another – because of their close proximity. It was the sixth run-out in Australia's last seven Test matches, of which Watson has been involved in three, each ending an Australian opening partnership. England, by contrast, have sustained not one such casualty; Trott's at Melbourne is the only close call that comes to mind.

Effective running between wickets is one of the most elusive cricket skills, and also one of the least practised. But it basically comes down to one thing: an understanding of, and a trust in, your team-mates. When you respond to a comrade's call, you are putting yourself in his hands as completely as at any time in the game. That is why good teams invariably run well, and why run-outs always seem to beget other run-outs. When understanding and trust break down in any community, the effect is contagious; a cricket team is no different.

It is a truism to say that England have retained the Ashes this summer because they have been the more skilful side. It is more illuminating to refine that statement by concentrating on the broader aspects of the visitors' superiority, which involve those that bind eleven cricketers into an XI, and make cricket into a game rather than simply a collection of biomechanical processes.

Bowl ten half-volleys to Watson and he would welly all ten through the covers for four – which looks good, is measurable, reproducible, and might lead to a defensible average, but is hardly the end of a cricketer's responsibilities to his team. When it comes to forming part of a unit that punches above its collective weight, Watson exhibits no extra dimension, none of the qualities that galvanise team-mates, light up a game or lift a crowd. He is about as good a cricketer as Australia has put in the field this summer – and he is still not very good.

7 JANUARY 2011

Day 5

Close of play: Australia 2nd innings 281 (84.4 overs)

As the morning waned, and the strains of 'The Last Post' reverberated again from Billy Cooper's trumpet, a disturbance of stumps at the Sydney Cricket Ground ended Australia's on-field agonies in the Ashes of 2010–11. The off-field agonies have barely begun.

At nearly two hours, the fifth day took a little longer than expected, but new balls have been England's sphere of influence this summer, and twenty-eight deliveries with a new one sufficed to see off the last vestiges of Australia's tail, and conclude a victory by an innings and 83 runs. When Michael Beer was the last wicket to fall, it was possible we had seen the last of him in Test cricket. Australia are not scheduled to play a Test match until August in Sri Lanka – there will be a lot of brooding between now and then.

Despite the overnight rain, Steve Smith and Peter Siddle resumed their overnight resistance on time, and brought up their 50 partnership after twenty minutes, whereupon one of the promised 'isolated showers' eventuated and the players dashed for the shelter of the pavilion – all save Tremlett, who allows nothing to disturb his steady, measured tread, and who wandered in some way after the umpires.

Tom Parker's groundstaff did well to limit the interruption to three-quarters of an hour, the ground announcer rather less well when he decided to reintroduce all the players by reference to their images and stats on the big screen. There truly is no limit to the insults heaped on the intelligence of spectators inside Australian Test grounds. Gosh, here's a picture of Alastair Cook with his arms crossed. After all, he's only batted thirty-six hours this summer so you might have forgotten him. The Barmy Army responded as if on cue to mention of Mitchell Johnson's name by launching into another of its growing repertoire of tributes to Super Mitch, then continuing as a kind of human karaoke machine, rifling through its songbook at random.

Finally they exulted in unison when Siddle holed out to Anderson off Swann in front of their lower terrace in the Trumper Stand. For those who enjoy such statistical curios, Siddle, by adding 86 in 131 balls with Smith, had participated in Australia's best partnership in consecutive Tests – which tells you as much as you need to know about Australia's ineffectual top order.

Smith pressed on to Australia's highest score, showing some of his much-lauded spark, while not quite dispelling the image one has of him of a boy waving around a bat too big for him. Tremlett took the new ball at 261 for eight, and Anderson promptly removed Hilfenhaus to give Prior his twenty-third catch of the summer. Within a blink of Beer's stumps being rattled, four of them were souvenired, the two containing stump cams being left behind – even in their ecstasy, the players never forget their debt to television.

Afterwards, Andrew Strauss looked as relaxed as he had with the bat on the second day, and was rather more expansive than usual, as befits the captain of what today became officially the world's third-ranked Test team. When discussing the task of managing off-field as distinct from captaining on, he sounded almost Obama-esque: 'People want to buy into something. People want to buy into the idea that we're going somewhere as a unit and we're not going to leave anyone behind.' You could not miss the allusion here to Paul Collingwood, to whom England gave every opportunity to succeed, and who has now repaid them by retiring with dignity. While his 83 runs in six innings do not suggest a player with much still to offer, England will miss his sticky palms at slip, responsible for nine catches, and demeanour in the dressing room, which caused his captain to describe him as 'very much the soul of English cricket'.

To Michael Clarke then fell the job of defending the indefensible, admitting that this was 'as close to the bottom as it gets', while adamantly dismissing talk of a 'crisis in Australian cricket', and claiming that this was 'as gifted as any team I have been a part of' – a rather remarkable assertion given that his era overlaps with those of Shane Warne, Glenn McGrath, Adam Gilchrist, Matthew Hayden and others too numerous to mention. But then, perhaps a deeper point lurked here, that these Australians have been gifted quite a lot, and were strangers to struggle when they found themselves involved in one. It is a condition that they may well have a chance to get used to.

7 JANUARY 2011
ASHES VICTORIES

Parallel Lives

When Cricket Australia's sloganeers prophesied that 'History Will Be Made' this summer, it's fair to say that they wouldn't have had this history in mind – history involving Australia as loser of three of their last four Ashes series, and of six of their last eight Tests.

But what does the history made here mean for England? For history's power is great. At the victory ceremony following events today, it was fascinating to note how reverently Andrew Strauss and his players treated the tiny replica urn that looked like it was worth all of $5, even bestowing gentle kisses on it, while swinging around the far more expensive Waterford Crystal trophy inaugurated by the Marylebone Cricket Club like a jerry can.

History tells us that since the routine of deciding the Ashes over five Tests was established in the 1890s, England have only defended the Ashes successfully in Australia on four occasions: 1928–29, 1954–55, 1978–79 and 1986–87. In both the latter two cases, Australian cricket was weakened and divided, by Kerry Packer and Ali Bacher respectively. Mike Gatting's wins here twenty-four years ago were his only ones as a Test captain.

Percy Chapman's tourists of 1928–29 rank among the very best in history: Hobbs, Sutcliffe, Hammond, Jardine, Larwood,

Tate and the inexhaustible left-armer Farmer White, who ploughed through 3,252 deliveries in those five Tests, compared to the 1,315 bowled by Graeme Swann in these. But the margin of the supremacy of that team, 4–1, is exaggerated by the fact that Australian Tests were then played to a finish. Strauss's team blew their opponents away innings after innings. Today was the first time Australia's batting had lasted longer than 100 overs since Brisbane, and then only just: 106.1.

The fairest, simplest and most illuminating comparison is with the team led by Len Hutton here fifty-six years ago. Like Strauss's men, they had beaten Australia by the odd Test with a win at the Oval fourteen months earlier.

Like Hutton, Strauss is a seasoned opening batsman. Like Hutton, Strauss arrived with the prior experience of being towelled up in Australia. Like Hutton, Strauss learned from that misfortune. Perhaps because they were accustomed to bearing its brunt at the top of the order, both saw the solution to Australian conditions as pace bowling.

Hutton's solution was Frank Tyson, who took 28 wickets at 21 on his tour of a lifetime. The 24 wickets at 26 taken by Strauss's solution, James Anderson, are actually the best in Australia by an England bowler since, even if Anderson is closer in method to Tyson's great partner Brian Statham: slim, whippy, untiring, unyielding.

Since Hutton's era, the effect of raw pace has been somewhat mitigated by the advent of the helmet and improved protective gear. It is swing that confounds modern batsmen, with their techniques built around a forward press, and addicted to the sensations of bat on ball. The relative success of the bowlers finding edges in this series is evinced by Matt Prior's twenty-three catches to Brad Haddin's eight.

What both Hutton's and Strauss's attacks also have in common is an orientation to economy, an end Hutton achieved both through the accuracy of his auxiliaries Trevor Bailey, Bob Appleyard and Johnny Wardle, and through slowing his over rate to a soporific degree. As *The Times'* venerable cricket correspondent John Woodcock has explained it, Hutton 'planned to keep Australia waiting, to make them fret, to get up their noses'.

While the expedient of deliberate tardiness and nasal insinuation was not open to Strauss, the latter's conviction that 'strangling your opponent' was a key to success down under contains an echo of the former's approach. So where Australia's most penetrative bowler Mitchell Johnson leaked runs at more than 4 an over, Anderson grudged less than 3. Where Australia's spinners took only five wickets and gave up 3.65 an over, Swann and Collingwood as England's relief bowlers claimed seventeen wickets and gave up a run an over less. Among Australian batsmen lacking patience and touch, inclined to go hard at the ball and to trust in their powerful bats to get them out of trouble, the effect was regular self-immolation.

The other advantage England have enjoyed this series has been their noisy, visible support. When Percy Chapman's team came here eighty-two years ago, they arrived with only a handful of wealthy camp-followers, who were treated almost as extensions of the touring team. These included the playwright Ben Travers, who, expecting that Chapman would be swamped by messages of support and patriotic injunction before the series, was amazed to find that the only message received by England's captain from HM Government was a tax demand from the Inland Revenue. 'England expects each man to pay his duty,' Travers told Chapman consolingly.

The staunchest group of supporters for Hutton's Englishmen was then their nineteen-strong press corps, one of whose number, Alf Gover of the *Sunday Mirror*, acted as the David Saker of his time by helping Tyson shorten his run, sharpen his pace and improve his stamina.

In days of yore, however, it could be a lonely life inside Australian cricket grounds for visiting cricketers. So the significance of the armies of spectators who have followed England this summer, Barmy and otherwise, cannot be under-estimated. They have made Australia a home away from home for their team, as was recognised today when Strauss's men made a beeline for the serried ranks of red and white on the lower deck of the Trumper Stand as soon as the presentation was over.

It wasn't a spontaneous gesture, for Andrew Flintoff's team did the same here four years ago – deserving no more, frankly, than a massed raspberry in return. But it was a heartfelt one. Not every day is history made, and it is an experience to be shared when it is.

7 JANUARY 2011
AUSTRALIA

Australia Versus Itself

Did the Australian public turn on their cricketers during this Ashes series? You would be forgiven for thinking so, if you took the increasingly florid tabloid newspaper headlines to be an accurate reflection of public opinion. The truth of this *annus horribilis* is probably subtler: that Australians never believed their cricketers were in with a chance in the first place.

The tradition, of course, is that England cricketers arrive to a chorus of detraction, following in the hallowed memories of the wharfies at Fremantle Gages in the 1930s who welcomed the ships carrying Marylebone teams by reminding them whose side Bradman was on with choruses of 'You'll never geddim out!'

Not this summer. Australian cricket's fall from its lofty estate since the Oval Test of 2009 might have been swift, but it has registered. Almost three weeks before this Ashes series commenced, a big nationwide online survey in News Ltd papers concluded that the home side had no chance of regaining the Ashes, that coach Tim Nielsen was a failure, and that heir apparent Michael Clarke was the wrong choice to succeed Ricky Ponting.

When Michael Atherton arrived in Hobart to report on the tourists' game against Australia A, he was shocked by the degree of local pessimism, at a stage on tours when Australians were normally at least rehearsing their *Schadenfreude*. And it seemed to communicate itself to Ponting's team early on, when Mitchell Johnson mumbled a complaint after the Gabba Test that most of the fans seemed to be English. The fans' retort seemed to be that Australia's cricketers should not expect support they had not earned.

Quite what engendered this fatalism? The simplest answer is realism. The cycle of retirements in the four years since the last Ashes here has rendered Australian cricket a succession of curtain calls, to the extent that there now seems a good deal more talent in the commentary box than on the field.

These characters have not been replaced, and their continuing visibility in various guises, from charity worker (Glenn McGrath) to human headline (Shane Warne), offers a ready basis for unflattering comparison. It was the dearth of salty humanity in current Australian ranks that led to Doug Bollinger's brief cult-hero status last summer, which soon petered out when he lacked the game to go with it.

Certainly, this current team is one to which locals find it difficult to warm. Wild vauntings of Phil Hughes or Steve Smith have convinced nobody, while reservations remain about Clarke, thought a little too self-regarding and self-involved for high office, and also Shane Watson and Mitchell Johnson, imagined to be principally concerned with hair and tattoos respectively. Cricket Australia are encouraging their players to use social media in communicating with fans, but what it shows more faithfully is how superficial is the acquaintance of the team and its public.

Only Michael Hussey, Brad Haddin and Peter Siddle of

the current XI are genuinely thought to be made of the right stuff. Administrators would kill for their own Graeme Swann – quick, gregarious, worldly and naturally funny.

The press, meanwhile, has actually been less capricious than usual. On the eve of the Perth Test, I had a conversation with a senior tabloid journalist, who admitted that he was under immense pressure from his office to condemn Ponting and his players in the most astringent terms, but that he was doing his best to resist. 'I don't know how much longer I can hold out,' he confided. 'They want names and they want faces. They want to know who to blame.'

When Australia capitulated on the first day of that Perth Test, the coverage was wickedly cutting. It wasn't 'Swedes 1 Turnips 0', but in years to come the back page of that day's *West Australian* may become a collector's piece. There they were, on the back page of the paper, the heads of Australia's selectors, bespattered with egg. The headline explained it all just in case: 'Egg On Their Faces'.

There was a little more egg to go round that evening after Johnson and Ryan Harris rock'n'rolled the visitors on a sporting wicket, but as a headline it has looked better by the day. For those who did in anticipation sense the weakness of the Australian team this summer, in fact, there is a perverse satisfaction to be derived from having seen it coming.

7 JANUARY 2011
ENGLAND

Stars among the All-Stars

In their green and golden age, Australian cricketers were apt to complain of never receiving the credit they deserved, results being customarily explained by reference to the weaknesses of opponents. Something similar may befall England's team in the Ashes of 2010–11 – think of it as the last of those reversals of traditional roles on which we have been musing all summer.

England seemed, after all, to do nothing spectacular. No batsman shredded an attack outright; of the mere three five-fors obtained, only one, Graeme Swann's in Adelaide, was in a winning cause. If anything, the high-explosive efforts were Australian, such as Peter Siddle's in Brisbane, Mitchell Johnson's in Perth. With the possible exception of the first day in Melbourne, England's cricket was like a series of controlled detonations at strategic intervals and locations.

So future generations may miss the overwhelming authority achieved by English individuals in this series; partly, too, because the players themselves were apt to underplay them. Alastair Cook's response to an interlocutor at Adelaide about the sweat of his long toil there was a kind of tour motif: 'I'm quite lucky – I don't really sweat that much.' Thanks for the ready-made headline, Cooky: England retain Ashes without breaking sweat.

Before the tour, Cook was an England player whose measure the Australians would have felt they had. In a gloating overview of the visiting team for the *Sydney Morning Herald* published on the eve of the Gabba Test, Stuart Clark dismissed him airily: 'Opponents around the world have realised he is predominantly a square-of-the-wicket player, and now bowl full and outside off stump as there is a question about his ability to leave the ball.'

Question answered, methinks: it was in the neglected art of leaving the ball that Cook gave his bat-on-ball-happy opponents a lesson. That flowed, however, from a confidence in his repertoire of strokes, and ability to dispose of the bad ball. It's when you're worried where your next run will come from that you play shots you shouldn't. Cook could be Sir Leavealot because he had the swordplay to go with it.

No other England player fits so seamlessly into the team's coaching structure. Andy Flower is a former close Essex team-mate; Graham Gooch is a former county coach. They have modified his technique, but in such a way that it remains his, and that he now understands his game more completely. They backed him through thin times, so that they have seen his character in adversity. These factors make a powerful combination.

Jonathan Trott began the Ashes of 2010–11 as the only member of England's top six without prior Australian experience. On the odd occasion, too, he looked overeager to play the pull shot, which thrice cost him his wicket on tour. Otherwise, he was the complete number three, despite having first been drafted into the position for the want of something better. He and Cook were the kind of batting combination that bring to a camp calm and order. The middle order could relax, bowlers put their feet up.

His outward phlegmatism notwithstanding, a passion seems to lurk deep in Trott. When he was left out of the Headingley Test of 2009, Andrew Strauss described his look as that of someone 'genuinely distraught'. He was the one England player who gave a hint of his team's latent rage at home last year by having a crack at Wahab Riaz. But in the main, that passion smoulders, summed up somehow in his technique: with his trigger movement forward, he always seems in danger of launching at the ball, yet somehow ends up playing exquisitely late, right beneath his nose. It is force under control. During his critical 168 not out at Melbourne, he never lost momentum despite the acutest self-denial.

What England's successes this summer have in common is that they were not players Australia would have spent much time worrying about in advance. Cook had had no impact on two prior Ashes series; Trott had struggled on bouncy wickets a year earlier. James Anderson? Before the tour, Australians remembered him mostly as the cannon fodder of four years ago, and a threat in the Ashes of 2009 only when clouds rolled in. Under cloudless Australian skies, Shane Watson and his top-order colleagues quite fancied their chances against him. Ahead of the series, Watson talked up Anderson's down-under record as a point in his team's favour: 'If he doesn't start out the way he wants to, those wounds can open up straight away.'

Watson's punditry proved as speculative as his calling. One of the most impressive features of Anderson's bowling in

2010–11 was his willingness to be struck for early boundaries in search of swing – he was like the proverbial spinner prepared to keep tossing it up even under attack. Anderson had some expensive opening spells among his successful ones, but he never lost faith in his ability to beat the bat with sideways movement, or his stomach for the contest. Even when Watson had another piece of him after Perth, chirping that Anderson's failure there as night watchman to protect Paul Collingwood had been 'one of my best moments on a cricket field', England's number one quick never stopped coming. Anderson's contribution as straight man to Graeme Swann's video diaries also made them among the tour's most successful partnerships. His deadpan retort to Swann in Adelaide – 'Excuse me, there's nothing wrong with being both informative *and* interesting, Graeme' – was perhaps the best line of the trip.

On preparing to face Chris Tremlett, meanwhile, Australia appeared to spend no time at all: indeed, the one aspect of Australia's preparation that Michael Clarke was later prepared to concede was deficient was the failure to train against 'tall fast bowlers', and they come no taller than Tremlett.

The reason, one fancies, was Tremlett's prior reputation for reticence, for temperament and body language that Shane Warne described as 'just a bit soft' and 'awful' respectively. Here, perhaps, we learned more about Warne than Tremlett, the Australian's deportment ideal being David Hasselhoff. From his first ball in Perth, Tremlett looked the part as a bowler, while remaining utterly impassive, even placid, between times.

Tremlett, in fact, might have been devised with batsmen accustomed to propping on the front foot and hitting happily through the line in mind. His ball to begin Australia's rout in Melbourne, forcing a skittish Watson on to the back foot and taking the shoulder of the bat, was the kind that sends a tremor through the dressing room – the hunters of Perth, it said, were now the hunted. Mind you, it was almost comical to contrast the consternation Tremlett induced in his own slips cordon with the total equanimity he exhibited himself, and the physical difference he opened up between the visitors and hosts. When 6ft 7in Tremlett walked past 5ft 7in Phil Hughes at the non-striker's end in Melbourne and Sydney, they seemed involved in different games, not just different teams.

England came to Australia shadowed by doubts about the efficacy of a four-man attack. They got a little lucky. Thanks to the unseasonally mild summer, fast bowling was not so physically extentuating as usual; the speed with which the tourists grew accustomed to rolling Australia over helped too, of course. Above all, though, it was thanks to Tremlett and also to Tim Bresnan that England were able to absorb the loss to attrition of Stuart Broad and Steve Finn: statistically at least, they were actually almost twice as effective, turning over 28 wickets at 21, versus 16 wickets at 39.

Yet in concentrating on the four statistical standouts of this England team, one is at risk of ignoring their most impressive quality, which was their strength-through-joy unity. After a rocky start at the Gabba, they caught superbly. Their ground fielding was electric, inflicting four damaging run-outs, while their own running between wickets was judicious, incurring not a single casualty themselves. Above all, they radiated confidence and pleasure in the contest.

This is not something for which England has been known down under. In a memorable passage in his autobiography, Adam Gilchrist described the air around Alec Stewart's team twelve years ago as 'the epitome of everything wrong with English professionalism', resembling 'office workers turning up for a dreary day behind the desk'. Thus it was not a space-filling sound bite when Flower said on England's departure that there was 'nothing to be afraid of in Australia', that it was 'one of the best places to go' and 'should be a lot of fun'. It meant also that when the Australians tried something similar before the Third Test, with Steve Smith describing his mission as being to 'come into the side and be fun', 'making sure I'm having fun and making sure everyone else around is having fun', it sounded as if the locals had simply exhausted other possibilities. A winning team will always be the happier one, but in this case happiness also seemed to beget success. For this, England deserve most credit of all.

FIFTH TEST   Sydney Cricket Ground 3–7 January 2011
Toss   Australia   **England** won by an innings and 83 runs

AUSTRALIA 1st innings			R	M	B	4	6	SR
SR Watson	c Strauss	b Bresnan	**45**	178	127	5	0	35.43
PJ Hughes	c Collingwood	b Tremlett	**31**	116	93	5	0	33.33
UT Khawaja	c Trott	b Swann	**37**	120	95	5	0	38.94
***MJ Clarke**	c Anderson	b Bresnan	**4**	25	21	0	0	19.04
MEK Hussey		b Collingwood	**33**	108	92	2	0	35.86
†BJ Haddin	c †Prior	b Anderson	**6**	16	13	0	0	46.15
SPD Smith	c Collingwood	b Anderson	**18**	79	53	1	0	33.96
MG Johnson		b Bresnan	**53**	84	66	5	1	80.30
PM Siddle	c Strauss	b Anderson	**2**	3	4	0	0	50.00
BW Hilfenhaus	c †Prior	b Anderson	**34**	86	58	3	1	58.62
MA Beer		not out	**2**	22	17	0	0	11.76
EXTRAS	(b 5, lb 7, w 1, nb 2)		**15**					
TOTAL	(all out; 106.1 overs; 423 mins)		**280**	(2.63 runs per over)				

FoW	1-55	(Hughes, 29.3 ov),	2-105	(Watson, 44.3 ov),
	3-113	(Clarke, 50.6 ov),	4-134	(Khawaja, 58.6 ov),
	5-143	(Haddin, 62.4 ov),	6-171	(Hussey, 79.6 ov),
	7-187	(Smith, 84.2 ov),	8-189	(Siddle, 84.6 ov),
	9-265	(Johnson, 99.5 ov),	10-280	(Hilfenhaus, 106.1 ov)

BOWLING	O	M	R	W	ECON	
JM Anderson	30.1	7	66	4	2.18	
CT Tremlett	26	9	71	1	2.73	(2nb)
TT Bresnan	30	5	89	3	2.96	(1w)
GP Swann	16	4	37	1	2.31	
PD Collingwood	4	2	5	1	1.25	

ENGLAND 1st innings			R	M	B	4	6	SR
*AJ Strauss		b Hilfenhaus	**60**	92	58	8	1	103.44
AN Cook	c Hussey	b Watson	**189**	488	342	16	0	55.26
IJL Trott		b Johnson	**0**	5	6	0	0	0.00
KP Pietersen	c Beer	b Johnson	**36**	82	70	4	0	51.42
JM Anderson		b Siddle	**7**	40	35	1	0	20.00
PD Collingwood	c Hilfenhaus	b Beer	**13**	63	41	0	0	31.70
IR Bell	c Clarke	b Johnson	**115**	292	232	13	0	49.56
†MJ Prior	c †Haddin	b Hilfenhaus	**118**	229	130	11	1	90.76
TT Bresnan	c Clarke	b Johnson	**35**	108	103	5	0	33.98
GP Swann		not out	**36**	48	26	3	1	138.46
CT Tremlett	c †Haddin	b Hilfenhaus	**12**	33	28	1	0	42.85
EXTRAS	(b 3, lb 11, w 5, nb 4)		**23**					
TOTAL	(all out; 177.5 overs; 730 mins)		**644**	(3.62 runs per over)				

FoW	1-98	(Strauss, 22.2 ov),	2-99	(Trott, 23.3 ov),
	3-165	(Pietersen, 43.2 ov),	4-181	(Anderson, 53.3 ov),
	5-226	(Collingwood, 68.3 ov),	6-380	(Cook, 115.3 ov),
	7-487	(Bell, 139.4 ov),	8-589	(Bresnan, 167.6 ov),
	9-609	(Prior, 170.6 ov),	10-644	(Tremlett, 177.5 ov)

BOWLING	O	M	R	W	ECON	
BW Hilfenhaus	38.5	7	121	3	3.11	(1w)
MG Johnson	36	5	168	4	4.66	(2w)
PM Siddle	31	5	111	1	3.58	(1nb, 1w)
SR Watson	20	7	49	1	2.45	(2nb, 1w)
MA Beer	38	3	112	1	2.94	(1nb)
SPD Smith	13	0	67	0	5.15	
MEK Hussey	1	0	2	0	2.00	

AUSTRALIA 2nd innings			R	M	B	4	6	SR
SR Watson	run out (†Prior/Pietersen)		38	50	40	7	0	95.00
PJ Hughes	c †Prior	b Bresnan	13	73	58	1	0	22.41
UT Khawaja	c †Prior	b Anderson	21	88	73	2	0	28.76
***MJ Clarke**	c †Prior	b Anderson	41	89	73	6	0	56.16
MEK Hussey	c Pietersen	b Bresnan	12	60	49	1	0	24.48
BJ Haddin†	c †Prior	b Tremlett	30	50	41	3	0	73.17
SPD Smith		not out	54	165	90	6	0	60.00
MG Johnson		b Tremlett	0	1	1	0	0	0.00
PM Siddle	c Anderson	b Swann	43	125	65	4	0	66.15
BW Hilfenhaus	c †Prior	b Anderson	7	14	11	1	0	63.63
MA Beer		b Tremlett	2	9	9	0	0	22.22
EXTRAS	(b 11, lb 4, w 3, nb 2)		20					
TOTAL	(all out; 84.4 overs; 369 mins)		281	(3.31 runs per over)				

FoW 1-46 (Watson, 12.4 ov), 2-52 (Hughes, 19.2 ov),
3-117 (Khawaja, 37.3 ov), 4-124 (Clarke, 43.4 ov),
5-161 (Hussey, 53.6 ov), 6-171 (Haddin, 56.3 ov),
7-171 (Johnson, 56.4 ov), 8-257 (Siddle, 78.3 ov),
9-267 (Hilfenhaus, 81.3 ov), 10-281 (Beer, 84.4 ov)

BOWLING	O	M	R	W	ECON	
JM Anderson	18	5	61	3	3.38	(1w)
CT Tremlett	20.4	4	79	3	3.82	(2nb)
GP Swann	28	8	75	1	2.67	
TT Bresnan	18	6	51	2	2.83	(2w)

Ashes 2011

Averages

	Mat	Inns	NO	Runs	HS	Ave	SR	100	50	0	4	6
England batting												
AN Cook	5	7	1	766	235*	**127.66**	53.26	3	2	0	81	1
IJL Trott	5	7	2	445	168*	**89.00**	50.39	2	1	1	52	0
IR Bell	5	6	1	329	115	**65.80**	56.14	1	3	0	38	1
KP Pietersen	5	6	0	360	227	**60.00**	63.94	1	1	1	50	1
MJ Prior	5	6	1	252	118	**50.40**	78.26	1	1	1	25	2
AJ Strauss	5	7	0	307	110	**43.85**	51.85	1	3	1	39	1
GP Swann	5	5	1	88	36*	**22.00**	88.88	0	0	0	9	1
TT Bresnan	2	2	0	39	35	**19.50**	32.50	0	0	0	5	0
PD Collingwood	5	6	0	83	42	**13.83**	46.62	0	0	0	8	0
CT Tremlett	3	4	1	19	12	**6.33**	36.53	0	0	0	1	0
JM Anderson	5	5	0	22	11	**4.40**	26.50	0	0	1	3	0
ST Finn	3	3	2	3	2	**3.00**	37.50	0	0	0	0	0
SCJ Broad	2	1	0	0	0	**0.00**	0.00	0	0	1	0	0

	Mat	Inns	O	M	R	W	Ave	SR	5	10	Ct	St
England bowling												
KP Pietersen	5	2	5.0	0	16	1	**16.00**	30.0	0	0	5	0
TT Bresnan	2	4	82.4	25	215	11	**19.54**	45.0	0	0	0	0
CT Tremlett	3	6	122.3	28	397	17	**23.35**	43.2	1	0	0	0
JM Anderson	5	10	213.1	50	625	24	**26.04**	53.2	0	0	4	0
ST Finn	3	6	107.4	9	464	14	**33.14**	46.1	1	0	2	0
PD Collingwood	5	6	31.0	6	73	2	**36.50**	93.0	0	0	9	0
GP Swann	5	10	219.1	43	597	15	**39.80**	87.6	1	0	6	0
SCJ Broad	2	4	69.5	17	161	2	**80.50**	209.5	0	0	0	0
IR Bell	5	-	-	-	-	-	-	-	-	-	3	0
AN Cook	5	-	-	-	-	-	-	-	-	-	5	0
MJ Prior	5	-	-	-	-	-	-	-	-	-	23	0
AJ Strauss	5	-	-	-	-	-	-	-	-	-	8	0
IJL Trott	5	-	-	-	-	-	-	-	-	-	1	0

	Mat	Inns	NO	Runs	HS	Ave	SR	100	50	0	4	6
Australia batting												
MEK Hussey	5	9	0	570	195	**63.33**	52.53	2	3	1	67	3
SR Watson	5	10	1	435	95	**48.33**	48.17	0	4	0	57	1
BJ Haddin	5	9	1	360	136	**45.00**	54.87	1	3	0	35	5
SPD Smith	3	6	1	159	54*	**31.80**	49.07	0	1	0	15	0
UT Khawaja	1	2	0	58	37	**29.00**	34.52	0	0	0	7	0
SM Katich	2	4	0	97	50	**24.25**	46.85	0	1	1	11	0
MJ Clarke	5	9	0	193	80	**21.44**	44.16	0	1	0	24	0
PM Siddle	5	9	1	154	43	**19.25**	56.41	0	0	0	15	1
MG Johnson	4	7	0	122	62	**17.42**	58.37	0	2	3	13	2
MJ North	2	3	0	49	26	**16.33**	36.02	0	0	0	7	0
PJ Hughes	3	6	0	97	31	**16.16**	38.80	0	0	0	11	0
RT Ponting	4	8	1	113	51*	**16.14**	51.59	0	1	1	14	1
BW Hilfenhaus	4	7	2	55	34	**11.00**	50.92	0	0	2	7	1
XJ Doherty	2	3	0	27	16	**9.00**	46.55	0	0	0	4	0
MA Beer	1	2	1	4	2*	**4.00**	15.38	0	0	0	0	0
RJ Harris	3	5	1	14	10*	**3.50**	37.83	0	0	2	2	0
DE Bollinger	1	2	2	7	7*	-	36.84	0	0	0	1	0

Australia bowling											
	Mat	Inns	O	M	R	W	Ave	SR	5	10	Ct	St
RJ Harris	3	4	83.4	19	281	11	**25.54**	45.6	1	0	0	0
PM Siddle	5	7	147.1	28	484	14	**34.57**	63.0	2	0	2	0
MG Johnson	4	6	136.3	22	554	15	**36.93**	54.6	1	0	0	0
BW Hilfenhaus	4	6	157.5	42	415	7	**59.28**	135.2	0	0	1	0
SR Watson	5	5	76.0	19	223	3	**74.33**	152.0	0	0	5	0
XJ Doherty	2	3	75.5	11	306	3	**102.00**	151.6	0	0	0	0
MJ North	2	3	38.0	3	110	1	**110.00**	228.0	0	0	1	0
MA Beer	1	1	38.0	3	112	1	**112.00**	228.0	0	0	1	0
DE Bollinger	1	1	29.0	1	130	1	**130.00**	174.0	0	0	0	0
MEK Hussey	5	1	1.0	0	2	0	-	-	0	0	5	0
MJ Clarke	5	1	3.2	0	13	0	-	-	0	0	3	0
SPD Smith	3	2	31.0	3	138	0	-	-	0	0	2	0
BJ Haddin	5	-	-	-	-	-	-	-	-	-	8	1
PJ Hughes	3	-	-	-	-	-	-	-	-	-	0	0
SM Katich	2	-	-	-	-	-	-	-	-	-	1	0
UT Khawaja	1	-	-	-	-	-	-	-	-	-	0	0
RT Ponting	4	-	-	-	-	-	-	-	-	-	4	0